SHOO
THE HiPI

I really enjoyed the book. It's compelling, h   , .ciataple and inspiring. Everyone should read it. It will fast become the go-to guide for everyone from students entering the digital marketing world to current profession-als wanting to improve their knowledge in this field. GEMMA BALM, SENIOR BRAND MANAGER, DIXONS CARPHONE

My mission in life is to drive up UK digital skills and empower the businesses we advise. Digital can be complex and sometimes overwhelming. This book focusses on what's critical to success. I've worked with Footprint Digital for many years and I'm thrilled that they've made their deep expertise accessi-ble. I'd recommend it to any of our clients. DEREK SCANLON, DIGITAL TRADE ADVISOR, DEPARTMENT FOR INTERNATIONAL TRADE

I loved "*Shoot the HiPPO: How to be a killer Digital Marketing Manager*" and was especially fascinated by Footprint's approach to Environment, Culture and Strategy. I would definitely recommend it to any online business seek-ing professional digital marketing support or anyone who is interested in enhancing their digital marketing skills. DARRELL HAYWARD, VICE PRESIDENT CONSULTING – APAC, FORRESTER RESEARCH

There is so much misinformation and poor advice around digital sustain-ability out there. Some of the courses and books I have read talk rubbish. This is different. Marketa and the team at Footprint have walked the walk and have real world experience in reducing the carbon footprint of web-sites. I love you guys and your philosophy and I'm excited to see digital sustainability featured in this book. ASIM HUSSAIN, GREEN CLOUD ADVOCACY LEAD AT MICROSOFT AND CO-ORGANISER OF CLIMATEACTION.TECH AND THE CLIMATE FIX PODCAST

As a senior lecturer of Digital Marketing, I have found this book fascinating. Alongside making the book thorough, the authors have also managed to make it approachable. It is the perfect bridge from the academic to the real world. The result is a book of great interest, for the most part easy to read and full of insights. I recommend it to all of my students. DR MAGED ALI, SENIOR LECTURER OF DIGITAL MARKETING LECTURER, ESSEX BUSINESS SCHOOL, UNIVERSITY OF ESSEX

Digital has always been fundamental to leadership. Be it in the public or private arena. This insightful book teaches lessons from the successes of the past, and spotlights the challenges and the opportunities for innovation as we move from the industrial age to the knowledge economy. DR PAURAV SHUKLA, PROFESSOR OF MARKETING, DEPARTMENT HEAD – DIGITAL & DATA DRIVEN MARKETING, SOUTHAMPTON BUSINESS SCHOOL, UNIVERSITY OF SOUTHAMPTON

What a great contribution to the field of Digital Marketing! I love Shoot the Hippo! This book offers a wealth of knowledge in an incredibly accessible and engaging manner. I will be recommending it to all my digital marketing students. DR FATEMA KAWAF, SENIOR LECTURER IN DIGITAL MARKETING, GREENWICH BUSINESS SCHOOL, UNIVERSITY OF GREENWICH.

I just finished reading Footprint Digital's new book "*Shoot the HiPPO: How to be a killer Digital Marketing Manager*" and I LOVE this book. I thought it was extremely easy to follow, it is a great tool. I love the tone of voice and the narration of the book. It was extremely laid back and relatable. Definitely get this book. 10 out of 10 recommended! JORDAN MITCHELL, MA, MS, DIGITAL MARKETING MANAGER, STONE NATURAL MEDICINE

Shoot the HiPPO is an essential resource for marketers that need to ramp up their digital marketing prowess. It is easy to follow and full of actionable insights that will help you to take your marketing from good, to great. Read this book if you want to learn from Footprint's decades of experience at the forefront of digital marketing. I highly recommend grabbing a copy. ANDY BARGERY FCIM, MARKETING CONSULTANT AND AGENCY ADVISOR, AGENCY SQUARED

As a digital marketing executive aspiring to be a digital marketing manager, "*Shoot the HiPPO*" tackles one of the most difficult challenges I have which is getting colleagues in the higher positions on side with digital marketing. I think Footprint do a great job in explaining and giving recommendations based on facts and figures rather than on gut feel. And the book really covers some key areas of Digital Marketing such as SEO, PPC, Websites and Digital Marketing. I therefore recommend any digital marketers to read this book. CHRISTOPHER TURNER, TECHNICAL MARKETING EXECUTIVE, KLIP-SPRINGER LTD.

"*Shoot the HiPPO*" is an act of massive generosity. It's an invitation from Footprint to sit down alongside them, share their experience and insights, and make them your own. They go out of their way to demystify the secrets of digital marketing with warmth, humour, and a great balance between technical knowhow and common sense. All their tips and suggestions are linked to broader business issues and decisions, so Digital Marketing

Managers can keep others onboard and make a real difference in their organisations. And, just like them, their words are fresh, real and approachable. Enjoy! SAM GUISE, BUSINESS WRITER, YOURSTORYMYWORDS

Overall, I really enjoyed the book and would highly suggest it to anyone in the field (or not in the field even)! Very informative and was not just your average informative marketing book. The anecdotes, quotes and exercises in between were captivating as it gave it character and broke up any dense areas. JULIE MORRISON, BA ADVERTISING MARKETING COMMUNICATIONS, GREENWICH UNIVERSITY, MARKETING ASSOCIATE AT ODIN ENTERPRISES, LLC

Thanks to you for the opportunity to read this "Shoot the HiPPO: How to be a killer Digital Marketing Manager". The book encapsulates the essence of Footprint and the author's passion for the media and enthusiasm in enabling others to achieve their best. I can appreciate how much work has gone into it and have found it a really useful & practical guide for digital marketing managers. SAMANTHA PEARCE, DIRECTOR, THE FINISHING POST DESIGN AND MARKETING CONSULTANTS

I really enjoyed this book. Good flow and easy to read and follow along. It is very relatable and I particularly like how the authors associate the topic to stories in their personal lives and other environments as well as in marketing. This helps make it easier to understand the concept and make it more memorable. I liked the head chef syndrome theory in chapter one and getting the right people in your team to do the right things, rather than trying to do it all yourself. ROCHELLE RHODES, SENIOR DIGITAL MARKETING EXECUTIVE – LONDON, ROBERT WALTERS

"Shoot the HiPPO" is probably the most entertaining marketing book I've ever read. It is a great combination of digital marketing theory and how to best execute digital marketing in the real world.

I can recommend reading "Shoot the HiPPO" to anyone who is interested in entering the field of digital marketing or wants to improve their skills and execute those in their company or at university. Super easy to understand and follow and great examples for execution. TINA GLAVANOVITZ, MARKETING DIRECTOR, IMPIBAG

I have woken up this morning and seen your YouTube video and heard your absolutely amazing news! Well done guys! I know we talked about the book a little while ago and know how much hard work has gone into making it a reality and seeing your enthusiasm about it is just infectious. I couldn't start the day without congratulating you all! ELIZABETH O'HANLON, DIGITAL MARKETING MANAGER, SCRUTTON BLAND

It's a God damn Bible for marketing and marketeers. I have been in marketing for over 25 years, worked with some of the best in my varied career and this book sums up beautifully, clearly and concisely the keys to unlocking and creating effective and successful marketing and marketing teams. Footprint Digital are the hidden treasure we all hope to find. I love their philosophy and the fact they practice what they preach! We searched long and hard for the right partners to deliver courses to hundreds of business leaders across our area and I have seen the impact their courses have had. You guys at Footprint have blown minds and expanded horizons and set expectations some didn't even know were possible. If I could recommend one thing for your business or if you are marketeer, no matter your time in the industry, it would be to "read this book", it should be made law! **SUE SIMMONS, EVENT COORDINATOR FOR SCALE UP NEW ANGLIA AND NEW ANGLIA GROWTH HUB**

It's great to see such an accessible and visionary book that not just helps readers harness the power of digital marketing, but inspires them to harness it for positive change! **TOM GREENWOOD, MANAGING DIRECTOR, WHOLEGRAIN DIGITAL**

"*Shoot the HiPPO*" is a fabulous read for anyone wanting to get up to speed with Conversion Rate Optimisation and User Experience testing. Tom's knowledge, expertise and deep understanding of the subject matter is as good as it gets. **DR PETER MOWFORTH, INDEZ LTD AND THE INSTITUTE OF ECOMMERCE**

This book is absolutely great. I expected nothing less from Footprint Digital their SEO, PPC & Conversion Rate expertise is second to none. The chapters discussing culture and sustainability are a real breath of fresh air. Whether it is how we work as a team or our impact on the environment we are together in this world and it is great to read a book that addresses how important this is. **WILL NEWLAND, DIRECTOR, SO BOLD**

Marketing is complex. It is so refreshing to find a book that lays out a digital marketing process in a fun and approachable way. You can waste so much time doing the wrong things. I recommend this book to Digital Marketing Managers that want to be more productive with the little time they have. **SARAH EDWARDS, DIRECTOR, MAKE IT CLEAR**

First and foremost, "*Shoot the HiPPO*" is an informative, practical book that takes a very human perspective on what it means to be an effective Digital Marketing Manager. This echoes through in the parallels it finds with nature – the human body, permaculture, fungal networks in forests, evolution – to explain a field that is decidedly not associated with nature. The chapter on sustainability further illustrates that any activity of any business ultimately takes place in a natural environment and that each of us can help to preserve it, even in the digital field. CHRISTIAAN MAATS, AWARD-WINNING DUTCH PRODUCT DESIGNER, ENTREPRENEUR, AND EDUCATOR

Refreshing, easy to read and surprisingly detailed in all the right places. I love the way you can jump straight to any chapter and get right up to speed in the latest thinking with some super relevant examples and insight. I found it hugely informative and a surprisingly good page turner! If you read this book, you'll never find yourself out of your depth! I love it!! JON EARNSHAW, FOUNDER & CHIEF PRODUCT EVANGELIST, PI-DATAMETRICS. VISITING LECTURER, UNIVERSITY OF HERTFORDSHIRE BUSINESS SCHOOL

Reading this book felt like every other interaction I've ever had with Tom and Tom – personable, full of enthusiasm, humour, good advice and encouragement. Who they are as people spills over into this book as they inspire you to try new things without fear of failure and spur you on to succeed in defining and achieving your goals.

In many senses "Shoot the HiPPO" is a manual for the modern marketer, full of exercises and checklists, whilst challenging you to ask the right questions and make data driven decisions. Frankly I'm worried that they've given too many of what should be their trade secrets and too much of their IP away in this book, but that is to the readers benefit! I wouldn't be surprised if "Shoot the HiPPO" is added to the reading lists of every marketing course and CIM qualification in short order!

Footprint Digital are my recommended agency in supporting clients with well researched digital marketing and SEO strategies. The team are knowledgeable, insightful, practical, responsible, and inspired. MELISSA WIGGINS, HEAD OF CLIENT STRATEGY, NETXTRA

I used to think I was doing a good job. I was cramming tasks into every minute of every day. I was super busy and if i'm honest a little burned out! "Shoot the HiPPO" helped me prioritise the important work and give things the focus they needed. It is such a better outlook and it has meant I deliver work I am proud of and I have become more productive and efficient with my time. ELEANOR HARRIS, MARKETING MANAGER, CBHC ACCOUNTANTS

The chapter on sustainability was such a welcome surprise. Who knew what an impact a website has on climate change?! I am now working through the recommendations to make sure that we reduce the carbon footprint of the site and work to become planet positive. It is such an important message and I feel pleased that I now have things I can do that make a difference. MUNTAZIR PANJWANI, DIRECTOR, VIBE AGENCY

I'm excited about people and businesses that try and make a positive difference in the world. When it comes to green tech so many organisations talk a good game but don't deliver. It's wonderful to see how this book can empower Digital Marketing Managers to make better choices and be the change they want to see in the world and positively influence those around them. ANN-SOPHIE BLANK, DIGITAL EXPERIENCE CONSULTANT AT IBM IX AND CLIMATE REALITY LEADER

"Shoot the HiPPO" translates the science of digital marketing in an authoritative and easily digestible narrative for new marketers and strategic leaders alike. Using relatable analogies this informative guide brings all components of digital marketing to life with practical guidance and engaging storytelling. The book introduces an open, honest and fresh approach as to how to navigate the jungle out there. This will no doubt be a well-thumbed reference guide for many. MARISA SLOPER, SENIOR MARKETING MANAGER, BENNETTS MOTORCYCLING SERVICES LIMITED

SHOOT THE HiPPO

How to be a killer Digital Marketing Manager

Tom Bowden and Tom Jepson

Published by

FOOTPRINT DIGITAL

First published 2020

By Footprint Digital Ltd.
1-3 Head Street, Colchester, Essex, CO1 1NX

© Tom Bowden and Tom Jepson 2020

Contributing authors Chris Green, Michael Scanlon, Marketa Benisek

Edited by Alexandra Eade, Kerry McCarthy & Sam Guise

Cover design by Andrew Sharman

Typeset by Euan Monaghan

Printed in Great Britain by IngramSpark

ISBN 978-1-8382781-9-9

For the sponges.

Your ideas, talent, and energy
mean everything to us.

Acknowledgements

All business journeys benefit from a healthy mix of assistance. Our business is no exception. Throughout this incredible journey we have learnt from others; in training, videos, seminars, conferences, books, websites, articles and a host of other mediums. Where possible, within these pages, we have sought permission to share the ideas that may not have originated in our own minds but have become part of our business philosophy. We have referenced, where applicable, the sources of this learning. If, for any reason, we have missed you and your contribution to our business journey, we offer you our sincere apologies and will endeavour to make this right in future editions of this book.

Our heartfelt thanks to everyone we have learnt from. Whether you know it or not, you are part of this amazing adventure.

Thank you to our co-authors Chris Green, Marketa Benisek and Michael Scanlon and for the significant contributions by Josef James. Thank you to our designer Andrew Sharman and our first readers, Bob Agnew, Lucy Agyrou, Shaakir Ahmed, Chris Ainsworth, Maged Ali, Rosie Baker, Gemma Balm, Andy Bargery, Kate Barrett, Taya Beleanina, Darren Bewley, Rachael Bilby, Sophie Braybrooke, James Coates, Alia Coster, Melissa Critchley, Nora Deme, Justine Duncan, Alexandra Eade, Eleanor Elam, Lewis Francis, Erica Gilson, Tina Glavanovitz, Ben Green, Khrieu Healy, Joanna Hetzel, Craig Hindmarsh, Alan Hoggard, Erik Jacobi, Emma Jennings, Fatema Kawaf, Anca Lazar, Nick Looby, Reuben Marshall, Rita Matias, Ben Matthews, Rebecca McKay, Hannah Meadows, Jordan Mitchell, Robin Moore, Julie Morrison, Elle Moss, Elizabeth O'Hanlon, Samantha Pearce, Raffaele Pieroni, Rochelle Rhodes, Dave Roscoe, Thomas Rowson, Paurav Shukla, Sue Simmons, Marisa Sloper, Chris Turner, Simon Welling, Kevin Wiles and Rich Wood.

We would like to extend a special thanks to our editing team Alexandra Eade, Kerry McCarthy and Sam Guise. George Orwell said, *"Writing a book is a horrible, exhausting struggle, like a long bout of some painful illness."*[1] Without your unrelenting support we would have succumbed and would not have a book to show for it.

---

1   Orwell, G. (1946) *Why I Write*. London, Penguin Books.

Full disclosure message regarding the tools, resources and software that we refer to in these pages.

During the years we have been in business we have amassed a wealth of knowledge and experience regarding the tools, software, and resources that have assisted us in all aspects of our day to day activities. Throughout the book we will refer to a number of resources for you to explore. We have no commercial involvement in any of the resources we suggest and will not benefit financially from their reference. We mention these, purely for your benefit, as we have found them personally useful over the years.

All profits go to providing opportunities for young people in Malawi.

Everyone deserves the opportunity to learn, play and grow. Building Malawi (www.buildingmalawi. com) provides opportunities for young Malawians through the construction of schools, libraries and sports facilities.

We are giving all the profits from *Shoot the HiPPO: How to be a killer Digital Marketing Manager* to Building Malawi (Registered Charity Number: 1145965). By purchasing this book, you are helping to provide pathways out of poverty for some of the poorest people in the world.

Thank you.

"Do the difficult things while they are easy and do the great things while they are small. A journey of a thousand miles must begin with a single step." **LAO TZU**

Contents

Preface

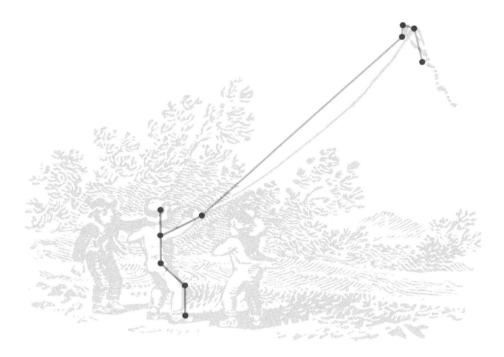

We set up Footprint Digital because we didn't want to 'keep clients quiet'. We wanted to do good work and be the best we could be; to be proud of what we do and to push ourselves to grow.

We strive each day to provide the perfect combination of technical expertise and collaborative human relationships to help people achieve things they never thought possible; to deliver exceptional digital marketing services that help people join the dots and make more money online.

We knew that nothing great was ever achieved without enthusiasm, and nothing great would be achieved alone. Our big-bang moment occurred when leading technicians, analysts, and marketers decided to join forces.

We knew then that we had to create an environment where talented people would be supported to do the best work of their careers and grow, both personally and professionally.

We are committed to providing opportunities to people at the start of their careers, to developing raw talent and being a safe proving ground where people can try things, share, and educate.

We are Footprint Digital.

— Footprint Digital's Little Pink Book (2019)

How to read this book

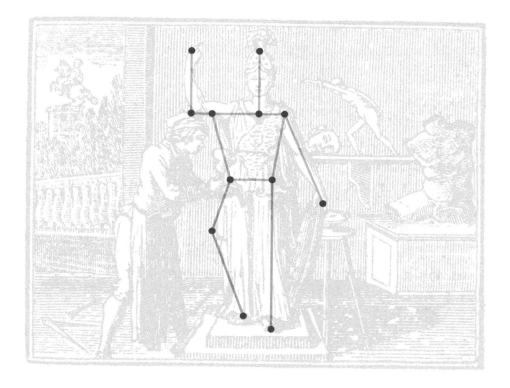

Crafting a winning digital marketing strategy is a bit like the sculpting of Michelangelo's David. We begin with a huge block of marble hewn from a quarry and work on a daily basis to refine and perfect a masterpiece. We invite you to grab a chisel.

This book was written to help Digital Marketing Managers find their way in the often confusing and overwhelming digital space. The book is formed in large part from a Digital Marketing Manager course that we have taught for the past five years (2015-19). It sets out to take away the noise around digital and help you join the dots across this complex and varied discipline.

The range of topics that we could have covered in this book is vast and the depth we could have gone into is great. To remain focused, and just present the things that we believe are really important, we asked ourselves the following question to decide what to include:

> "If I only had two days to teach each topic, what would I focus on to help a Digital Marketing Manager do their job well?"

We also kept the following rules in mind:

1. All of the lessons must be practical as *"a strategy is only real when it is realised"*.
2. The concepts must be universal and relevant to any business.
3. The book must be to the point and focus only on the most important information.

We've done our best to keep this book as simple and jargon-free as possible. Each of the chapters start with a story that brings the broad concept of the chapter to life. The main part of the chapter is a theoretical lesson. The chapters also include a range of practical activities which we hope will help bring the lessons to life and make them more applicable to your business.

The book can be read in different ways. It is structured in a logical order and, unlike many business books, the stories included in each chapter make it readable from end to end. You can also use it to dip into topics that you are particularly interested in. We also hope that you will return to it as a point of reference to help structure your thoughts.

The first few chapters outline the challenge faced by Digital Marketing Managers and some of the things that we believe are the foundation of success in the role. The latter chapters are more tactical and deliver detail on some of the core digital marketing channels.

This book shares methods that we have found effective over the years. We invite you to feel emboldened and expand upon these foundations. There is no red tape to stop you improving the way the work is done.

We hope that *"SHOOT THE HIPPO: How to be a killer Digital Marketing Manager"* will become part of your day-to-day life, your 'living book' with page corners folded, notes scribbled throughout, and full of makeshift bookmarks.

We hope you find it useful.

— Tom Bowden and Tom Jepson

Reasons for this book

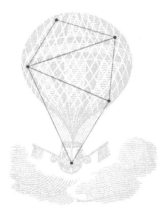

We believe that there is nothing you can't achieve

> *"The greatest crime in the world is not developing your potential. When you do what you do best, you are helping not only yourself, but the world."* **ROGER WILLIAMS**

In the early days of Footprint Digital, founder Tom Bowden travelled to Morocco with his wife to climb Mount Toubkal in the Atlas mountain range. After they took their final purposeful steps to the peak of the 4,167m mountain they sat down, unclipped their icy crampons and exhaled big plumes of breath into the clear, cold air. A metallic frame marked the summit. Ragged shards of cloth and national flags were tied to it and these rippled noisily in the wind. They stared down into the silent broad expanse of snow capped mountains in the valley below. They had done it.

One by one fellow climbers joined them. Each took a moment to gather themselves. Some paused to lean on one knee as if to mutter a prayer. Some stood tall, arms out, chin to the sky and heaved in lungfuls of air. Others, collapsing under exhaustion, slumped to their bottoms and leant against their rucksacks like exhausted toddlers with their legs splayed out in front of them. Slowly each recovered and raised their heads to take in the incredible view.

Once they had enjoyed their personal moment of triumph, they turned to congratulate one another. A group formed and everyone chatted excitedly.

Within the cluster was Bouchra Baibanou. A hush came over the crowd as she explained that she wanted to be the first Moroccan woman to climb *The Seven Summits* (the mountaineering challenge to climb the highest mountains of each of the seven continents).

Middle-aged, female and without an abundance of wealth, half of the group dismissed her immediately. They claimed that she was *"too old"*, that she didn't have enough money and *"could women manage to climb mountains like Everest?"*. The moment of silence that followed those words echoed down the valley like a crack racing through ice.

Tom's wife's eyes darted at the chauvinist. Tom felt a flush of warmth in his face. This was his moment to issue a damning and witty defence that would gallantly put the sceptic in his place. Indeed, a better man might even have punched him, but, being not very adept at that kind of thing, Tom instead took the approach of a cowardly playground friend. He waited for the hubbub to calm down and for the bully to retreat. Tom's chivalry returned as soon as the doubter became a tiny dot against the snow hundreds of metres below.

Alone with Bouchra they took a moment to tell her how cool they thought she was. *"There is nothing you can't achieve,"* they said. Of course, she didn't need to be told, but, she took the statement with the warmth by which it was intended and smiled a large sparkly eyed good-natured smile that was as memorable as their day's achievement would be. At that moment they made a commitment to support her.

At the time the 'agency' was just two people working from a kitchen. There wasn't enough money to go around. Yet, in spite of this, and buoyed by Bouchra's enduring spirit, some money was found and Footprint Digital was proud to support Bouchra with a small financial contribution.

Bouchra had already reached the summit of Kilimanjaro (March 2011), Mont Blanc (June 2012), L'Aconcagua (January 2014), and Denali (June 2014). In the short few years after they met, Bouchra climbed Puncak Jaya (November 2015), Everest (April 2017) and, true to her word, completed the seven summits with Mount Vinson in 2018.

Not bad for someone who had been dismissed by the group as *"too old"*, *"too poor,"* and female.

We are proud to have supported Bouchra. Knowing that she achieved her dream gives us warm tingly feelings of joy. Our financial contribution barely made a dent on the whole, but, as she later explained what meant more to her were our voices of encouragement. She knew she had people in her corner. People that were there for her. Because, when you're taking on a monumental challenge, that is the most important thing.

We also learned a lot through the experience. It helped us see that the role of catalyst is our core purpose in the world. We exist to encourage and support people as they take on adventures in their life. We take great pleasure in enabling others to realise their brilliance, fulfil their promise and achieve greatness.

Bouchra Baibanou is a real inspiration to us. We love her optimism and her refusal to give in to the barriers in her way. We're motivated by people that also believe that, *"there is nothing that you can't achieve"*. It is those people we want to work with. We look for that belief in our team, our partners, our suppliers, and our clients. We now look for it in you.

"SHOOT THE HIPPO: How to be a killer Digital Marketing Manager" is written to remind you that there is nothing that you can't achieve and enable you to achieve greatness.

Bridge the gap from the academic to the real world

> *"I can't learn anything from you, I can't read in some f*ckin' book."*
> **ROBIN WILLIAMS AS SEAN MAGUIRE IN GOOD WILL HUNTING (1997)**

A university lecturer asked us if we'd come and deliver a lecture to her masters course. *"They've studied marketing for the last three years and are extremely well-versed in the theories and principles of marketing,"* she said. *"But, what is it like in the real world?"*. We explained to the students that all you have to do to be successful at marketing is *measure what you do* and then *test it*. That is, try some things, measure if it works and try some other things based on what you learned. Approaching all marketing activities with this outlook of continuous improvement is the key to success. Only half-joking, we suggested that, equipped with this wisdom, they needn't to worry about the rest of their academic course.

To demonstrate this philosophy, we created an interactive quiz showcasing the results from some tests we've run over the years. We'll come back to this in more detail in our chapter on CRO, but for now here are some of the potentially controversial and counter-intuitive results:

- Beautiful pages with limited information do not convert as well as ugly pages that use the right language.

- Slick sales language does not convert as well as messaging that addresses concerns a customer has about buying something (something we call the customer anxieties).
- Bright white contact forms do not convert as well as forms with lots of information and coloured form fields.

Conventions are so routinely torn up through testing that the more we test the less we feel we know. In the decision making process, human instinct often does not serve us well. Our own biases are our enemy and, unfortunately, it is almost impossible to escape them. Customers never fail to amaze us with what they prefer.

There is no substitute for the experience gained through this kind of real world *live* work. Universities expertly equip their students with marketing theory, but, without access to active clients it is far harder for lecturers to give students the experience of what it looks like, smells like, or tastes like in the real world. This is a problem. A problem elegantly articulated in the *"Good Will Hunting"* quote[1].

This book sets out to show how to apply academic theory in the real world. We want to equip these brilliant young minds with practical tools for success, to support marketers to make fact-based decisions and not be swayed by personal opinions, and enable them to bring their knowledge and enthusiasm into the world. So you can try things, deliver better results and have lots more fun.

"SHOOT THE HIPPO: How to be a killer Digital Marketing Manager" is for anyone that is looking to bridge the gap from academia to the real world. It will help you create campaigns that are expansive and fun by understanding how to measure what you do and test your marketing activities.

Have the freedom to do the best work of your career

> *"I have been impressed with the urgency of doing. Knowing is not enough; we must apply. Being willing is not enough; we must do."*
> **LEONARDO DA VINCI**

We started our careers at a company reckless enough to throw us in at the deep end. This was a stroke of luck. From day one we were producing work for large, demanding corporate clients and we were responsible for

---

1   Bender, L. et al. (1997) *Good Will Hunting.* Buena Vista Home Entertainment.

the results we achieved. We didn't have specialist training and didn't really know what we were doing. It should have been terrifying, but we didn't know any different. It was through this weee I'm-freewheeling-down-the-hill-with-the-stabilisers-off freedom that we really learned our trade.

People in that company made ground breaking discoveries about how search engines worked. The company quickly became an industry leader and the money followed. It wasn't all a utopia. With freedom comes waste and errors and when the agency peaked at seventy employees the lack of structure became its undoing. Clearly there is a middle ground. But, as an enthusiastic young recruit it was a great environment in which to learn.

Very few organisations provide anything like the opportunity we were given. A young fiery graduate that is full of raw brilliance is likely to get plonked in a corner, and encouraged to do the equivalent of filing for years, before they are given any level of freedom to express themselves. Years later when their moment arrives enthusiasm has long since drained away. Cue drab lifeless work. This is a massive shame for both the business and the individual.

We hope this book can help address this challenge. At Footprint Digital we strive to build a team that says: *"I am proud of what I do, and I am supported to do the best work of my career"*. We have tried to create a culture in which people can learn, play, and grow. We're able to operate this way due to the great faith we have in our team. Or, rather, due to the confidence that our team members exhibit. Their ability and authority shines through. We in turn loosen the shackles to the point that they are almost entirely auton-omous. If you regularly get results management will trust you. Confidence creates trust which allows for freedom. We hope this book will give you puff-out-your-chest levels of confidence so that your boss will fast track your filing years.

This book is only useful if you apply the ideas in it. Results only occur when you change things. *"A strategy is only real when realised"* is the credo that we live by. No matter how sophisticated your plan may be, the only thing that matters is what gets applied. We aim to have clients, shareholders, bosses, and colleagues who say: *"Thank you for helping us achieve things we didn't think were possible"*. The reality of being a Digital Marketing Man-ager is that you are expected to make the impossible possible. This can only be achieved through bold action. We have made this book practical in the hope that it inspires bravery within you.

"SHOOT THE HIPPO: How to be a killer Digital Marketing Manager" is a prac-tical, to-the-point guide to help you take action and apply theory to get results in the real world.

It is time to understand how one person can fulfil the creative, analytical, technical, tactical, and strategic expertise required for online success and bring your talents to the world.

Chapter 1: Shoot the HiPPO

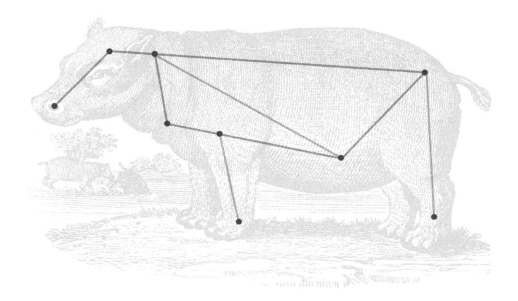

A true hippo story

A friend of Tom Bowden runs a wonderful charity in Malawi. They were work-ing in a small village next to a reservoir where an aggressive hippo lived. The hippo had killed a number of people in its long life and, fearing for the safety of the local children that were soon to attend school there, he decided that the organisation would pay to have the hippo relocated. He met with the Malawian minister for wildlife and explained the predicament. He suggested that the hippo be moved to a sanctuary or game park or some such lovely retirement home. The minister looked him in the eye, shrugged and said "Just shoot the hippo, it will save us all the bother". He then turned around to continue his work developing policy. My friend left in disbelief.

Please don't worry, the hippo in this story was unharmed. The charity direc-tor did not take the advice and instead *"took the bother"* and relocated the hippo to a wildlife sanctuary. Many years ago, when I was first told this story, I was appalled. How could the minister be so heartless? How could he be so cruel?

As I aged and became jaded by the experience of being a Digital Marketing Manager I recognised that there was wisdom in the advice of the callous government minister and came to better understand the minister's no non-sense approach. There have been countless times, when sat in meetings, that the phrase *"Just shoot the HiPPO"* has rung loud and clear in my head. It has stuck with me and become a wayfinding beacon to which I return to when projects have become strung out and lost.

What have I got against HiPPOs?

Hippos are irritable, territorial and aggressive. Despite being vegetarians and mainly eating grass, hippos are responsible for more deaths in Africa than any other mammal. In spite of these characteristics (and perhaps because I share some of them!) I find hippos to be quite lovely, majestic creatures, worthy of our love and adoration. It is another type of HiPPO that I take objection to…

In 2014, global online retail sales reached $1.3 trillion annually. However, almost 96% of website visits end with no consumer purchase. This low con-version rate worsens when consumers switch to mobile devices[2]. This data is over five years old, but there is little data to suggest this has changed significantly since.

So, why are there still so many terrible websites? The technology available to us is better than ever, yet we consistently fail to create websites that are intuitive for humans. The key to understanding why lies in another question: *Who should decide what your website looks like?* Should it be your designer, developer, marketing team or strategist? Of course the answer should be 'your customers'. More often than not the decision is made by:

The Highest Paid Person's Opinion. The HiPPO.

This term, first coined by the brilliant data guru and Google Analytics evan-gelist Avinash Kaushik[3] is the HiPPO I object to.

Let's be clear. I do not have an issue with the individual. In successful proj-ects there needs to be a decisive lead. Decisions need to be made. The issue lies in *how* these decisions are made, not *who* makes them. Too often these decisions are made by *opinion, not data*. Gut feel, not facts.

---

2   McDowell et al. (2016) An examination of retail website design and conversion rate. *Journal of Business Research*, Volume 69, Issue 11, Pp 4837-4842.
3   Kaushik, A. (2006) *Seven Steps to Creating a Data Driven Decision Making Culture. Occam's Razor.* [online] Available at: https://www.kaushik.net/avinash/seven-steps-to-creating-a-data-driven-decision-making-culture/ [Accessed 28 April 2020]

We have everything at hand to make informed decisions and are equipped with incredible tools that allow us to understand what customers really want. Avinash Kaushik also put it beautifully when he said, *"We have access to more data than God wants anyone to have"*. It is the reliance on gut feel or personal preference, decisions that rely on emotion instead of data, that we take issue with. The *opinion*, not the individual.

Think of the times that the Highest Paid Person's Opinion has wreaked havoc in business. How many hours, days, and weeks of frustration could have been saved if decisions around design were led by customer data? How much money would the world be making online if websites were built in response to what customers want rather than internal opinion? How much more enjoyable would it be to create them?

Businesses that do make informed decisions are always more success-ful than those that don't. Therefore we have made it our mission to help those individuals and, by association, their organisations become data-led (use data to inform their decision making). Doing so will improve business results, remove clashes brought about by differing opinions and, best of all, make life better for those that use the resulting products.

Why do we let HiPPOs run around causing chaos? Why do we let them stifle progress? We have the knowledge and power to prevent this. We can't stand aside and let this continue. We must tackle it. Our response is meta-phorically to: *Shoot the HiPPO*.

Informed rebellion starts with you

> *"Every revolution begins with a single act of defiance."*
> **MAHATMA GANDHI**

Chances are you may have read the HiPPO concept and experienced that moment of creeping dread where you realise that, on occasion, you have been the HiPPO. You have put forward strong opinions and made gut deci-sions without using data or testing your hypotheses. The truth is we all do it all of the time.

So, as much as you will battle the obstacles around you, we hope that your journey of a thousand miles will start with a single introspective step. That your first act of defiance will be to overcome your own natural inclination to make opinion-based decisions.

We hope you will feel galvanized to go against the standard way of doing things and approach your work with a new spirit of informed rebellion. It starts with you.

Become a HiPPO hunter

Are you fed up of having to justify every single landing page, ad text, design, or user experience recommendation you make? Are you sick and tired of the HiPPO telling you that it should be pink / aligned centrally / emphasised more / include an image of Cliff Richard because the HiPPO's Grandma thought it would be a good idea? Are you mad that changes are made without being tested?

Through this book we aim to empower you to make better decisions, so you can focus on the right marketing mix for your business, make your website easy to use, AND provide an enjoyable experience for the user. We also offer lots of methodologies to help you understand your organisation's environment and influence its culture, so that you can achieve buy-in from the entire team, but especially the HiPPO.

The challenge of overcoming HiPPO-led decision making is twofold. As Digital Marketing Managers we must know how to:

- Use data to make better informed decisions.
- Influence the environment and culture around us so that these informed decisions are adopted and applied.

This book will show you how to:

- Analyse performance.
- Locate areas for improvement.
- Create change.

Your ultimate aim is to use data to *Shoot the HiPPO.*

Activity – Take the HiPPO-Critic Oath.

Don't let the HiPPO prevent progress. Follow the fundamental rules for shooting HiPPOs:

- I vow to **arm myself with every tool at my disposal.**
- I promise to **use customer insights to make decisions.**
- I promise to **present findings in the simplest way possible** (bullet points rule!).
- I promise to use the insights to **make changes.**
- I will **NEVER let the HiPPO dictate what we do.**

Signed:

_____

A new recruit in the war against HiPPOs.

Chapter 2: The Head Chef syndrome

> *"Alice laughed: "There's no use trying," she said; "one can't believe impossible things." "I daresay you haven't had much practice," said the Queen. "When I was younger, I always did it for half an hour a day. Why, sometimes I've believed as many as six impossible things before breakfast."* **LEWIS CARROLL**

Tom Bowden and his wife bought a new kitchen. In that moment, they decided that it would be a good idea to have people over for dinner to celebrate this monumental stride into adulthood. It will be lovely, they thought. We'll be the best hosts...

The day arrived. Before they knew it, they were running out of time. The inner countdown clock was rapidly ticking. Blind panic had set in. It was just moments before everyone was due to turn up. Tom was running around the house. Hide the clutter, lay the table, change a lightbulb, stop the pots boiling over, be quiet dog! Wipe the worktop, oh no, did we get enough booze? And, just as his wife stepped into the shower, the doorbell rang. Why are people early?!

The evening continued in a similar state of distraction as they played host, chef, waiter, bartender and cleaner – more time spent thinking about the cooking than in the moment with their friends. When they collapsed on the sofa at the end of the night, they realised that they didn't get to be part of their own dinner party. They sat and wondered where it all went wrong.

This familiar domestic scenario poses an interesting business challenge. Our first question? How on earth do the big restaurants do it? I was stressed out by ten people. What's it like if you have to feed 50, 100, 200 a night? Thinking about this business challenge gives you a taste of how we are going to redefine the real-world role of a Digital Marketing Manager. The person who needs to achieve the impossible.

What makes a restaurant great?

Great restaurants make sure they are clear about who they exist to serve and what their customers should expect before they even get to the restaurant. They are clear about what they are better at than other restaurants. We call this *positioning*. Great restaurants also have fantastic *products* and clearly defined menus.

Another defining feature of great restaurants is that they are brilliant at resourcing the right specialist team members to bring the entire dining experience together. It isn't one person playing Head Chef, host, waiter, bartender, cleaner, sous-chef, pastry chef, saucier, and pot wash.

Much like running a restaurant, Digital Marketing is an activity that requires specialist multidisciplinary team members to work together. It is a complex challenge. To illustrate how problematic it is, we developed the following model. It shows the wide range of activities a business needs to think about to drive new customers to their website.

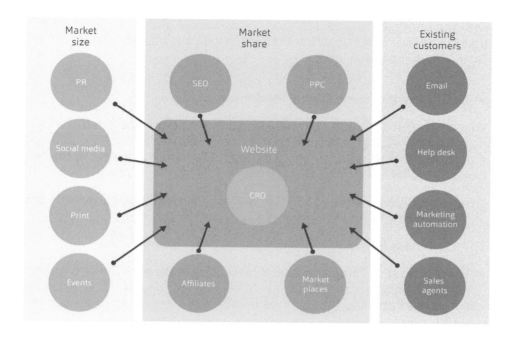

This model shows the need for the business to have clarity around their:

- **Vision** – where are we going?
- **Positioning** – where do we sit in the market?
- **Targeting** – who do we exist to serve?
- **Segmentation** – who are the customer groups we are targeting and why?
- **Product** – what do we sell?

The business then needs to think about:

- **Marketing Distribution** – which channels will we use to communicate?
- **Data Analysis** – how will we measure performance?

Beyond this the business will choose a range of activities or methods of interacting with clients. In terms of strategy these could be categorised as:

- **Market size activities** – those that increase the size of the market.
- **Market share activities** – those that win work from an existing market.
- **Existing customer activities** – those that engage and re-engage the customers you already have a relationship with to maintain loyalty.

It is easy to see that this is too much work for one person. Even for the most experienced Digital Marketer, covering all of these activities cannot be done with the depth, time, and attention they deserve. Yet our research shows that this is exactly what businesses, perhaps your bosses, expect of their Digital Marketing Managers.

Head Chef syndrome in Digital Marketing

We call the placing of too many tasks on a single person *the Head Chef syndrome*. Chances are that you've seen it or experienced it. But how common a problem is it? What does being a Digital Marketing Manager in the real world look like?

To answer this we looked at 100 Digital Marketing Manager job adverts and analysed the tasks and skills defined in the job descriptions.

This is what we found:

- **There is no such thing as a Digital Marketing Manager** – There is no consistent definition of what a Digital Marketing Manager is. There is a huge difference between roles and responsibilities listed in job descriptions.
- **Within the role there is a conflict of skill sets** – Job descriptions often expect candidates to exhibit competencies and skills that, whilst not mutually exclusive, are often difficult to find in one person. Candidates may be expected to be both strategic and tactical, to be great technically and in communication. To be creative and analytical.
- **There is confusion between marketing and sales** – Many job descriptions include a range of tasks that should sit in a sales role, such as expecting marketers to sell and attend networking events.

Take a look at this list we compiled. Here we show a selection of some of the common tasks that were typically included in the Digital Marketing Manager job role. Whilst the path to becoming a Digital Marketing Manager is often not linear, some of these skills may be picked up as a Digital Marketing Executive or Officer which are entry level positions; however, some of them are not marketing skills at all. The tasks require a broad range of skills, many of which are difficult to find in one person. To demonstrate this, we've added a column for the category we would put the task in, and another column for the skill needed to fulfil it.

Task	Category	Skill
Networking with a range of stakeholders;	Networking	Interpersonal
Working closely with third party companies to implement campaigns;	Manage agencies	Management
Communicating directly with the end consumer;	Sales	Sales
Managing Social media activity. Twitter, Facebook, Instagram, LinkedIn etc.	Social media	Social media
Developing and managing the production of marketing materials, including leaflets, posters, flyers, newsletters, e-newsletters;	Marketing materials	Creativity
Updating the company's website and presenting the analytics internally;	Website updates	Coding
Using software to design marketing materials;	Design	Design
Writing and proofreading copy;	Proofing Content	Copywriting
Liaising and managing designers and printers;	Manage agencies	Management
Organising photo shoots;	Manage agencies	Management
Planning the effective distribution of marketing materials;	Strategy	Strategy
Maintaining and updating customer databases;	Database	Organisation
Organising and attending events: conferences, seminars, and exhibitions;	Events	Events planning
Conducting market research, customer questionnaires and focus groups;	Market Research	Research
Developing marketing plans and strategies;	Strategy	Strategic planning
Managing the marketing budget;	Budget	Financial
Evaluating marketing campaigns;	Reporting	Understanding and relaying results
Monitoring and reporting on competitor activity;	Competitor Research	Research
Supporting the business development team and other colleagues.	Sales	Direct sales and closing leads

It's unrealistic for one person to have a significant depth of knowledge in all of these areas. Let alone deliver all of the work in each discipline. Imagine being asked to complete all of these tasks and being expected to have all of those skills. How many people do you know who are experts at graphic design, copywriting, and budgeting? Even seasoned Digital Marketers would struggle to demonstrate this range of skills. Yet, typically, businesses try to fill these roles with people in the early stages of their career in the salary bracket of £18,000-32,000. A rare few may be able to deliver. But, to be effective across all of these tasks, with the time allocated to a single person's role, is impossible.

Businesses are unwittingly setting up their Digital Marketing Managers *and* their businesses to fail

It seems absurd that any business would expect someone to be capable of all of this. But, that is exactly what is happening. The result is that the Digital Marketing Manager cannot do a good job, and the business does not achieve the results it expects.

The role has a high churn rate. The Digital Marketing Manager often leaves the company feeling unfulfilled, or is relieved of their position. They are then replaced with another who is burdened with the same impossible challenge. And on it goes.

The research shows:

- Digital Marketing Managers are given roles that are impossible to do well.
- There are not enough qualified people to meet the demand for Digital Marketing Managers.
- Unrealistic expectations are setting up employees, and businesses, to fail.

The expectations put upon this role are unrealistic, unsustainable, and damaging to both the employee and the business. Things need to change. It's time to redefine the role of a Digital Marketing Manager.

Redefining the role

Let's take another look at the unrealistically long, and diverse, list of capabilities that employers expect from someone taking on a Digital Marketing Manager job role. This time we have broken it down into the following categories:

Fundamental to the role	Part of the role	Not part of the role
• Strategy • Reporting • Finance/Budget • Management	• Marketing materials • Events • Storytelling • Creativity • Copywriting • Market research	• Networking • Sales • Social media • Website updates • PPC • Database • SEO

The responsibilities shown above as *Fundamental to the role* take priority, they are non-negotiable. Those that are *Part of the role* are desirable and if you find someone with these strings to their bow, snap them up. Those shown as *Not part of the role* require specialist support. Breaking the role out and finding specialists for parts of the campaign will yield far greater results.

To illustrate what this might look like we stripped away the unnecessary skills, leaving us with only the essentials:

Task	Skill
Input on product development	Management
Agency appointment and management	Management
Manage production of marketing materials	Management
Understanding where the company sits in the market	Research
Developing brand stories	Research
Overseeing development of strategic marketing plan	Strategy
Carrying out strategic marketing plan	Strategy
Analysis, measurement and reporting	Reporting
Budget management	Finance

By removing tasks such as sales, coding, or database management from the role the Digital Marketing Manager can focus their attention on their main priority: ensuring that the strategy is being executed effectively.

Let the chef be a chef

The most successful Digital Marketing Managers are generalists. They know a little about all the component parts of an effective campaign and have a great understanding of how each discipline can benefit the whole. They make sure that the business has a clear understanding of the brand goals, the brand messaging, and the ideal customers for the business. The Digital Marketing Manager then joins the dots. They build a team with the right specialists in the right roles to make this happen smoothly, successfully, and better than it ever has before.

Let the chef be the chef. That in itself is a challenging role. Then look at how to resource the tasks that fall out of the scope of that role.

The right people doing the right things

If you want your Digital Marketing Strategy to succeed you need to get the right people doing the right things. With your Head Chef overseeing, managing, coordinating, and joining the dots there is the need for team members with specialist skills to fulfil the remaining tasks. To deliver an exceptional meal a Head Chef will lean on specialists such as pastry chefs, sauciers or expediters (the person that makes sure meals are perfectly presented before they leave the kitchen).

For your marketing *pièce de résistance* you will need to resource specialists in disciplines such as SEO, PPC, CRO, analytics, design, video, code, and copywriting. This will mean that all of the work can get done. As the remaining tactical tasks are completed by specialists we may also assume that they will be of a higher standard that if fulfilled by the Digital Marketing Manager.

Resourcing this range of capabilities is a challenge. If you are a large company with a big pot of money the solution is easy. But smaller organisations need to achieve the long term benefits without the painful initial outlay.

There are two responses to this challenge:

1. Recognise the long term value of getting this right and find more money.
2. Be selective with what you choose to focus on first and build a team of specialist agency or freelance partners that you can scale up or down depending on the volume of support you need at any given time.

Footprint Digital's outsourced Digital Marketing Managers

At Footprint Digital we equip businesses with bold digital marketing strategies that position them as market leaders. You don't hire a full time accountant to complete your year end accounts, instead you outsource it to a chartered accountant at a rate proportional to the work required. In the same way you can hire one of our experienced team members to execute the marketing strategy and scale this up or down dependent on the volume of work required.

Our Digital Marketing Managers have comprehensive knowledge of a broad range of marketing disciplines. The key thing is they are not expected to carry out every aspect of every task. Their job is to oversee, manage, coordinate, and join the dots.

They are not dissimilar to the Head Chef who can budget for two hundred meals, organise a team to ensure stock levels are right and make sure that the plates are clean, warm and ready for a precisely timed dish of five parts.

Our Digital Marketing Managers:

- Have excellent management and financial skills to oversee any external marketing agencies and the work they produce.
- Manage the budget of marketing plans and are expected to provide a marketing perspective on new products.
- Are outstanding researchers and strategists, so they can manage the development and roll out of a marketing plan.
- Use research – a vitally important skill – to successfully shape campaigns.
- Have the strategic ability essential for seeing the big picture, even when getting into the nitty gritty.
- Can review and analyse the success or failure of a digital marketing campaign.
- Utilise strong reporting skills to not only judge the success of a campaign, but also to examine the granular data and find out the reasons *why* – usually using software like Google Analytics.

"SHOOT THE HIPPO: How to be a killer Digital Marketing Manager" is a practical guide to empower you to do all of these things.

So, what should it feel like to be a Digital Marketing Manager?

For the individuals that will lead this Digital Marketing revolution there are a few qualities that we believe will be the new currency.

- **Be a sponge** – be a sponge, not a stone. Knowledge is not power, the pursuit of understanding is. Whatever position you hold, be open and receptive to change. Absorb everything that you can, never stop learning and share what you learn on the way.
- **Shoot the HiPPO** – use data to measure and test your own work so that you can become empowered to try things by securing the full support of those higher up in the organisational hierarchy.
- **Be more human** – use technology to make businesses more approachable, more human, and to improve experiences for customers.
- **Help connect the dots** – observe the whole and join the dots across everything.

- **Grab a chisel** – craft a winning culture. Do not shy away from the challenge of shaping your environment.
- **Don't be an island** – digital success is dependent on a team. Get everyone engaged and empower others.

If you are strategic, put the right team in place and measure and test everything you do, then there is nothing that you can't achieve.

The moral of this chapter? A great Head Chef wouldn't run around the kitchen blindly chucking in ingredients whilst simultaneously washing pans and doing the wages. A Digital Marketing Manager shouldn't be made to take this approach either. You can't cook a delicious meal if you don't have a great menu, the right team and the time to put it together on the plate. You can't serve a satisfying digital marketing campaign without knowing how to combine all of the right ingredients.

Better management has the potential to give birth to great new things

For my wife's birthday last year, I did things differently. I made her a cake (which I was very proud of), but that's where my involvement ended. In a moment of genius I believed in the impossible – that we could throw a party and enjoy the experience. I practised what I now preach and outsourced the catering. A wonderful chef came in and took care of the food preparation. Thanks to her we could relax, enjoy the company of our guests, and we all had a lovely night.

Nine months later, we had a little baby boy.

Imagine if, in your business, you were relaxed, engaged, and open to doing things differently. What new adventure could you bring into the world?

> **Activity – Rewrite your job role and define the tasks that you need specialist support with**
>
> Which are best suited for a Digital Marketing Manager?
>
> Which would need to be given to an expert/specialist?

Chapter 3: Go with the flow

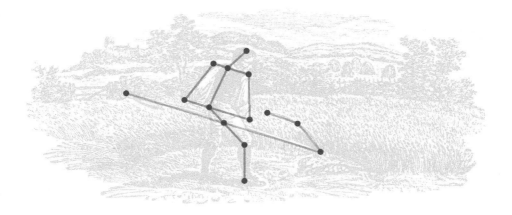

> "Let reality be reality. Let things flow naturally forward in whatever way they like. From wonder into wonder existence opens." **LAO TZU**

What is the natural pattern?

Masanobu Fukuoka (1913-2008), author of The One Straw Revolution[4], was the eldest son of a rice farmer. He lived on the Japanese island of Shikoku. As a result of being brought to the brink of death by acute pneumonia he experienced an epiphany: "Humanity knows nothing at all. There is no intrinsic value in anything, and every action is futile, meaningless effort". Having come to this realisation he returned from his scientific and academic work on plant pathology to labour in the fields on his family farm.

Fukuoka took time to observe the "natural pattern". He discarded the complexities of modern farming and instead of "adding things to nature" he developed a method of 'farming by subtraction'. He wouldn't till the land or use compost and instead of flooding his rice field and adding fertilisers, he let weeds grow. This approach cooperated with nature rather than trying to "improve" upon nature by conquest. He called this style "do nothing farming". He did all that he could to minimise artificial tasks to build a harmonious relationship with nature.

---

4   Masanobu, F. (1978) *The One Straw Revolution.* New York, New York Review Books Classics.

Despite his neighbours believing him to be mad, this method, latterly known as permaculture, was extremely effective and the yields of his farm far exceeded those achieved by agribusiness.

Nothing goes to waste in nature

Masanobu Fukuoka was not against work, he was against *unnecessary* work. The principle lesson of *Permaculture* is that successful agriculture doesn't require arduous labour, what it needs is awareness, observation, connection, and persistence.

If one was to observe the makeup of a forest you will see this in action. You will note the layers of the forest. Root crops can grow alongside flowers, shrubs and trees of various sizes, with each plant providing nutrients for each other. The leaves that fall become mulch and feed the forest floor. There is never a need for any tilling or man-made intervention. Nothing goes to waste in nature. Waste is a human concept.

If planned well, and working alongside the natural pattern or rhythm of nature, it is possible to grow a rich and diverse food forest with yields far greater than any commercial farm.

The principles of permaculture as an agricultural technique follow this philosophy. As do the principles of *effective* Digital Marketing Management.

Our lives as Digital Marketing Managers are just as connected as the examples of Masanobu's farm or a natural forest. If we understand what's happening around us, we can make better and more informed decisions, find new ways of being more efficient and adapt to the changing needs of our customers. But, in today's fast-moving and ever-changing world, it can feel counterintuitive to find the time to just sit back, observe what's happening in the environment around us, and reflect on it.

The natural pattern of things in digital marketing

> *"Keep in mind, that the first person to go to Mars is in school today."*
> **TONY ANTONELLI, LOCKHEED MARTIN**

It is said that the first person who will travel to Mars is in school today. There is no school curriculum that can teach you what you need to know to travel to Mars. So how on earth will they prepare for it? The same can be said for the future of digital marketing. If we look back 25 years, there was barely an internet and hardly any mobile phones. Let alone Google, Amazon, Facebook, Ebay, Instagram, LinkedIn, Wikipedia, Snapchat, WhatsApp and more. There was no school then that could have prepared you for what was to come. Fast forward another 25 years. Imagine the changes that are to come. How can you prepare?

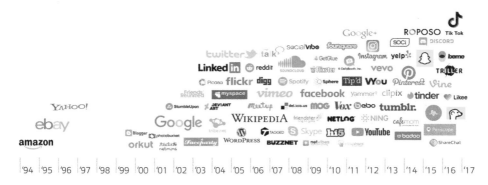

Moore's law of more

> *"Our industry does not respect tradition – it only respects innovation."*
> **SATYA NADELLA, CEO MICROSOFT**

We live in a new world where technology is bringing about exponential change at an exponential rate. Moore's Law states that overall processing power for computers will double every two years.[5] A similar growth curve is seen across the digital marketing discipline. Digital is constantly changing. It invariably becomes the Digital Marketing Manager's job to successfully

---

5   Moore, G, E. (1965) *Cramming more components onto integrated circuits* (PDF). intel. com. Electronics Magazine. [accessed April 1, 2020].

navigate this rapidly changing environment on behalf of a company or brand without wasting precious resources, such as time and money.

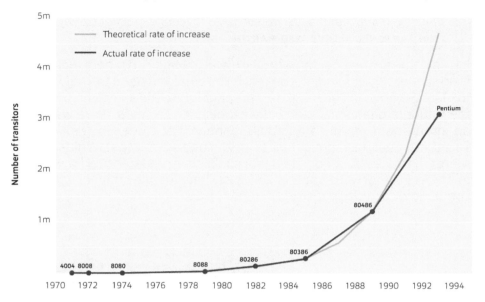

Whilst our parents' careers were defined by their diligence to traditional methods, our careers will be defined by how open and receptive we are to change, to observing the new pattern of things, and to adjusting our thinking and actions. If we want to reap a bountiful harvest without wasting precious energy on what doesn't work, we can't stand still – innovation is now a minimum requirement for survival.

But to do this, it is going to require a fundamental change in business organisational structure. To succeed, businesses need to be more agile and able to react. The Digital Marketing Manager needs to help create an environment within which change is welcomed and brave decisions can be made.

I.T. Wins

> "I.T. Wins" **SIR CLIVE WOODWARD**

It was an unexpected end to an after dinner speech, when England World Cup winning rugby coach Sir Clive Woodward concluded: "I.T. Wins". For a man known for motivating and organising humans at the top of their game to conclude that the key to success was I.T. was somewhat surprising. His view was sound. I.T. Systems will vastly outperform humans at many things.

The organisations that adapt quickest to benefit from the processing power at their disposal will be the ones that gain competitive advantage and 'win'.

And we know, it is the Digital Marketing Manager's job to encourage the adoption of technology within an organisation. In the digital space this means being able to: measure it, test it, and then share what we learned with everyone involved.

Internet Schminternet

"It doesn't matter to me if we're a pure internet player. What matters to me is to provide the best customer service. Internet Schminternet.

If we're not one of those important lasting companies born of the internet we will have nobody to blame but ourselves and we will be extremely disappointed in ourselves.

I believe that if you can focus obsessively enough on customer experience, selection, ease of use, low prices, more information to make purchase decisions plus great customer service... If you can do all that you have a good chance.

If there is one thing that Amazon.com is about it is excessive attention to the customer experience. End to end. " **JEFF BEZOS, 1999.**

This quote, taken from an interview with Amazon's Founder and CEO Jeff Bezos in 1999[6], demonstrates how irrelevant the medium through which you support clients is. **It is about excessive attention to the customer experience and wherever that leads you.** We believe this to be true. Therefore, it is vital that your approach (including your digital strategy) is open, flexible and able to pivot with the changing nature of the online or digital environment.

How we adjust to the changing environment around us

"It's a lot easier to sell something that people are already in the mood to buy." **SETH GODIN**

---

6   Bezos, J. (1999) *Jeff Bezos In 1999 On Amazon's Plans Before The Dotcom Crash* [online] Available at: https://www.youtube.com/watch?v=GltlJO56S1g [Accessed 28 April 2020]

An example of this is our response to the changing landscape within digital marketing. In the past few years, businesses have recognised the need to equip themselves with a digital understanding to help build a strong online presence and reach a wider audience. They have done this by hiring Digital Marketing Managers, which led to an organic and significant demand for these roles.

However, as discussed in the *Head Chef Syndrome* chapter, there is no standard job description for the Digital Marketing Manager role and, there is no recognised path or qualification to become one. Take, for example, the process accountants follow to become chartered as a benchmark. Although there are some equivalent courses, digital marketing has yet to professionalise in the same way. It is also clear that universities don't equip graduates to walk out of academia straight into these roles. Most Digital Marketing Managers are coming into the role from a diverse range of academic disciplines and accumulating their knowledge on the job.

This change of environment presented us with the opportunity to provide help. We responded by developing education products that help upskill Digital Marketing Managers (including this book). We also support businesses with this challenge by enabling them to outsource the Digital Marketing Manager role to our team without having to hire additional team members.

We have adapted to the changing environment while remaining aligned to our vision to help every business in the world achieve more. Flexibility has enabled us to further our purpose and fulfil our passion of sharing our knowledge to help others understand the digital world.

The markets around you and the needs of your customers will change quickly. The message for Digital Marketing Managers is that the products you offer have to adapt to the environment that you exist in. Pay excessive attention to the customer experience; wherever that leads you. To do this, observe, measure and learn about the environment around you.

Open your eyes and prepare to measure, test, and adapt

> John Tuld: *"Let me tell you something, Mr. Sullivan. Do you care to know why I'm in this chair with you all? I mean, why I earn the big bucks?"*
>
> Peter Sullivan: *"Yes."*

> *John Tuld: "I'm here for one reason and one reason alone. I'm here to guess what the music might do a week, a month, a year from now. That's it. Nothing more."*

The character of John Tuld from the film *Margin Call* describes his value being in his ability to guess what the future may bring. Successful business strategies (like receivers in American Football) speak of the concept of standing where the ball is going to drop. Far from being an abstract intuitive skill, a great Digital Marketing Manager observes the market and environment within which the organisation exists, and gains a greater understanding of the bigger picture, to identify where the competitive advantage is.

Just like Masanobu Fukuoka, a talent scout, or an outstanding sports person, a great Digital Marketing Manager won't find success using the same old techniques to get the same old results.

What's the takeaway? **Stop blindly wasting time and energy**. Adapt, measure, and test to stay ahead. Open your eyes to the ever-changing environment around you and go with the flow.

Learn to observe your environment

To achieve real, significant, and lasting results with better yields, we would do well to adopt the principles of permaculture: observing, interacting, integrating, and producing no waste. To do this, we must be in the context of the whole, and work with the way things are.

Consider the following questions. How much awareness do you have of the digital environment your business works within? Broaden your understanding of the whole by investigating the following:

- **What is the natural pattern for your customers?** What are their needs now? What will they look like in 3, 5, 10, 25 years?
- **What is the natural pattern across your industry?** What does the playing field look like now? What has the competition been up to? What's around the corner? What will it look like in 3, 5, 10, 25 years?
- **What is the natural pattern within your organisation?** How well will your organisation adapt to change? How brave can it be? What will it look like in 3, 5, 10, 25 years?
- **What is the natural pattern of the technology you utilise?** Are you aware of all of the systems and tools your organisation uses? How will these need to change in 3, 5, 10, 25 years?

- **What is the natural pattern of the products you offer?** Do you have an understanding of all of the products that your company offers? How will your product offering need to change? What will it look like in 3, 5, 10, 25 years?

> ### Activity – Observe your environment
>
> Work through the questions above. Your answers will put you in a position to build a well informed strategy.

Chapter 4: Craft a winning culture

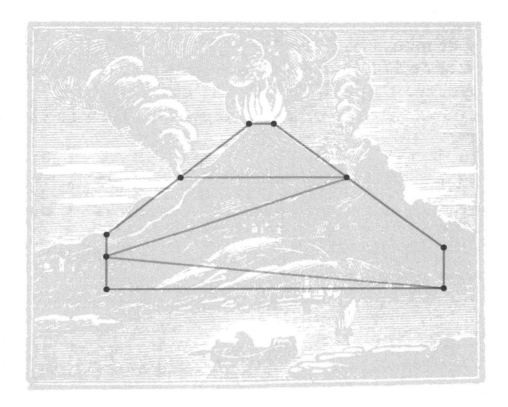

> "It's not the strongest of the species that survives, nor the most intelligent that survives. It is the one that is most adaptable to change."
> **CHARLES DARWIN**

Sometime between the years 1000 and 1600, a group of people known as the Moriori left their home, New Zealand (and their kinsmen, the Māori), and set sail, heading east into the great unknown.[7]

For days and days, sailing across a stormy ocean, they did not pass a single speck of land. Finally, after 500 miles, they spotted some distant islands on the horizon. The travellers named them Rēkohu, or "Misty Sun". Today these

---

7   King, M. (2017) *Moriori: A People Rediscovered*. New Zealand, Penguin Random House.

are known as the Chatham Islands. These rocky outcrops on the edge of the world would become their home.

Unlike the moist, warm environment of their former home – well suited to growing food for a large population – Rēkohu was an inhospitable land only capable of supporting a couple of thousand people.

Life was hard, and often short. There was only just enough to eat. The Moriori had to adapt. Thus the Moriori renounced warfare and agreed to cooperate with one another. They adopted a form of pacifism they called 'Nunuku's law'. They embraced a hunter-gatherer culture on their tiny island because it couldn't support crops of any kind and shared what they gathered amongst their community.

The Moriori had been used to resolving disputes with violence, even death. But being so remote, and with such a small population and only the simplest of weapons, it became apparent that they needed to resolve disputes in another way. If physical conflict was truly necessary, it was agreed that men could hit one another with tupurau, poles the width of a man's thumb and a couple of feet in length. But the moment blood was shed or skin broken, they were obliged to stop.

It was these and many other cultural changes that allowed the Moriori to survive for hundreds of years on this inhospitable outcrop.

In 1835, five hundred Māori made the journey from New Zealand to the Chatham Islands. Here they met the Moriori. The Māori, armed with guns and axes, proceeded to slaughter the Moriori "like sheep". In just a few days most of the Moriori population had been killed. Some of those who were killed were also cooked and eaten, a Māori custom common to mainland disputes over control of crops and farmland. Those who had not been killed were enslaved, separated from their families, and prohibited from marrying.

The Moriori and the Māori, with the same culture and language, were once virtually identical. But in the space of only a few hundred years the Māori had become adept at fighting, whilst the Moriori mastered pacifism. The story of the Moriori demonstrates the significant impact our environment has on our culture. The culture of both communities was shaped by the need to survive, to adapt to their surroundings, and to make the most of the available resources. It is a story that is often used as an example of *determinism*[8] which is the theory that all events are completely determined by previously existing causes. The opposite of which is *free will*.

---

8 Encyclopaedia Britannica. *Determinism*. [online] available at: https://www.britannica.com/topic/determinism [accessed 28 April 2020]

What can we do at an individual level to shape the culture within which we work?

In this chapter, we show you how you can contribute to creating a culture that supports people to be their best, and do the best work of their career. We show you how this seemingly impossible task is possible. We will take a look at what they do at Google and equip you with a range of management tools which you can use to help your teams. It is simpler than first imagined and the impact will propel you to achieve results that you never thought possible.

What is an effective culture?

> *"Never doubt that a small group of thoughtful, committed, citizens can change the world. Indeed, it is the only thing that ever has."* **MARGARET MEAD**

We define culture as the unspoken rules that are followed within the organisation, often understood as, *"the way things are done around here"*.[9] It is possible to achieve good results within a toxic culture. But, if you really want to achieve exceptional digital marketing results, an effective culture is key.

Every culture that exists will be different and there is no universal blueprint for what a culture *should* be. We have observed that the best digital results come from high performing teams that are 'in it together' to achieve a common purpose. There are some characteristics that we see in effective digital teams. They are full of people who:

- Are on a journey together.
- Are happy and love going to work.
- Feel safe to try things.
- Are willing to make mistakes.
- Feel cared for.

---

9   Bower, M. (1966). *The Will to Manage: Corporate Success Through Programmed Management.* New York, McGraw-Hill.

- Are challenged to improve.
- Are empowered to make decisions.
- Feel encouraged to be themselves.
- Have relationships between team members based on trust.

> "If you get the culture right, most of the other stuff will just take care of itself."[10] **TONY HSIEH**

As a Digital Marketing Manager it is very normal to feel that these things are out of your control. The culture or 'way things are done around here' is usually determined, consciously or not, by the values of the owners or senior management (the HiPPO). We know that many company cultures do not currently foster the spirit of openness and endeavour crucial to digital success. This can be an incredibly frustrating situation for Digital Marketing Managers.

Whenever we propose that a Digital Marketing Manager should be responsible for bringing about change to 'the way things are done around here' it strikes fear into everyone. Both management and Digital Marketing Manager alike. But we believe that anybody – on any team, at any rank, at any level – can be a leader and can have a positive impact on those around them. The first criterion for being a leader is that you have to want to be one.[11]

Overcoming dominance hierarchy

It is understood that in any human social group a hierarchy is formed. Hierarchies form quickly and spontaneously[12] through nonverbal and verbal communication and often without us being conscious of it happening. What is unique to humans is that people attain positions not only through *dominance* (force or force threat) as seen in the natural world, but also through *prestige* (freely conferred deference).[13]

---

10 Hsieh, T. (2010) *On a Scale of 1-10, How Weird are You?* [online] The New York Times, accessible at: https://www.nytimes.com/2010/01/10/business/10corner.html [accessed 9th November 2020]
11 Flynn, G, cited by Sinek, S. (2020) *The Tail Can Wag the Dog.* [online] available at: https://www.youtube.com/watch?v=Qg7smyaXdrI [accessed 28 April 2020]
12 Koski, J et al. (2015) *Understanding Social Hierarchies: The Neural and Psychological Foundations of Status Perception* [online] Available at: https://www.ncbi.nlm.nih.gov/pmc/articles/PMC5494206/ [Accessed 28 April 2020]
13 Henrich, J., and Gil-White, F. J. (2001) *The evolution of prestige: Freely conferred deference as a mechanism for enhancing the benefits of cultural transmission.* Evolution and Human Behavior, Volume 22, Pp 165–196.

The challenge with leadership by dominance in the digital space is that it shuts down the creativity of the group. Matthew Syed, a former English number one table tennis player and author of Bounce and Black Box Thinking, puts it beautifully when he says *"Dominant leaders who are dominant in meetings, are dominant when executing, dominant when evaluating... are a disaster for their companies."*

When managed by dominance, people, without necessarily realising it, don't say what they think. They say what they think the leader wants to hear. So the collective intelligence of the group merges to unconsciously mirror the brain of the leader.[14] That might be effective for types of work that don't require creativity, but, this style causes a lack of diversity of thought and is a disaster for activities that do require creativity, such as digital marketing.

> *"Leaders who don't want to listen will eventually be surrounded by people who have nothing to say."*[15] **ANDY STANLEY**

What is encouraging for Digital Marketing Managers is that humans attain high social status, not only through force or threat, but also through freely conferred deference: *prestige*. We look up to and follow people who we admire and respect. This admiration is won through traits such as wisdom, empathy, example, or wise leadership. This is where, by taking steps to *Shoot the HiPPO*, a high-performing Digital Marketing Manager can take their team on the journey and gain social status within the work hierarchy. Crucially, great leaders have the capacity for both *dominance* and *prestige* and are adept at using either at the appropriate time. Start with a gentle informed rebellion and see where this first step will take you.

Dignity in keeping with the role

In Kazuo Ishiguro's novel The Remains of the Day[16], the lead character is a butler called Stevens. Reflecting on the definition of what makes a great butler he states,

---

14 Syed, M. (2020) *Diversity and creative thinking – the power of rebel ideas* [Podcast] Available at: https://podcasts.apple.com/gb/podcast/eat-sleep-work-repeat/ id1190000968?i=1000471564042 [Accessed 2 May 2020]
15 Stanley, A. (2011) Tweet on @AndyStanley account [online] available at: https://twitter. com/AndyStanley/status/103841035108630528 [accessed 9th November 2020].
16 Ishiguro, K. (1989) *The Remains of the Day*. Boston, Faber.

> *"The great butlers are great by virtue of their ability to inhabit their professional role and inhabit it to the utmost; they will not be shaken out by external events, however surprising, alarming or vexing. They wear their professionalism as a decent gentleman will wear his suit: he will not let ruffians or circumstance tear it off him in the public gaze; he will discard it when, and only when he wills to do so, and this will invariably be when he is entirely alone. It is, as I say, a matter of 'dignity'."*

Alas, the story is a tragedy. Stevens is so entrenched in his role of butler that he maintains a neutral persona in everything he does. So committed to upholding this unwritten code he represses his true feelings about everything. He maintains his dignity in keeping with the role of butler, but this comes at the cost of pursuing marriage to the woman he loves. He ends the story alone and questions with regret the decisions he made in his life.

Don't be like Stevens. Don't be a silent, subservient butler. Take on the leadership role. With the spirit of *Shooting the HiPPO* in mind, a Digital Marketing Manager must recognise the strength of their own *free will* and change this apathy within themselves. Once you have made that first step you can then take concerted efforts to improve the cultures within which you work.

The tail can wag the dog

> *"The right man sitting in his house and thinking the right thought will be heard a hundred miles distant."*[17] **CHINESE ADAGE**

We recognise that for a Digital Marketing Manager to feel responsible for bringing about change is daunting. The first thing to accept is that you can't control what you can't control. That is to say, if the overall culture is so toxic and driven from the top down then it is best to recognise that and instead focus your efforts on the space that you can influence. Think about how you can contribute to making things better within your sphere of influence. How can you make things better for the people around you? Your team, your colleagues, your partners, your agencies, your boss?

> *"Be the change you want to see in the world."* **MAHATMA GANDHI**

---

17 Wiseman, R. (2019) *Shoot for the Moon: How the Moon Landings Taught us the 8 Secrets of Success.* London, Quercus Publishing.

Change does not have to be grand and total, it can be small and incremental with even small improvements having a ripple effect on the whole. Entrepreneur and internet personality Gary Vaynerchuk[18] considers his role as a boss is to serve his people, not the other way around. If you commit to making those in your sphere of influence feel supported, cared for and able to be themselves you will soon find that they love coming to work and the results will inevitably follow. In larger organisations word will get out, people will want to be on your team and some of the things you put in place will be adopted elsewhere.

Start small, but, don't doubt that your actions can be a catalyst and lead the way for the rest of the organisation. The tail *can* wag the dog.[19]

Fortune favours the brave (and agile)

> "Man is not fully conditioned and determined but rather determines himself whether he gives into conditions or stands up to them. In other words, man is ultimately self determining.
>
> Man does not simply exist. But always decides what his existence will be. What he will become in the next moment. By the same token every human being has the freedom to change at any instant." **VIKTOR E FRANKL**

The organisations that will still be here in 10 years time will be those that are able to respond and adapt to change the fastest. They are unlikely to be organisations that leave innovation to the leaders at the top of the hierarchy. The organisations with top down hierarchical structures are likely to fail because the bottleneck constricts the pace of innovation.

---

18 Schawbel, D. (2016) Gary Vaynerchuk: Managers Should Be Working For Their Employees. [Online] available at: https://www.forbes.com/sites/danschawbel/2016/03/08/gary-vaynerchuk-managers-should-be-working-for-their-employees/?sh=205afca62008 [accessed 28 April 2020]
19 Sinek, S. (2020) *The Tail Can Wag the Dog*. [online] available at: https://www.youtube.com/watch?v=Qg7smyaXdrI [accessed 28 April 2020]

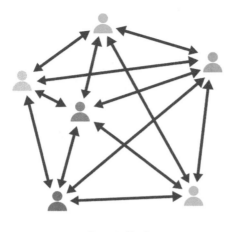 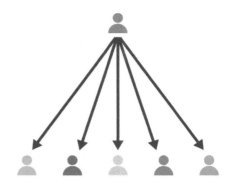

Decentralised
Peer-to-Peer

Centralised
Command and Control

Blockbuster is the poster child for failing to adapt to the rise of technology. Whilst they stood still Netflix moved from mail order film rentals to the online live streaming and entertainment production behemoth that they are today. The momentary delay where the person at the top asks *"should we do something about this?"* opens the door to the plucky upstarts that don't care for the traditional ways.

This is where a brave and agile Digital Marketing Manager has a chance, through positively influencing the culture of their team, to influence the entire company to become more innovative and successful – providing great returns for all involved.

We need more daring leaders

"The future of leadership is braver leaders and more courageous cultures." **BRENÉ BROWN**

Brené Brown is a researcher and storyteller, famous for her work around vulnerability and shame. If you haven't watched her TED talk on 'The Power of Vulnerability'[20], go and watch it now. It's one of the most watched TED talks ever and for good reason.

---

20 Brown, B. (2011) *The Power of Vulnerability* [online] available at: https://www.ted.com/talks/brene_brown_the_power_of_vulnerability [accessed 9th November 2020]

In her book, *"Dare to Lead"*[21], Brené explains that,

> *"Leadership is not about titles or the corner office. It's about the willingness to step up, put yourself out there, and lean into courage. The world is desperate for brave leaders. It's time for all of us to step up."*

Many of us may think that the word 'leader' equates to top management positions and a six figure salary. But in reality, it's far from that. Brené talks about one specific example when she was invited to talk to the teams in the Fortune 500 companies. They would call her and say, 'Hey, we loved your TED talk! Could you come and talk to our team? We'd really appreciate it if you didn't mention vulnerability or shame, though.' She would smile and say, "Okay, what do you want me to talk about?". And the answer would always be the same: innovation, creativity, and change.

> *"Vulnerability is the birthplace of innovation, creativity and change."*[22]
> **BRENÉ BROWN**

Being innovative, creative, and trying to change things *cannot* be done without being vulnerable. If you want to create something that never existed before, it takes a lot of courage, uncertainty, and risk of failure.

Solving problems or coming up with new solutions requires Digital Marketing Managers to become leaders in every sense of the word. As Brené states in her Dare to Lead podcast[23],

> *"We have to create cultures in which brave work, tough conversations and whole hearts are the expectation and where armour is not necessary or rewarded."*

---

21 Brown, B. (2018) *Dare to Lead: Brave Work. Tough Conversations. Whole Hearts.* London, Vermilion.
22 Brown, B. (2011) *The Power of Vulnerability* [online] available at: https://www.ted.com/talks/brene_brown_the_power_of_vulnerability [accessed 9th November 2020]
23 Brown, B. (nd) Dare to Lead with Brené Brown [podcast] Parcast Network. available at: https://open.spotify.com/show/3oEPsPKDhPVoNNL7pH5db6?si=x4dw5xBKROO5pdA3Lodb1A [accessed 9th November 2020]

Let's be clear. Courage and leadership skills are not things that we are born with. They are things we can all learn. We just need to be willing to show our true selves, be brave, and lean into courage. If we do that, we can make a whole lot of difference not only at work, but in our personal lives, too.

Create a culture where people have the freedom to get things wrong

> *"Business should view people not as resources but as sources."*
> **JOHN MACKEY**

Change means risk, mistakes, and failures. Businesses need to be brave and look beyond today. Standing still – as we have seen with the way the digital environment is naturally evolving – is not an option. Businesses need to adopt a level of trust and belief in their teams that has never been seen before. This will expose businesses to short term risks. But, it will mean that they will be around to laugh about their minor mistakes years down the line.

Successful organisations need to build teams of smart creatives[24] who have the freedom to get things wrong. Everyone in the organisation will need to contribute to making the organisation better. Everyone needs to feel welcome to lead innovation. To help this happen, individuals will need to have a growth mindset and be receptive to change. Organisations will need to create psychologically safe environments where team members feel accepted and respected and free to make mistakes.

Few organisations have crafted cultures that operate with this level of expansive freedom. We encourage you as the Digital Marketing Manager to introduce this way of working within your sphere of influence and encourage those above you in a hierarchical structure to take note of the positive impact this kind of culture delivers. Embrace this challenge and see it as part of your role. As well as having a happier team the commercial results will soon follow.

Innovation requires breaking the norms

> *"You can't solve a problem on the same level that it was created. You have to rise above it to the next level."* **ALBERT EINSTEIN**

---

24 Schmidt, E. et al. (2014) *Google: How Google works* (First edition.) New York, Grand Central Publishing.

If you want to have results that you've never had before, you are going to need to do things in a way you have never done them before. Most organisations that stagnate will reach a point where they focus their efforts on simply doing more of the same things – just think back to chapter three, 'go with the flow', where we examined the story of the one straw revolution. Think about the farming methods Masanobu Fukuoka turned his back on, and how his innovative approach delivered higher rice yields with far less effort!

Businesses running on automatic pilot are preventing substantial improvements with their tunnel vision. This is understandable when you consider that they are only continuing to do what originally brought the organisation success. The Digital Marketing Manager is in a great position to lead innovation. If, within your sphere of influence, you can create a culture where ideas and experimentation are encouraged, in which there is freedom and safety to try new things, even if they don't turn out all that well, you will soon find that your team really pushes boundaries and achieves things out of the ordinary.

Help your management team connect the dots and understand how this is achieved and they will soon buy into the successes you are having and want them replicated across the organisation.

How to change a toxic culture?

> *"Culture is more important than vision. Some leaders have great vision, but have created a toxic culture where that vision will never happen."* **PHIL COOKE**

Imagine working in an environment where the energy and morale are so low that it pulls everyone down. People are not enjoying their jobs, they're frustrated, bored, and unhappy. How could one person make a difference in such a toxic culture?

> *"We can learn to love what we do, even if at the moment, we may not be doing exactly what we love."* **FISH!**

Believe it or not, the answer may be found in a fishmongers. Seattle's famous Pike Place fishmongers is notorious for its fun, bustling atmosphere and its great customer service. But it hasn't always been that way. *"Fish!"*, a book by Stephen C. Lundin, Harry Paul, and John Christensen[25], explains how they turned gutting fish in a smelly fish market from a dreary place to work to an uplifting, vibrant workplace by applying four simple lessons. It is a story about finding the deep source of energy, creativity, and passion that exists inside each of us.

The four simple lessons, a so-called Fish Philosophy from the Pike Place fishmongers are:

1. **Choose your attitude** – we have the power to choose our attitude in *any* situation. Think about who you want to be while you do your work. You can either decide to be bored and unhappy, or you can decide to be the person who's bringing in a positive vibe with them. Ultimately, the choice is yours.

2. **Play** – having fun while you work is energising. Think about ways how you could have more fun and create more energy in your team? It could be as simple as enjoying a cuppa and a casual chat with your teammates every Friday at a specific time. This way, you could learn more about your teammates and create something to look forward to every week.

3. **Make someone's day** – Try to find creative ways how to engage your customers. Involving others and working to 'make their day' is a great way to make good stories that your customers will remember for a long time afterward. Think about your customers and how can you engage them in a way that will make their day?

4. **Be present** – some of us may feel that we went from being fully connected to being rather disconnected. If you want to bring a positive change to your organisation, you need to be present. Try to interact with your team and your customers. Listen to them and talk to them as if they were your friends.

If you decide to change the toxic culture in your organisation, first of all, well done for being so brave. Solving a problem like this will require you to become a brave and courageous leader.

The foundation of a successful team is Psychological Safety

> *"The only way to discover the limits of the possible is to go beyond them into the impossible."* **ARTHUR C. CLARKE**

------

25 Lundin, S et al. (1998) *Fish!* New York, Hyperion.

Following on from concepts developed by american scholar Amy C. Edmondson in her book *"The Fearless Organisation"*[26], Google ran some research into the characteristics of successful teams in their organisation.[27] They concluded that *how* a team works together matters more than *who* is on the team. Teams that work together always outperform teams with better individual performers. They reported that so-called 'safe' teams outperform others by 2:1.

Google's research states that effective 'safe' teams exhibit five dynamics. Like a hierarchy of needs,[28] the foundation of this is psychological safety. The list below represents a hierarchy of five dynamics, with the most important first:

1. **Psychological safety** – This is considered the foundation of a successful team. Can you be human, authentic, and be your whole self in your team? Do teammates feel safe to take risks and be vulnerable in front of each other?

2. **Dependability** – Can you trust your team members to get things done on time and hit the high bar that you set? Or do you feel you can't leave it to others? If it is the latter this will lead to bottlenecks in work and frustration.

3. **Structure and clarity** – Does the team have clear roles, plans, and goals? The roles must be structured, but not too structured to stifle change.

4. **Meaning** – Is work personally important to team members? Does it mean something at an individual level?

5. **Impact** – Can team members see the impact of their work? The work that team members do matters and creates change.

Psychological safety is therefore the most important element for an effective team. Google recognise three components of psychological safety:

1. **Voice** – Do I have a voice and when I say something am I heard? Do I feel like I belong?

2. **Trust** – Can I trust other people with both my personal and business things?

---

26 Edmondson, A. (2018) *The Fearless Organization: Creating Psychological Safety in the Workplace for Learning, Innovation, and Growth.* New Jersey, Wiley.

27 Sakaguchi, M. (2019) *Creating Psychological Safety in the Workplace. A Think with Footprint guest lecture.* [online] Available at: https://www.youtube.com/watch?v=H0-2Wfk8n3M [accessed 28 April 2020]

28 Maslow, A, H. (1943) *Hierarchy of Needs: A Theory of Human Motivation*

3. **Inclusion** – Do I feel included?

Are you encouraging voice, trust, and inclusion within your sphere of influence?

How to set the tone for psychological safety

To create an environment where colleagues do not feel embarrassed, rejected, or punished for speaking up:

1. **Admit your own fallibility** – Let people know that you don't know everything so that they feel welcome to contribute.
2. **Remember that work is a series of learning problems** – Accept that things will go wrong and welcome errors and mistakes as opportunities to make things better. It is far more fun to work on a challenge of discovery.
3. **Ask more questions and welcome all ideas** – In meetings don't dismiss ideas or thoughts, encourage them. Instead of 'how can we make that happen?' Invite more contributions from everyone.

Of course, maintaining this environment is not easy. You must consistently work at it to ensure your team feels safe. At the beginning of the project you could set the tone by asking the entire team for three things they bring to the project and three things they each want from the project. You could also invite the team to read this chapter and complete the Amy C. Edmonson 'Psychological Safety team survey.'[29]

Partners, not suppliers. The story of Mercedes and Petronas

Building a team that can deliver success is as much about the shared goal, vision, and motivation as it is about the component competencies of each team member. This fundamental observation is often entirely overlooked when procurement teams select their suppliers. Think about this model when you build relationships with your digital suppliers. Can you turn your suppliers into partners?

Let's take the example of Formula 1 car manufacturer Mercedes and fuel supplier Petronas.[30] In a conventional business relationship the Mercedes

---

29 Edmonson, A. (1999) *Psychological Safety and Learning Behavior in Work Teams.* Administrative Science Quarterly, Volume 44, Pp 350-83).
30 This lesson was shared with Tom Bowden by Stephen Kavanaugh of Critica.

procurement team (P) will compete with the Petronas sales team (S) to battle over the best contract terms:

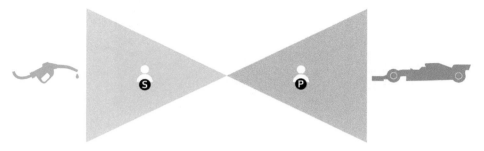

Each year one or the other may win and achieve a marginal gain for their respective organisation. One year Mercedes may drive down the Petronas' price by 5% and next year vice versa. The issue is that this transactional relationship does not serve the vision and aspiration of each of the organisation's leadership teams.

Here is why:

Imagine that instead of the sales and procurement team beating each other for the best deal, that the two organisations understood their aligned visions and worked together so that each could achieve theirs.

First, at board level, the organisation directors would need to explain to each other what they are each trying to achieve. In this case Mercedes want to have the best car in the world and Petronas want to develop the best fuel in the world. At board level (B), there is an alignment in vision between the two organisations. They both want to be the best. Can there therefore be a better way of working together?

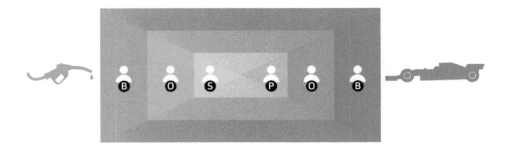

P Procurement
S Sales
B Board
S Operations

How could both organisations work together to achieve their visions of becoming the best? It follows that if Mercedes want the fastest car in the world they will need the best fuel in the world. Petronas can produce the best fuel in the world for Mercedes. To be able to develop the best fuel Petronas needs to understand the specifications of the Mercedes engine. The world beating results will be achieved if both the Mercedes and Petronas operations teams (Ops) work collaboratively. If this is done then both teams will succeed. At this point they can move beyond a supplier relationship and become a partner. The commercial agreements also become easier as the shared success is far greater.

This move from a supplier to a partner mentality is a shift in culture that drives innovation and success on both sides.

Cultivating connection

"In nature we never see anything isolated, but everything in connection with something else which is before it, beside it, under it and over it." **JOHANN WOLFGANG VON GOETHE**

We are social animals. As much as bees need to be part of a hive; we need to feel we are part of a tribe. The alternative is not good. Social disconnection has a negative impact on health, and feeling disempowered can make a person feel depressed. Creating a workplace culture that fosters belonging, acceptance, trust, health, education, and wealth will not only benefit your organisation but it will also contribute to a more peaceful, empathetic, and compassionate society.

Is the organisation you're in working to create positive change in the workplace so that people feel 'happier'? What can you do at an individual level to help cultivate connection?

The importance of relationships

"Relationships are all there is. Everything in the universe only exists because it is in relationship to everything else. Nothing exists in isolation. We have to stop pretending we are individuals that can go it alone." **MARGARET J. WHEATLEY**

Everything we do is dependent on us building exceptional relationships. Relationships are the centre of our universe. The sun to our planets. A driving force that keeps us all together. If we were to draw a diagram of concentric circles detailing what is most important to us, relationships would sit bang in the middle. Good relationships allow us to make things happen and make the job enjoyable. Good relationships prevent us from being culled by a competitor.

To be a really good Digital Marketing Manager you need to be an expert at building relationships.

10 Steps for building strong relationships

Good relationships start with you. Being a person who can listen, be open, and be receptive to feedback will lay the foundations for building beautiful bonds with colleagues and customers.

At Footprint Digital we build relationships by supporting each other in a variety of ways:

- Through good things and bad.
- Being a critical friend.
- Thinking long term.
- Being supportive.
- Encouraging one another.
- Clear communication.
- Developing understanding.
- Through shared goals.
- Creating a safe space.
- Respecting one another.

The following selection of exercises can help you do the same.

1. Figure out what makes for a good relationship

What is a good relationship? Defining it helps you to understand and implement it, so form a list of all the things you want and need in a business relationship.

Here is ours:

- Communication
- Trust
- Honesty
- Constructive
- Alignment
- Common Vision/Goals
- Equality
- Understanding of roles and responsibilities
- Respect

These are just a few of the things that constitute a good relationship. Don't be afraid to alter it to better reflect the values of your business. Try to make it as extensive as possible. How could you measure how effective you are at each of these things within your organisation? As a business obsessed with figures, data, and analytics, we work to find a way to measure the success of our relationships. This can be complex, or as simple as asking each other for feedback and including feedback surveys at the end of our emails where people can leave a quick review of how we've done. Encourage all feedback to be delivered in the context of *"open, honest, and fair"*.

2. Contemplate the Trust Bucket

Relationships are measured by trust. The more trust there is, the stronger the relationship.

Think of a bucket into which your actions are poured. You have to work hard to fill the bucket. Beware that even the smallest breakdown can erode trust; once there is a hole you have to work doubly hard to maintain the relationship.

Work hard to maintain the trust bucket.[31]

3. Create an environment that is open about mistakes

The best conversations to have with your team occur when they feel comfortable enough to discuss mistakes openly. Encourage the team to operate under the principles of open, honest, and fair[32] in all communication.

If you or your team make a mistake in your work then take the time to think about it, address it, and use it as an opportunity to learn. Then take that lesson forward with you and make sure that the same mistake isn't made again. Ensure that everyone knows it's okay to be wrong because this allows you to work as a team, fix mistakes together, and grow.

If you or your team are not getting things wrong or making any mistakes when working on marketing campaigns then chances are that you are not growing or testing your limits. To encourage your team to be able to push their boundaries it is important to foster an environment that is open to experimentation, tries new things, and is supportive of those brave enough to take controlled risks.

That is not a free pass for people to be sloppy, but if they do make a mistake in pursuit of trying something new, they should be supported. Social media consultancy NixonMcInnes went one step further and introduced a monthly

---

31 Tom Bowden was shown this 18 years ago when he was a soccer coach for Major League Soccer in the USA. He was at a training weekend with them and a coach educator drew it on a whiteboard as a way of describing how important it is to give children confidence and reassurance and how one tiny criticism from the coach can make a hole that would take a hundred compliments to re-fill.

32 Rosling, J. (2013) *More money More time Less stress.* London, 1Fish 2Fish.

'Church of Fail' where innovation is fostered by celebrating its employees' mistakes in a monthly ritual.[33]

4. Build critical friendships

> *"Genuine friendship cannot exist where one of the parties is unwilling to hear the truth, and the other is equally indisposed to speak it."*
> **MARCUS TULLIUS CICERO**

Surround yourselves with critical friends and perform the role of a critical friend. The motivation is always to help the other person thrive.

A critical friend can be defined as a trusted person who asks provocative questions, provides data to be examined through another lens, and offers critiques of a person's work as a friend. A critical friend is also someone who discreetly lets you know that you have a bit of lunch on your chin rather than letting you sit through an entire meeting unaware.

5. Delegation not abdication[34]

> *"When we do for those in need what they can do for themselves we disempower them."* **ROBERT T LUPTON**

The easy route can lead to loss of power and prevent self sufficiency. Do not do anything for anyone that they can do for themselves. You are stealing from them when you do. Likewise, a Digital Marketing Manager should work hard to empower people that they delegate work to by briefing well and training them as well as maintaining responsibility for the end result. Do not relinquish responsibility when delegating.

---

33 Buchanan, L, Inc. (nd) *Welcome to the Church of Fail* [online] available at: https://www.inc.com/magazine/201311/leigh-buchanan/nixonmcinnes-innovation-by-celebrating-mistakes.html [accessed 28 April 2020]

34 Gerber, M. (2001) *The E-Myth Revisited.* New York, Harper Business, Harper Collins.

6. Choose to be a victor not a victim

> "The greatest relation-
> ships are built on Blame,
> Evasion, and Denial"
> **SAID NO ONE EVER!**

OARBED[35] is a communication framework which sets
out the choices that we can
make, helping us know how to act in a situation.

The choice is simple – you can either stay above the line and be a victor or
sink below and be a victim.

Accept your responsibilities, take ownership and be accountable for your
actions and you will find your life full of rewarding, healthy relationships.

7. Beware the drama triangle!

When relationships within a business start to break down, it can lead to
instability and ineffectiveness. This is why it is essential for a Digital Marketing Manager to be aware of the ways a relationship can degrade, and be
equipped to prevent it from descending into a self-perpetuating spiral of
drama as a result.

The *Karpman Drama Triangle*[36] explains
how conflict can escalate, illustrating how
people caught in a disagreement assume
one of three roles:

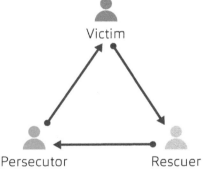

* **Persecutor** – usually blaming, repres-
  sive, and critical, attacks a victim over a
  problem.

35 Original Source Unknown. (nd) *Where Do You Sit? Above The Line Or Below The
   Line?* [online] available at: https://peopleleaders.com.au/above-or-below-the-line/
   [accessed 28 April 2020]
36 Karpman, S. (1968) *The Karpman Drama Triangle – Fairy tales and script drama
   analysis* [PDF] available at: https://karpmandramatriangle.com/pdf/DramaTriangle.
   pdf [accessed 6th November 2020]

- **Victim** – feels oppressed, having had their rights trampled. They feel they have lost power and are dependent.
- **Rescuer** – a third party, usually someone who tries to 'fix' problems and who may be an enabler for the victim.

These roles are not static though. As the rescuer 'saves' the victim, they may start to attack the persecutor, therefore turning them into the victim. Over time this can escalate, and turn into a vicious cycle from which it is impossible to escape. When you recognise these behaviours in yourself then take a moment to reflect, be aware it is a pattern and adopt a neutral position. It is harder to take a wider team on this journey with you, but, if you can model a better way of behaving it will have a positive impact on the culture.

8. The authenticity t-shirt

There is massive value in being able to bring your whole self to work. Nick Looby, author of *"Modern Zombies: How to Stay Ahead of the Horde and Communicate Your Way to Incredible Success"*[37], advocates that you create a space within which your team can be their authentic selves. Working with the Footprint Digital team, we undertook an exercise called 'the authenticity t-shirt'.

Trust, rapport, and strong relationships come from authentic interactions; but who are you really? The activity invites you to ask yourself, *Who are you really?* And also question whether this 'authentic self' is the one who communicates at work.

If you wore a t-shirt that represented who you are, what would it say? The activity will help you to write down yours and share it with your colleagues. Your authenticity t-shirt is a reflection of who you genuinely are.

If your colleagues wore one what would their t-shirt say? Be the real you and allow everyone in the team to be true to themselves and your team relationships will strengthen.

> ### Activity – The Authenticity t-shirt
>
> Sum yourself up in three words – would your friends be able to recognise you by your t-shirt alone?

---

37 Looby, N. (2017) *Modern Zombies: How to Stay Ahead of the Horde and Communicate Your Way to Incredible Success.* London, Feet on the Ground Training Ltd.

9. Taking life's journey together: personal goal setting

It is rare that we take the time to consciously reflect on our lives. Invite your team to score out of 10 their level of satisfaction against the following criteria:

- Health.
- Wealth.
- Friends and family.
- Giving.
- Learning.
- Adventure.

This is for the individual to keep to themselves and is not something that needs to be shared.

Once they have scored each criteria, ask them to make a list of three things they are going to do to improve.

10. How do you like to receive praise?

Shari Harley, author of *"How to Say Anything to Anyone: A Guide to Building Business Relationships That Really Work"*[38], shares a funny story about the impact of how to deliver praise.

A popular cleaning lady at a huge international organisation had been working for the organisation for 25 years. Everyone loved her and were hugely appreciative of her work. As it was her 25 year anniversary, the management decided to honour her at the huge glitzy company annual awards ceremony. With thousands of people in attendance, they brought her up on stage to give her an award. She was so overwhelmed by the experience that she needed to take the next two weeks off work with anxiety. It transpired she would have been much happier with a bunch of flowers and a 'well done' from her boss.

Do you know how everyone on your team likes to receive praise? Make it your job to find out and use this information to make people feel special in the way that suits them.

---

38 Harley, S. (2013) *How to Say Anything to Anyone: A Guide to Building Business Relationships That Really Work.* Texas, Greenleaf Book Group Press.

Let's go fly a kite

As you can see, creating a culture of connectivity, collectiveness, and kindness in a team can be done without the intervention of 'the boss', even if you are part of an organisation with a top-down hierarchical structure.

If you have seen the film "*Mary Poppins*", you may interpret her role as being to help support and raise the Banks children. The accompanying film, "*Saving Mr Banks*"[39], makes it clear that she is not there for the children. She is there to save Mr Banks from his obsession with work and money to become more playful.

A good Digital Marketing Manager is able to recognise that the power to effect change for the better is in their hands. We invite you to become more like Mary Poppins. You may see your role as being there to serve those in your immediate team, but also strive to take the management team on the journey to a happier more effective culture.

Do the following activities to kick-start this process:

Activity – Vision and values

1. As a team, define the values of your organisation and create a culture handbook so that this can be explained quickly with colleagues, suppliers, and customers.

2. Build your digital team ensuring that you have a shared vision and psychological safety.

---

39 Hancock, J et al. (2013) *Saving Mr Banks*. Walt Disney Studios

Chapter 5: Define business goals

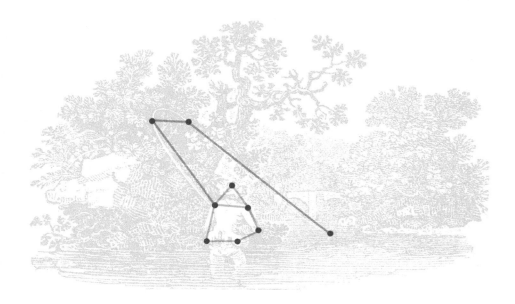

> "If you don't know where you're going, any road will take you there."
> **GEORGE HARRISON**

In the early 1970s, Yvon Chouinard, author of "Let My People Go Surfing: The Education of a Reluctant Businessman", and founder of the outdoor clothing brand Patagonia, accidentally stumbled across an idea that would revolutionise the industry.

Growing up, Yvon was notoriously hopeless at whatever he turned his hand to. That is until he discovered climbing in 1953 aged 14. The excitement and intensity of rappelling down the sides of sheer cliffs meant that Yvon was instantly hooked. As he got older, Yvon became more involved and climbing became his way of life.

At the time it was common that climbers used the British style of climbing. The focus of this style was to hammer safety supports into the rock and to climb up these fixed routes (often in the fastest way possible). Yvon noticed the damage this was causing the rock faces. Yvon was environmentally conscious and he aspired to 'leave no trace' on nature. So he began making his own equipment that could slot into rock crevasses and be removed after use. This was less harmful and enabled climbers to leave nature as they found it.

This new equipment soon became popular with fellow climbers. His passion to look after the environment soon turned into a business. He began supporting himself through the sale of his equipment, travelling around the country, climbing by day and forging by night.

In 1970, on a winter climbing trip in Scotland, he bought a rugby shirt to wear while climbing. Built to withstand the brute force of a rugby match, the top withstood the climb and the collar prevented hardware slings from cutting into Yvon's neck. He knew he was on to something. This impulse purchase would change his life. Back home, Yvon's new choice of climbing gear caught on – and before he knew it, a brightly decorated rugby jersey with a good collar was in high demand by his climbing clients.

Yvon ordered jerseys from Umbro in England. They sold out. He then ordered from New Zealand and Argentina. They sold out too. The Chouinard team saw that clothing was a way to support their equipment business. As the clothing side to their company grew, they decided it needed its own unique name. In 1973, Patagonia was born. A name they described as one that brings to mind "romantic visions of glaciers tumbling into fjords, jagged windswept peaks, gauchos and condors".

Since their inception, Patagonia has spent decades perfecting their product. It has researched different materials, colours, working environments, and environmental ethics. These are products it is proud of and products that are true to the vision of protecting the environment.

Today, Patagonia is one of the world's leading environmentally friendly clothing brands but the company reaches far beyond clothing – it is committed to teaching and training the next generation of environmental activists. Patagonia is doing this to continue their mission; to find a solution to the ongoing environmental crisis.

Your goal is to change things for the better

Businesses always start for a reason. More often than not, those that deliver enduring success are built on the foundations of wanting to create a better world and to change things for the better. This can be in a small way or a large way. Finding the language and articulating that desire into a vision, purpose, and goals enables teams and the world to buy into the organisation and therefore fulfil its aspirations. To do this, you need to know how to ask the right questions and find the power of *Why*.

The power of *Why*

In his book *"Start with Why: how great leaders inspire everyone"*[40], Simon Sinek, author and motivational speaker, articulates the challenge of connecting to your audience using a model called the golden circle. He uses the example of Apple computers, explaining how audiences may often connect with *Why* Apple do what they do, rather than focusing on the *What* and *How* – the descriptive explanation, the features of the products.

Flipping the focus from *What* you sell to *Why* you exist is a powerful method of connecting with customers and clients. For Yvon Chouinard, the *Why* was to follow the philosophies of writers such as John Muir and Henry David Thoreau: to explore and enjoy nature, but leave no trace. He was powered by this purpose. It led him to, reluctantly, build a huge outdoor brand through which he promotes the protection of the environment.

The beauty and the power of 'finding your *Why*' is that once you know *Why* you do things, you will recognise what drives you in life. Once you have found the words to describe it, you are able to recognise whether *What* and *How* you spend your time in this world is aligned with what is truly important to you. This can help you make decisions that lead to greater fulfilment in your life.

In business, if you know your why, your messaging will become clearer and you won't need to waste any energy on trying to figure out what to do or say. Everything will be more clear and driven by a single purpose.

Activity – Articulate the why

Can you articulate the:

- *Why* of the business you represent?
- The *Why* of your role as a Digital Marketing Manager?
- Your personal *Why*?

---

40 Sinek, S. (2009) *Start with Why: how great leaders inspire everyone.* London, Penguin.

Be curious

> *"I cannot teach anybody anything. I can only make them think."*
> **SOCRATES**

Being curious and asking questions are two fundamental skills in life (not just as a Digital Marketing Manager). There is an art to asking as few questions as possible and still gaining the information you need. There is also an art to knowing when to challenge and pursue answers that are not forthcoming. The adage goes: *"Good students answer questions. Great students question answers."*

We have observed that most marketing campaigns that fail unravel because of a lack of the right kind of exploration at this initial hurdle. Often this is because the teams involved do not feel brave enough to ask, or have the right questions to probe their management teams with. It is also often because Digital Marketing Managers do not see this as part of their role.

At Footprint, we believe that even asking unassuming questions has the power to spark critical thinking, and get 'I'd never thought of that' kind of responses. *"It's not the answer that enlightens, but the questions"* as Eugene Ionesco put it. Digital Marketing Managers need to ask probing questions of those around them in the business. This will result in greater insights and make it much easier to create a successful strategy.

We utilise the Socratic method to unearth great truths and weed out contradictions:

> *"The Socratic method is a form of cooperative argumentative dia-logue between individuals, based on asking and answering questions to stimulate critical thinking and to draw out ideas."* **WIKIPEDIA**

Whilst asking any question will result in greater insights, knowing the right questions to ask will enable the Digital Marketing Manager to excel in their role, and for the team as a whole to contribute to a successful strategy.

Digging for goals

The Digital Marketing Manager's role is to live the brand, breathe the brand, and be the brand. To be able to do this, it is vital to learn as much as possible about the brand and understand the goals of the organisation. What follows is a series of questions that will help you understand these and unearth the hidden gold beneath.

We developed these questions to help us quickly get a picture of where a business is at and how we might be able to support it. The important thing to note is that these 'questions' are delivered as part of a fluid and natural conversation that usually takes no more than an hour. Your role is to set the environment so that the person you are talking to is able to be open, honest, and fair. Then you must listen, take notes, and learn.

Start by opening the conversation with seemingly unassuming questions like: *"How are you? How's business?"*. Then ease through the following:

Business background and history

These questions help us discover more about the business, its history, and *why* it exists.

- Please tell us a little bit about the history of your business.
- How did you get into this line of work?
- What led you to set up the business?
- Where do your competition usually get things wrong?

Business goals

It's time to probe for the numbers that are critical to the business. We want to learn whether the business is growing, shrinking, or staying the same as well as discovering its commercial vision. Through these questions we will also understand how target-orientated the team is. Remember that the person you're asking may not know the answers but the important thing is that they are challenged to think about them.

- What are the targets or objectives for your business?
- What does the business need to achieve this year?
- How is that different from the previous year and the year before?
- If you could describe in one sentence what 'making it' would look like for your business, what would it be?
- How do you want others to describe your business?
- What do you want to be doing in five years?

Website goals

Where does the website factor in the business's day-to-day? Usually, sales and lead-generation are pretty crucial, but websites can (and should!) operate in many other ways.

- How does your site help you achieve your business goals?
- How does the website help generate leads and/or revenue (i.e., online sales, enquiry forms, brochures, etc)?
- What roles/purpose does the website play for the business?
- Who do you expect to use the website?
- What do you want them to be able to do?
- How can the website add additional value to the customer?
- What could the website do better?
- Is the website performing as it should?
- How much revenue/how many leads does your website need to drive this year?

- If your website were a person, what job description would you give it? i.e. sales, customer service, marketing, technical support.

Conversion goals

This is where we talk details on what a new lead/sale is worth to the business and, crucially, how much can be invested to acquire it. Please note that the emphasis isn't on getting 'hard' numbers here but the conversation around conversion costs can be very revealing and can inspire the person being asked to go and calculate the answers.

- What is the target Cost Per Acquisition (CPA) for the project?
- How much can be invested to make a sale?
- What's your average customer/transaction worth to you?
- Of your existing marketing, how much do you pay for a new/sale (CPA)?
- Do you know your current conversion rate?
- What percentage of enquiries are converted into sales?
- How long does it take for an enquiry to become a sale?
- How long does a customer stay a customer?
- Do you know the average customer lifetime value?

Customer goals

Understanding who you are marketing to is the foundation of any digital strategy. Here we learn more about the profile of the 'perfect customers' for a business. This profile includes who stays a customer the longest, who is the most profitable and more importantly, who can get the best results from the product or service.

- Within your current set of customers, which are your favourites?
- If your business was made up of a greater proportion of your favourite clients, what would it look like?
- What characteristics do your favourite customers exhibit?
- Tell me about a project/sale that went really well recently.
- Who's your longest-serving client? Why do you think this is? Are they profitable to you?
- What work, in an ideal world, would you want less of?
- Where are your target customers, geographically?
- Where are your target customers, digitally? I.e. do they prefer to use your website or certain social channels?
- What anxieties/fears do your potential customers raise when they talk to you?
- What major challenges do you overcome for your customers?
- What do your customers really need?

Product or service goals

It almost goes without saying, but getting a deep knowledge of the products and services you will be marketing is crucial. You need to understand what's on offer, how it works and who would be interested in buying it.

- What are the key products and/or services that are particularly important to your business?
- Which is your best selling?
- Which is your most profitable?
- Which do you want to sell more of?
- Have you got any new products/services coming soon?
- If you could name any products/services you want to offer – which your competition already provide – what would they be?
- Why and when do you think potential clients/customers are lost?
- Why have clients left?

Sales messages

This is where we aim to gain an understanding of the sales messages that the business feels are effective. Now is not the time to say if you like them or not (we will appraise and re-visit these later on). It can be especially helpful to speak directly with the sales and customer services team as they deal with the day to day rebuttals of sales objections. This is often so much part of their second nature, that it is not applied to their website or marketing materials. Senior management can often be too detached.

- What makes your company great?
- What do you like to shout about?
- Are there Unique Selling Points and phrases that are important for your company to convey?
- How is your product/offering different from what's out there already?
- What are you most proud of about your product/service?
- What do potential customers really want?
- What do your customers like about you?

Competitors

Who does the business believe their competitors are? This will help to understand who the business measures themselves against.

- Who are your five main competitors? What do they do well? What can you learn from them?
- Who's leading in your industry/niche/vertical?
- Which competitors have good websites?
- Which competitors would you say have bad websites?
- Where does your competitors' web traffic come from?

Roles and responsibilities

Who runs the marketing, the website, and the related activities will differ heavily, although understanding this is crucial to a campaign's success.

- In your organisation, who is responsible for making the website a success?
- Who are the key personnel?
- Who will make technical changes in the business?
- Who are the other stakeholders?

- Who currently runs the marketing?
- Who publishes content on the blog?
- Who's responsible for the website when it goes wrong?
- Who built the current website?
- Are any 3rd parties involved?

Keyword goals

This is more of a search marketing question – information which will help inform the SEO (Search Engine Optimisation) and PPC (Pay Per Click) campaigns in the future. Asking these questions will help you to understand what the business *thinks* they need to target. These answers are likely to change during the keyword research process.

- What are the most important keywords to your business?
- Do you know what keywords your customers use when searching for your services on Google/other search engines?
- What would you search for?
- Have you ever done paid search (PPC) before? Do you have access to the account and keywords used?
- Do you have Google Search Console (GSC) access? If so, do you ever check the data?
- If you have worked with an agency previously, do you have any old tracking reports?

Tracking and system goals

How well does the business track current website and marketing activity?

- What is the status of tracking on the site?
- Are phone calls being tracked?
- Do you use a system to store leads and enquiries?
- Is Google Analytics or another web tracking service installed on your website?
- Do you know how many purchases/enquiries/downloads happen through the website each month?
- When a potential customer gets in touch, do you ask them how they found you?
- Do you know which marketing channel works best for your business?
- Do you have a CRM?

Other marketing activities and existing documentation

Think of these as bonus questions, usually for businesses/brands who have invested more in marketing previously. You generally have to use your own judgement here as to what you ask for.

- What previous marketing activity have you done? Please supply any existing documentation you think might be useful including which channels were used, which performed best, and why.
- Do you have any previous print work (brochures/leaflets/magazines/fliers)?
- Do you have brand guidelines?
- Do you have Tone of Voice guidelines?
- Have you ever established buyer-personas? Do you already have customer segmentation data?
- Do you attend trade shows? Utilise email marketing? Use Social Media?

There are many more questions you *could* ask, but the above will help you cover the most important. It is also worth noting that these questions also form the brief for the subsequent project, carrying out a Digital Marketing Audit.

Just remember you don't *have* to ask each one, especially if previous answers have already covered it, and you can always come back and dig deeper if you feel you need more insight. After all, much like Yvon and his impulse buy, you may not know where this is all going until you stumble across that nugget of gold!

Activity – Asking business questions

Perform the business questions above on the business you represent or reach out to a local business, or a friend or family member who runs their own business. Approach them as their new Digital Marketing Manager – they will likely enjoy the opportunity to talk about their business.

- How did you get on?

- Reflect on how you felt asking the questions and how your interviewee answered them.

- What would you try differently next time?

Chapter 6: Audit and prioritise

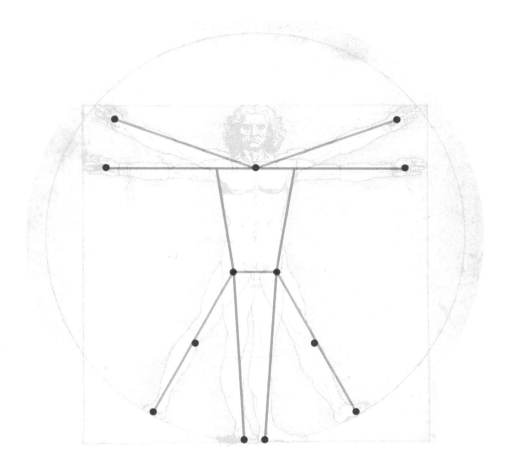

> *"Learn how to see. Realise that everything connects to everything else"*
> **LEONARDO DA VINCI**

The physio room

I've reached an age where there are players on my football team that are literally half my age. I'd been struggling with my shoulder. Something just wasn't right so I went to the physio to have it looked at.

"Hmm", he said looking at me, head cocked to one side. "Can you sort my shoulder?", I asked. "Give me a massage? An injection?"

"I could", he said, "but... it's actually your left ankle..."

"I don't think so... it's my shoulder that hurts!"

"Well, you see", he said. "Your muscles all interrelate. When your thigh contracts, your hamstring relaxes. Yin and yang. What's happening here is that your ankle is weak. All of the muscles around it have hardened and are compensating for the weakness. As a result, your gait has changed. You are hitching to the left. This means your lower back muscles are working extra hard on the left and to counter this, your right shoulder blade is working extra hard to stay in position. This is causing knotting and is why you're in pain. Let's work on your ankle and your shoulder will soon ease up."

I was blown away. It all made absolute sense to me. I thought back to an ankle twist a year ago. I knew it, but I'd not had the perspective to see it myself.

Six months of exercises later, I was better than ever.

Overwork one set of muscles and you'll run the risk of damaging others. Don't pay attention to your diet, or exercise, or mental health, or your teeth, or your physical wellbeing, then your entire system suffers. Busting an ankle, or having a frozen shoulder, does not have to stop a body from functioning but the chances of being able to perform at full potential is drastically reduced.

The same is true for your website and digital marketing. Ignore areas of your online presence and your business won't perform as well as it could. A structured, thorough, data-led appraisal of your marketing performance is the key to knowing exactly what your strengths and weaknesses are and, subsequently, where you should invest your time and resources.

Just like the physiotherapist, you should not take your own initial self diagnosis as the truth – we don't with our clients, new or existing. You need to conduct a full examination to find the actual problem. This means setting your own prejudices aside and using facts to prescribe the right course of action. We achieve this via, what we call, the Digital Marketing Audit (DMA).

What makes a website great?

So, what is 'good'? Any form of assessment or appraisal is done against a series of predefined criteria. If you want your website to be great, you first need to decide what the characteristics of a great website are. Of course, this is a subjective activity and everyone is likely to come up with a different set of criteria depending on their preferences and the purpose of the website.

> ### Activity – Consider three of your favourite websites
>
> What makes them so good? What characteristics do they have?
>
> Make a list of these. Then rank them in order of importance.
>
> Assess your website against this list. Does it have the characteristics to be great?

Get hooked on spotting greatness

Chances are, you may come up with a list of things that make any website great. It is likely to include some of the following:

- Guides you through the site
- Clear navigation
- Trusted brand
- Everything is understandable
- Great quality and up-to-date content
- Simple layout
- Lets you shop by your goal
- It's fun!
- Has personality
- Inspiring Imagery
- Strong call to actions
- Sets expectations (e.g. delivery times)
- Easy to complete tasks (i.e. forms)
- Testimonials are visible and credible
- Draws you in
- Looks nice/aesthetics
- Clear message
- Customisation which helps you
- Practical
- Mobile optimised
- Fosters a community

- Easy to use
- Trustworthy
- Fast to load
- Useful
- Helpful
- Free, valuable content
- Clean design
- Engaging
- Social
- On my side
- Enables you to set email reminders
- Great reviews
- Easy add to basket
- Frictionless payment/checkout
- Learning
- Customer services
- Reviews
- Recommendations
- Inspiring
- Has great content
- Easy delivery options

Make it part of your routine to note down websites or Apps which provide a great experience. Whether it is functionality which works really well, content which delights you, or something that is interesting where you didn't expect it.

Minimum expectations

You may note from the exercise above that we have high expectations for every website we visit. Customers are unforgiving when these expectations are not met. Sites like Amazon and Google do an incredible job of giving the user what they want and, while it may be daunting to have them as the benchmark, Digital Marketing Managers must rise to the challenge. To have a well-designed, user-friendly, multi-functional website is a bare minimum. You may not have the money, resources, or skills of behemoths like Amazon but you will need to find a way.

The first step is to find out where best to focus your energy for the fastest and best returns. This is where the Digital Marketing Audit comes in.

The Digital Marketing Audit

A marketing audit is best thought of as an inspection of your brand's marketing. It is an investigation into what is working, what isn't working and ultimately where things can be improved. The principle is to get as much information as you can from as broad a spectrum as possible. This will help build a picture of the whole and equip us with lots of useful data to inform our decision making and enable us to *Shoot the HiPPO*.

The Digital Marketing Audit could include a wide range of mini-audits across the full range of activities you are undertaking and, crucially, also include things you are not doing. There is overlap between digital and offline marketing, as an audit without a digital focus will be unfit for purpose and vice versa. We take the approach of trying to get as close to observing the whole picture as possible whilst also not drowning in data or experiencing paralysis by analysis.

The following is an example of some of the reports we produce at Footprint in a standard Digital Marketing Audit. It is common that we expand upon these or explore some areas in more depth in relation to activities the client is currently undertaking. So don't see this as an exhaustive list but rather a solid starting point.

You will note that even what we would consider a basic audit includes a huge amount of data from a wide range of sources. It is also time consuming and as a minimum we commit 24 hours to the process. That investment of time is worth it as the audit guides the future strategy and becomes the foundation of everything to follow.

We break the digital marketing audit into a series of mini reports that include:

- Investment Payback Report.
- Tracking Audit.
- Google Analytics Analysis.
- Initial Keyword Research and Position Benchmark.
- PPC Account Feasibility or Existing Account Audit.
- SEO Technical Audit.
- Competitor Analysis.
- Spellcheck, Readability, and Accessibility.
- Social Media Review.
- Content Marketing Review.
- Backlink Report.

- Content Audit.
- UX (User Experience) Audit.
- Influencer Report.
- Digital Carbon Audit.

Let's explore each of these reports and the questions we hope to answer with each. Everyone's audit process and tools will likely differ, but if you start with the questions you need the answer to, the rest of the process is much more approachable.

1. Investment Payback Report

In this report we analyse the impact we estimate we may have on the business. By quantifying the potential returns in advance, it helps make better decisions about where to invest. This report answers the following questions:

- What is your approximate Market Share?
- What is the current website conversion rate?
- What would the impact be if traffic increased in 10% increments?
- What would the impact be if the conversion rate increased in 10% increments?
- What would the impact be if both traffic and conversion rate increased in 10% increments?
- What is it worth to your business to increase traffic and conversion rate?
- How much are you investing into digital marketing?
- What is the payback period for your investment into digital marketing?
- What is the net present value of future cashflows (cash)?
- What is the net present value of future cashflows (impact on valuation of the business)?

These questions can be daunting to approach. But, there are many online calculators that can help you calculate these reports.

2. Tracking Audit

To make effective decisions, it is important to be equipped with accurate data. Through this audit, you need to check a range of data collection and analytics platforms to see if they are configured correctly.

We advise setting up the tracking to capture everything you can. Even if you do not use all of the information now, it may become useful in the future.

Answer the following questions to assess how well set up the website tracking is. The objective is to answer 'yes' to all of these questions or to mark it as redundant if it is really not relevant to the work you are doing.

Item	Done (or N/A)
Is Google Analytics (GA) set up?	
Is Google Search Console verified?	
Is eCommerce tracking set up?	
Is phone call tracking set up? (tracking "tel:" link clicks and/or dynamic call tracking)	
Have you set up filters for bots, spam, multiple views in GA?	
Is your live chat tracking set up? Are you feeding the data into GA?	
Are "mailto:" events configured? So you can see email clicks in GA	
Is email tracking set up? So you can track your email campaigns in GA	
Is video tracking set up? So you can see video plays in GA	
Are all of your goals being tracked in GA? Whether these are contact forms, transactions, phone calls or more.	
Have you integrated with 3rd party data sources? For example Hubspot form submissions being captured in GA	
Are downloads being tracked as events in GA?	
Is event tracking set up for outbound clicks in GA?	

If you're not sure how to check each of these things, then there is a wealth of support on our website and across Google.

3. Google Analytics Analysis

This is the report in which we review how people have used your website. That is, the actions they have taken whilst on the site. This includes things like where they have come from (ie, referral from other site, Google search, direct visit), how long they stay on your site and what actions they have taken whilst on your website.

Google Analytics is a tool that is often too powerful and overwhelming for its own good. There is endless data which can be refined and viewed in a myriad of different formats.

The following questions help you get a top-level snapshot of how your website is performing. To make the most out of this section, it is advised you gain access to the Google analytics account and investigate as you go. Through answering these questions, it is hoped that you will diagnose something that is worthy of further investigation.

- **Where is your traffic coming from?** Organic, Direct, Referral, Paid, Social, Email, or Campaigns?
- **Is your website engaging enough?** Look at Bounce Rate, Pages Per Session, and Session Duration.
- **Which pages are letting my site down?** Pivot landing page volumes using bounce rate and bounces against the site averages to find the pages that most let you down.
- **Is your mobile experience engaging?** Compare mobile bounce rate, pages per session, session duration and page load time with desktop performance.
- **Should I translate my site into other languages?** Use the language report to see visitor figures in different languages.
- **Should I be doing more to keep people coming back to the website?** Search 'count of sessions' in the main search bar to see how often people come back.
- **Which traffic sources are driving the most revenue to my business?** Look at the goal report and view goals by source/medium to see which marketing channels are working best for your bottom line.

Google's own GAIQ (Google Analytics Individual Qualification) is a great way to get to grips with how to get the most out of GA, but using the search functionality – typing what information you're looking for – is a great starting point.

4. Initial keyword research and position benchmark

'Keywords' are the words (or phrases) people type in when searching for things online. Keywords are one of the foundations of any digital marketing strategy. Identifying popular keywords helps you to understand the ways in which people may find you, your products and services. This knowledge will help you focus your content, on-page optimisation (SEO) and how you target paid search (PPC) campaigns.

In the Digital Marketing Audit, the goal of keyword research is to understand which keywords may be important for your business. It will also help you understand where you sit within the current market and what you *could* achieve.

At this stage, it is intended to be a snapshot to give you an insight. Whilst thorough, it is not an exhaustive piece of research designed to form the campaign strategy (this comes later).

The basic steps to finding the right keywords to use include answering the following questions:

- What would you type in?
- What do your customers call your service/ product?
- What keywords are you already using on the website?
- What keywords are your competitors using?
- What variants could you use?
- Is spelling important for your audience location/dialect? E.g. Jewelry vs Jewellery

With this information, we use Google Keyword Planner and Google Trends amongst other tools to discover related keywords and the estimated monthly search volume for them. This data provides the 'size' of the market, with which you can then approximate the traffic this will drive to the website if you rank in position 10, five or even position one.

Once we have this data, we refine this list and then use a rank tracking tool to benchmark where you are currently ranking for each keyword within Google.

Use a rank tracking tool such as Moz, Ahref, or SEMrush (which often have free trials) to check all of the keywords that you have found and see where you currently rank for each in Google. With this you see how many of these are on the first page (position 1-10), second page (position 11-20), third page (position 21-30), fourth page (31-40) and beyond.

This will help prioritise where to focus your efforts. Anything ranking on page two usually provides the greatest opportunity to drive additional traffic in the shortest time – something we call 'low hanging fruit'.

Look at those areas where you think you could deliver results fastest. Typically these are the keywords which are ranking on the bottom half of page one and the top half of page two.

Activity – Further reading

Read more about keyword research in the SEO chapter later in this book.

5.1 PPC account feasibility audit

Paid search is a hugely important part of any marketing campaign as it is the most controllable and predictable method of reaching the right target audience at the right time. But, it can be one of the most costly if not set up and managed correctly.

Before you spend money advertising you need to conduct a feasibility audit to understand if the money will be well spent or not. Most platforms (like Google Ads or Facebook) make it very easy to spend your budget but don't always make it as easy to ensure you get the best return on your investment (ROI).

Key questions we ask as part of the feasibility audit:

- How much are you willing to spend on a sale/lead?
- How big is the potential market (i.e. what is the average monthly searches or how big is your audience)? Are there enough people looking for what you're buying?
- What is the average cost per click (as approximated by Google/Facebook)?
- How much can you afford to spend per day? Can you get enough clicks per day to make paid search worthwhile?
- What is your current conversion rate – what % of visitors purchase/contact you?
- If you don't have conversion rate data, are you confident that when a potential customer lands on your website they can easily purchase/get in touch? Compare your site to your competitors if you're unsure.
- Based on your conversion rate and cost per click data, will the return on investment be worthwhile for your business?

The data provided by Google's Keyword Planner or Facebook's Ad Manager is not always 100% accurate, but it will quickly highlight whether you can undertake paid search cost-effectively within this space. If the initial result does not look hopeful, don't automatically rule it out, you may simply need to change your target keywords or target audience.

5.2 PPC account audit

Whilst the feasibility audit builds a picture of the *appropriateness* of paid search for your business (assuming you are not already doing it in any meaningful way), the account audit reviews the actual *performance* to date.

There are many, many questions we would ask as part of a paid search account audit and very often these can vary depending on which platform the campaigns are being run through.

The following list is based on whether you're using Google Ads/Facebook and the principles can be applied to almost any advertising platform.

- Are you able to accurately track when users buy/contact/convert from your adverts? Is the tracking working?
- Are there clearly defined budgets? Is performance being constricted too heavily by budget?
- Are the campaigns set up with appropriate bidding strategies/goals?
- Are the campaigns set up with appropriate audiences/keywords in mind?
- Are the campaigns set with an optimal time of day, geographic, language and device settings? Are you speaking to the right people, in the right place, at the right time?
- Is the account set up with appropriate network targeting? Are you confident that when your users see your ads, they are willing/able to act as desired?
- Are ad groups grouped by common themes?
- Is the ad creative compelling and relevant to the target audience/keyword?
- Do your ads offer clear value to the audience? How does it compare to your competitors?
- Is ad creative being tested and the freshness maintained?
- Do the adverts include keywords, calls to action, and sales messages?
- Do the adverts direct people to a relevant landing page?
- Is the landing page compelling? Is the content related to the ad which the user clicked on?

This list could continue, there are hundreds of different facets you need to check as part of a thorough audit. Each small setting which is not promoting the best-possible performance will compound all the other areas of non-performance. Even if the issues seem small in isolation, together they can have a significant impact.

As part of an audit there are some particular questions you can ask to gauge the level of cost (or missed opportunity) which can help direct your optimisation efforts.

Over the last year look at your ads account, establish what your average cost per conversion is, then look at:

- How much have you spent bidding on non-converting keywords? Look under the 'search terms' if checking in Google Ads.
- How much have you spent on sending traffic to broken (404'ing) or inappropriate landing pages?

Take that wasted ad spend and divide it by your current cost-per-conversion – assuming you had an optimal campaign that's how many more sales/ contacts you would have received.

> **Activity – Further reading**
>
> Read the full chapter on PPC later in this book to learn more.

6. SEO technical audit

The SEO technical audit benchmarks your website's current technical compliance and presents a clear series of recommendations and improvements which are needed.

The audit can range in breadth and depth, but we work to produce a representation of the site's health, so we can easily compare pre and post audit scores.

To rank well in search engines you must:

- Provide a technically sound website which search engines can 'see' and navigate easily.
- Provide content which helps the user complete the task that they set out to do when they started the search.
- Provide signs of trust and authority. These are usually external signals (often links) used to verify whether the content on the website is supported by other trusted sources.

The SEO technical audit that we run at Footprint Digital looks at over 200 factors. These are too many to list, but we do cover lots of them in more depth in the chapter on SEO.

- Broadly-speaking, we would consider the following areas as part of an SEO audit and approach it with these questions in mind:
- How well is the site built?
  - How many errors are there?
  - How easily can search engines crawl the website?

- Does the website contain target keywords? This is so search engines can see the themes/topics the website is trying to rank for. Check for your target keywords in the following areas:
  - In the page <title>
  - In the headings (<h1><h2><h3> etc)
  - Within the content itself
  - In image filenames and ALT tags
- How fast is page load speed? Is the site fast for search engines and users?
- Is the website mobile-friendly? Does it provide the best experience to Google's mobile crawler?
- Are there any obvious signs of penalty from Google? Usually because you have acted against their webmaster guidelines.

The main focus in this audit are the 'on site' elements – those which are under your direct control. We recommend breaking out the Backlink audit into its own investigation. See more below.

The real importance of an audit is not just to surface a list of things which are 'wrong' or 'broken' but also to produce a plan to grow your footprint and online visibility. Think of the process as compiling a list of opportunities and new initiatives.

Activity – Further reading

Read the full chapter on SEO later in this book to learn more.

7. Competitor positioning review

There's an old joke about outrunning a bear. Two campers hear a bear and one starts running. *"What are you doing? You can't outrun a bear."* says the other. *"I don't have to. I just have to outrun you."* is the reply.

Everything is relative within marketing. There is an argument to say that you don't have to be perfect, you just have to be better than the rest. So we look at our sites and whether they are 'good' or 'bad' in relation to their online competition.

To conduct the analysis, choose five competitors and review their sites against yours in the following areas.

- Homepage.
- A product or service page.

- Contact us form.
- Brand strapline.
- Unique selling points.
- Homepage introductory copy.
- The amount of Calls to Action (CTAs) and their quality.
- Whether testimonials are used.
- Visible awards, qualifications, accreditations, and associations.

By doing this, we aim to answer the following questions:

- If a user were to visit you and any of your competitors online, which website would provide the best first impression?
- Whose site presents products and services in the best way and why?
- Which website is fundamentally easier to buy from?

What's really important here is that you are auditing the experience for any points of friction and suggesting ways to remove them.

At a minimum, we expect the outputs of this analysis to form a lively discussion around where the opportunities lie and where the current competitive advantage is. Nothing inspires a business to change/invest in marketing more than this kind of process!

8. Social media review

Within social media marketing, it's far too easy to build the wrong stats or be completely unaware of the true potential you have. You may need to make some decisions on how best to spend your time and understand what 'good' really looks like.

As part of a social media audit process, we would typically want to know the answer to the following questions:

- How many followers do you have on each platform?
- Which platforms do you post on?
- How frequently do you post messages?
- Which are the most commonly used hashtags?
- What level of engagement (likes, comments, shares etc) do you achieve relative to your following?
- Do you engage in conversations through your social platforms?
- Is the level of engagement with your posts growing, stagnant, or declining?

- Are there any social media platforms which are abandoned or have out of date creative?
- Is the information about your company accurate and up to date for each platform?

It's with this knowledge that you will need to re-assess how you are using social media and how this needs to change to work with your new marketing strategy.

> ### Activity – Further reading
>
> Read the full chapter on Social Media later in this book to learn more.

9. Backlink report

The backlink audit is where we investigate how other websites link to yours. The creators of Google grasped early on that the way to understand which website was the 'best' for any given search could be determined by the number and quality of backlinks (links) from other websites. Each link was seen as an endorsement.

In the years since, the SEO industry has been based largely on building links to influence rankings. Google takes a dim view of links that are built to manipulate its systems and as such we find it hugely worthwhile to audit the links to a website to ensure that none go against Google's guidelines or are likely to cause trouble in the future.

Running this audit requires access to tools which can identify the links pointing back to your website. Tools like Majestic, Ahrefs, SEMRush, and SISTRIX are paid options and recognised by the industry, but Google Search Console can also provide a view of the backlinks you need to be conscious of.

Whichever method you choose to capture this information, these are the questions you need to ask yourself:

- Are many of the websites linking to you recognisable brands?
- Do most of the links come from websites based in the territories you serve? Or failing that, at least territories that speak the same language.
- How many of the websites linking to you have low or no trust scores? (backlink tools like Majestic provide scores to depict levels of trust).
- Is the anchor text (the clickable text which the link is based on) unrelated to your product or brand? Even more crucially, is any of this anchor text

based on irrelevant or malicious things like prescription drugs, gambling, pornography etc?

Some of the above may appear daunting initially, but the picture we're trying to build is one of trust. The more trustworthy your backlink profile, the better your website will perform.

It is important as part of this process to compare your own website with the competition – these are the people you need to be able to beat.

10. Content audits

Perhaps the most broad of all of the audit types, if you work with anyone within the marketing world they would approach a content audit differently. We break audits down into three broad areas, but naturally the scope of the audit depends on the goal.

Content success

If we were auditing content for 'success' we'd typically be looking at the content for its ability to generate traffic, links, shares and new business. If you are starting a new content strategy this helps to ensure you are taking all the learning forward with you. What level of engagement has the content received from social media?

- How many backlinks (see below) has the content received?
- How much traffic has the content generated and from which sources?
- What were the outcomes after people viewed the content?

Broadly-speaking, any evidence of the content being talked-about is a really strong signifier of a successful campaign.

Content appropriateness

When we think about appropriateness of content, we generally think about how well it talks to the target user(s). Typically this kind of audit would be run by a copywriter or a strategist who is able to get into the mind of the intended audience and can judge what has been written.

- Does the content answer my question?
- Can I see my needs or anxieties met by the content?
- Do I have to work hard to read and understand the content?
- Is the content sincere?
- Is the content of an appropriate length for the platform?

This is a highly subjective audit, and really requires a solid understanding of your target audiences.

Content accuracy and site accessibility

Lastly, accuracy – which can come in many forms, but spell check, sentiment analysis, and readability can all be focused on here.

If the copy on your website is hard to read or full of spelling errors people will not stay and engage in what you have to offer. As well as being important to users this is also important to search engines.

Review how easy it is to read your website and whether the spelling and grammar is accurate.

- Is your site free of spelling errors? – Use a tool like InSpyder to spell check your site.
- What is the readability score for your site? – Use a tool like Hemingway App or Grammarly to assess readability.
- Does your website achieve accessibility standards? – Use a tool like W3C to check if your site achieves web accessibility standards.

Even without the ability to check all your content quickly at scale, running some manual checks across key pages on your website is worthwhile.

11. Influencer Report

Get in the know about who you should know in your space – an influencer report can jump-start that process.

We often find that businesses we work with know who their competitors are, but not who the *influencers* are. However, knowing exactly what someone's influence is on an industry and on consumers can be tough to gauge without extensive research.

You can speed up this process, tools like Buzzsumo and Sparktoro can quickly help you answer these questions:

- Who writes and posts about content within my industry or subject area?
- Of these people, who has the largest following and gets the highest engagement?
- Which hashtags are particularly relevant within this space, and how engaged are they?
- Who, out of the influencers, has a blog or website and is more likely to work with me to publish my content?

Using this data, our report will then give you your top targets to start reaching out to. Create mutually beneficial relationships with these people and leverage their impact for your marketing strategy.

12. Digital carbon audit

Many people don't realise that everything we do online has a carbon footprint, including our websites.

More and more businesses see the importance of working towards more sustainable and carbon-conscious ways of operating, which is why we have created the Digital Carbon Audit.

For those who are serious about having a 'green' website and leading the way in their industry, the following tools are ones we use to help people understand how they can make a positive impact for the future.

- **Ecograder.com** – this website carbon calculator was developed by a US-based web development agency called Mightybytes. It helps you calculate your site's carbon footprint and it also offers some useful tips on things to improve.
- **websitecarbon.com** – another great website carbon calculator developed by Wholegrain Digital, a London-based web development agency. They help you calculate the weight of your site and how much carbon is emitted each time someone visits a page.
- **Google Lighthouse** – this is a useful tool we can access through Chrome browser. It checks the performance of your site and you can also use this tool to set a performance budget and track the progress over a period of time.
- **Safari Energy Impact** – This tool is only available to Mac/Safari users and it allows you to run an energy impact report in real time on any given URL.
- **Page Speed Insights** – page speed is very important for digital sustainability. The less time it takes to load your website, the less energy is consumed. Use this tool to check the speed of your site.
- **Webtest.app** – this is another page speed tool and it's powered by renewable energy. It allows you to use a 'green' tool to test the 'greenness' of a website.
- **The Green Web Foundation** – this is a non-profit organisation with a mission to run the entire Internet on renewable energy. You can use their URL checker on https://www.thegreenwebfoundation.org/ to see whether a website is hosted on a green host or not, or you can also install

The Green Web plugin on Chrome to see which sites are 'green' when browsing the internet.

We will further discuss the principles of a 'green' website and how to approach improving them in Chapter 19.

Activity – Further reading

Read the final chapter of this book on digital sustainability to learn more.

Time for a cuppa

If you find the idea of conducting a Digital Marketing Audit intimidating, don't worry! It's normal, and understandable. There's a mind-blowing amount of data and insight that is born out of it. What's more, if you do it well, it will produce a (very) large list of tasks and things to do. But that is the point. These audits will become your roadmap and something you turn to again and again. It is what you have to do if you are going to make sure you are focusing on and fixing the right things.

Imagine what would have happened if the physio administered an injection to the supposed injured shoulder instead of identifying and resolving the issue with the ankle.

You cannot fix a problem without first identifying it. So pop the kettle on, have a cuppa and get on with it. You'll be glad you did!

Activity – Digital Marketing Audit

Perform a digital marketing audit incorporating as much information as you can find. Or, contact the Footprint Digital team to get us to perform one for you!

Chapter 7: How the web works

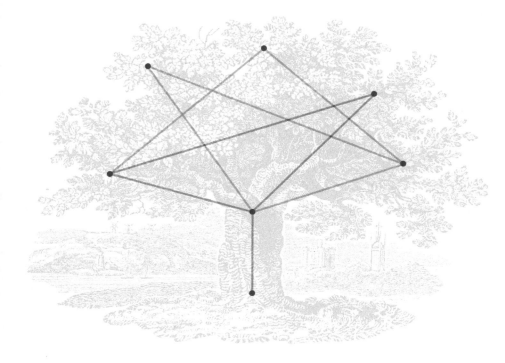

> "It has been said that something as small as the flutter of a butter-
> fly's wings can ultimately cause a typhoon halfway around the world."
> **AUTHOR UNKNOWN**

The hidden life of trees

*"What I had stumbled upon were the gnarled remains of an enormous
ancient tree stump. All that was left were vestiges of the outermost edge. The
interior had completely rotted into humus long ago — a clear indication that
the tree must have been felled at least four or five hundred years earlier."*[41]

*How can a tree cut down centuries ago still be alive? Without leaves, a tree
is unable to perform photosynthesis, which is how it converts sunlight into
sugar for sustenance. The ancient tree was clearly receiving nutrients in some
other way — for hundreds of years.*

---

41 Wohlleben, P. (2017) *The Hidden Life of Trees.* Glasgow, William Collins.

Peter Wohlleben's 'The hidden life of trees' is a fascinating insight into the life, death and regeneration of trees. It explains how trees live like human families with their tree children and how, as a collective, they create an ecosystem that mitigates the impact of extreme heat, wind, and cold. It also reveals a fascinating mystery of how trees in forests, through interconnected roots and complex fungal networks, operate as an extended nervous system connecting multiple trees as one. Through this they support one another by sharing nutrients with the weak and dying, they communicate to one another about environmental risks by releasing chemicals, and are even said to have the ability to talk to one another.

The unseen, ever-changing, interrelated tree networks are not unlike the internet. Or rather, the internet is not unlike the ordered chaos of the natural world: hidden, complex, and with an incalculable number of different factors contributing to the whole ecosystem.

The (world wide) web or internet is ubiquitous and inescapable. You may not need to understand how the web works to use it, but to understand your audience, the mechanics of paid search, tracking, and search marketing, a firm grasp of the fundamentals will give you an edge.

Like the underground world of forests, it would be impossible to document and grasp a clear picture of how the web functions in its entirety. Instead we will focus on the principles.

What is the internet and what is the web?

The Internet and the Web are not the same thing – you wouldn't be the first to think that was the case though.

The internet

A single computer can be connected so that it can communicate with another. When a collection of computers is connected, this is known as a network of computers. The internet is best thought of as a collection of networks.

The internet's origin dates back to the 1960s, when the US military created a network called ARPANET as a communication system and backup for all of the information they collected and stored. It was originally interacted with via a command prompt interface, which limited its use largely to academic institutions, government organisations, and businesses.

In 1990, Tim Berners Lee created HTML (Hypertext Markup Language) to create user-friendly websites. Rather than typing in commands to access data, the World Wide Web was born, providing a more graphically-friendly way of interacting with the information stored on the internet.

The web

The term 'web' originated because each web page or website is connected with hyperlinks, aka links. When visualised at scale, the links between each page and website is said to look like a (spider's) web of content.

The internet and web are all fundamentally built on relationships. Hardware (in the form of large computers known as servers) is networked together, with the web overlayed on the top to help users navigate from one space to another.

How the web works

When you want to connect to a server on a network to view its content, you need to direct your own device (be it a mobile, phone, laptop, TV or other) to that server by inputting its address.

An IP (internet protocol) Address is the unique address used to identify a computer on a network. Think of it like a telephone number: for communication to work you need to have a phone number that is unique to you and not shared by anyone else.

Like telephone numbers, IP addresses are hard to remember, so websites are provided with Domain Names to give a more memorable address to access the information on that server.

Activity – IP addresses

Type 216.58.206.132 into your web browser, what happens?

To ensure that all the various networks which make up the internet agree that a Domain Name matches an IP address, a Domain Name System (DNS) is used. This is quite simply an address book of websites which is looked up when someone enters an address into their browser.

Once you've typed in the name of the website you want to visit, and the DNS looks up the IP address it needs, it then connects to the web server. When the connection is established they then 'agree' on the language they will communicate with, defined by an HTTP (Hypertext Transfer Protocol) message. Assuming the server is happy, it sends a 200 (Okay) message

– these response codes are also particularly important for Search Engines and therefore Search Engine Optimisation (SEO) which we will cover soon.

It's easiest if you think of web servers and your web browser (i.e. Chrome or Firefox) 'talking' to each other. The web server serves you the content, then you interact via the browser to send instructions, to receive new content, or to send information to be processed.

Billions of these conversations between servers and clients (typically people, but not always) take place on any given day.

How URLs work

A URL (Uniform Resource Locator) is a unique identifier used to locate something on the internet. It is also referred to as a web address.

URLs are essential for search engine spiders (the code which Search Engines like Google use to collect information on the web). Search Engines use URLs to discover content, by first finding the location the content resides on and then requesting it. URLs consist of multiple parts – including a protocol (commonly HTTP or HTTPS) and domain name – that tell a web browser how and where to retrieve a resource.

Understanding the makeup and structure of a URL is therefore very helpful in SEO for knowing how content will be organised and optimised. Therefore URLs should always be as concise and accurate as possible.

Anatomy of a URL

Below, you can see the typical parts that are used to make up a whole URL. A URL's anatomy can be very simple or it can include many component parts.

1 Protocol	**Keyword priority**	**SEO tips for URLs**
2 Subdomain	Observed Google priority of keyword placement	• Use **subdomains** carefully. They may be treated as separate entities, splitting domain authority.
3 Domain	1. Domain	• Separate **path** and **page** keywords with hyphens.
4 Top-level domain	2. Subdomain	• Anchors may help engines understand page structure.
5 Folders/paths	3. Folder	• Keyword effectiveness in URLs decreases as URL length and keyword position increases.
6 Page	4. Path/page	
7 Named anchor		

① Protocol	**Popular TLDs**	**Popular ccTLDs***	**Popular extensions**
② Subdomain	**.com** - commercial	**.cn** - China	**.htm** - Static HTML
③ Domain	**.net** - infrastructure	**.de** - Germany	**.html** - Static HTML
④ Top-level domain	**.org** - non-profit	**.uk** - United Kingdom	**.php** - PHP code
⑤ Page/file name	**.edu** - schools	**.nl** - Netherlands	**.asp** - ASP code
⑥ File extension	**.info** - informational	**.eu** - European Union	**.aspx** - ASP.NET
⑦ CGI parameters	**.biz** - small business	**.ru** - Russian Federation	**.cfm** - ColdFusion
	.name - personal site	**.ar** - Argentina	**.jsp** - Java code

*ccTLD = Country code TLD

Finding websites

How users discover a website (or the brand attached to it) has changed dramatically over the last 30 years – and will likely continue to do so at an ever-increasing rate.

In the early life of the web, there was much more expectation on the user to find the right website for themselves. People shared web addresses with one another, websites presented long lists of addresses, and people referred to physical, printed directories such as *"The Good Web Site Guide 2001"*[42] which were much like the phone book.

Search engines – the doorway to the web

Search Engines were basic in the early days, and retrieving the right websites was hit and miss. Over a 10 year period they developed dramatically, becoming more effective and taking their place as the default tool for web users across the globe.

Google's dominance in the search market was hugely significant in changing the face of the web and the way we all consume information online. Their focus and dedication to building the strongest algorithms has set the standard and made the internet accessible. The onus to remember the address of a website is gone. Typing in something close to what you are looking for into Google (or Bing) will usually get you to where you are going. As Google and other search engines have become more sophisticated, they may even have a better idea of what you're looking for than you do.

---

42 Edmonds, G. (2000) *The Good Web Site Guide 2001: A-Z of the best 1000 web sites for all the family.* London, Orion.

In addition to Google, there are myriad other sites that also act as search or discovery tools – like Amazon, Youtube (although this is owned by Google), Facebook, and Instagram, to name just a few. Each of these businesses extend far beyond the website. They have applications (Apps) which install directly to your phone, TV, car, speaker, fridge, and more. They integrate with one another and with other services, sharing (and selling) information, and creating links you aren't even aware of.

The web, as we know it, is almost unrecognisable from when Tim Berners-Lee created it. He still insists it hasn't realised its full potential and he is not totally happy with how it has grown and developed[43]. This network of networks is a living and breathing thing. Whatever we currently understand about it is unlikely to stand still. The pace of development will continue to quicken.

The future of the 'web'

For those who remember a time pre-internet, the 'world wide web' would have conjured up images of typing in website addresses, and the sound of a dial-up modem squawking as it connects to an analogue mobile network. This idea (and sound), no matter how nostalgic for some, is thoroughly a thing of the past.

High-speed internet and mobile data connections will likely continue to grow at a staggering rate, changing the content we can produce and the complexity of the websites and applications which will deliver them. Running in parallel with this development is the increased power and sophistication of mobile devices. Just 50 years after we sent a man to the moon, we now carry devices 100,000 times more powerful.

App downloads grew from 84 billion in 2016 to 105 billion in 2018.[44] Mobile device usage has now overtaken desktop and laptop usage. More of the world is accessing the internet on the go than ever before. The rise of the app has reduced the emphasis on websites, and given us yet more opportunities to engage with brands, and brands with customers. The emergence of The Internet of Things and developments such as 5G mean that the only thing you can be sure of is that websites and apps

---

43 Guardian (2017) *Tim Berners-Lee: I invented the web. Here are three things we need to change to save it* [online] available at: https://amp.theguardian.com/technology/2017/mar/11/tim-berners-lee-web-inventor-save-internet [accessed 28 April 2020]

44 Iqbal, M. (2019) *App Download and Usage Statistics.* [online] available at: https://www.businessofapps.com/data/app-statistics/ [Accessed 28 April 2020]

will continue to grow and evolve – the line between the two is already becoming blurred.

Whatever the future holds, for those looking to speak to their audience with the right content at the right time, the opportunities are vast.

Chapter 8: Establish your brand's identity

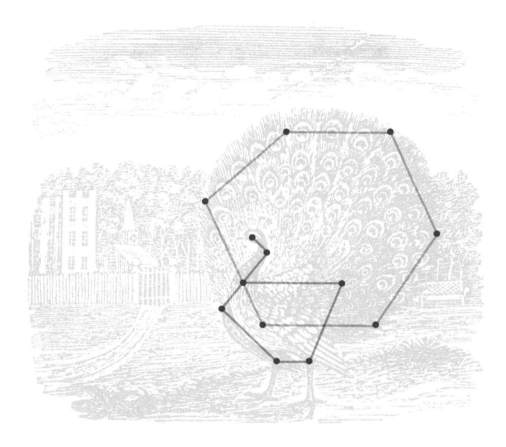

The Apple story

Early personal computers were built by technicians for technicians. Steve Jobs changed that. Apple obsessed about user experience and their designer-centric approach allowed them to build elegant and user-friendly products. But, their success is down to far more than that.

Jobs was a marketing genius. He understood the power of stories and crafted them around ideals that enabled customers to buy into a collective purpose. For many Apple consumers, he established the identity of the brand as something beyond just its physical products.

Apple marketing campaigns focused on what Apple represents, rather than being heavily laden with features and benefits. Jobs marked his return to Apple with the "Think Different" campaign that associated Apple with unconventional, visionary thinkers such as Albert Einstein and Mahatma Gandhi. As well as challenging people to 'think different', it was also an open invitation to those that identified with the idea to join the Apple brand.

When Jobs recruited Pepsi executive John Sculley to run Apple, he famously asked "Do you want to sell sugar water for the rest of your life or come with me, and change the world?" By crafting a story of what the Apple brand is about, beyond the technology, he created a fluid company that could adapt and respond to the changing marketplace.

What is a brand?

Businesses are in a constant state of flux. Customers and team members come and go. As do products and services. So what really is a brand? If you take away its clients, team, and products – does it cease to exist? How do brands that have been around for hundreds of years still consider themselves the same business?

Brands are a fiction. They are the stories that are told. A well written story is enduring and enables thoughts, ideas, and values to sustain throughout time.

Apple is a brilliant example of a well crafted story that represents something beyond its products. Being able to clearly define what your brand thinks and believes will enable customers to connect with you and understand what to expect, making for an enduring business.

This chapter will show you how you can produce a tangible document that articulates the core language of your brand to communicate this to your team, customers, partners, and the world.

Find your voice, find your message, find your platform

At its core, marketing is very simple. Marketing is delivering the right message to the right people at the right time. The skill is applying this simplicity in a very complex environment.

The most successful brands in the world have a very clear proposition that their audience can connect with. Defining and crafting this message and ensuring that it meets the needs of its audience is called 'brand positioning'.

Positioning your brand starts with understanding what you want to say to the world. You need to find your voice, find your message, and find your platform.

Be yourself, there are enough other people

Brands must be authentic. The temptation for brands and organisations is to sanitise themselves for the world – this is a mistake. Brand positioning must be undertaken with a commitment to absolute authenticity. The result must be a reflection of who you are, connected to the reality, rather than a statement of who you'd like to be. Constantly acting like the brand you want to be (without becoming it) is costly, time-consuming, and can appear disingenuous.

The art of authentically *"giving a sh*t"*

When we did our own brand positioning exercises, it brought up some choices that made us a little uncomfortable. We felt our authentic identity might not play well in the big wide world and we had to ask ourselves what we are about.

The first example of this is the phrase 'give a sh*t'. This is the value that everyone in the entire Footprint team connects with the most, and it provokes the emotive response that feels right to our team. The goal to 'help every business in the world achieve more' has been questioned by people outside of our organisation who feel it comes across as somewhat pompous and fluffy. 'Be a sponge' to explain the appetite for personal growth and absorption is a vital concept for us, but to some implies 'sponger' meaning lazy, a taker of things that are not deserved. 'We believe in people' has been criticised as being 'lofty' and 'idealistic'.

Although they're contentious, all of these values are a true reflection of our authentic selves. Instead of shying away from them, we have decided to embrace them. Promote them. Be proud of them. For some, our values and who we are will be a turn off. For others they may be endearing.

Brand positioning

Brand positioning is the process of developing a distinct position in the market in the eyes of the customer. To get there we use strategic brand communications – a term that connects a collective of questions such as:

- Why does the brand communicate?
- What does the brand want to achieve?
- To whom does the brand need to communicate?
- What does the brand need to communicate?
- How and where will the brand communicate?

It is primarily concerned with what the brand is going to say to the world and where it will say it – a roadmap for finding the brand's voice, message, and platform. The most successful brands in the world have a very clear proposition that their audience can connect with. Great brands then ensure that this message is delivered consistently across all of their chosen marketing channels and media, as well as being ingrained and understood by everyone within the organisation.

Brand positioning means different things to different people. The extent to which this activity is done depends on the size and aspirations of the brand. If a multinational company wants to introduce a new brand to the market they might put a team of 30 in a room for two years and design every element of the brand. Smaller businesses, on the other hand, may just buy a new domain, design a logo and *"see how it goes".*

The Brand Positioning Document – an asset no Digital Marketing Manager should be without!

At Footprint we define the vision, product, and positioning of the brand in a simple and accessible Brand Positioning document. This document exists to achieve alignment for everyone involved with the brand before it's communicated to your team, customers, partners and the world. It is intended to be a starting point and something that everyone will contribute to and work with.

Although we advocate investing as much time as possible into this process, we've honed our approach to get to the quickest usable output with the least amount of time.

We have condensed the document down to eight distinct focus areas which we present as different pages in a document or slides in a PowerPoint.

We look at the following areas:

- **History** – define the story of how the brand got to where it is today.
- **Why** – investigate the core reason for the brand to exist.
- **Vision** – articulate what the brand wants to achieve in the world.
- **Goals** – define what the brand intends to achieve. Looking at non-commercial, commercial and website goals.
- **Values** – what are the values of the brand?
- **Audience** – who does the brand exist to serve?
- **Products** – what products does the brand offer? Do these work cohesively to create a funnel that graduates customers?
- **Territories** – where does the brand serve?

Done correctly, a Brand Positioning Document is an eye-opening process, a source of provocation and investigation throughout your business. We aim to tackle this challenge with a few short activities delivered in workshop style sessions that last around 45-90 minutes each.

Activity – Tell your story

Write down the story of the brand you represent. How did it come to be what it is today? This could be as simple as a descriptive statement that would be found on the 'about us' section of the website. Usually it states the date when the company began, the story of the founders and the reason for the inception of the company. Think back to Yvon Chouinard, and the story of Patagonia.

Ours is as follows:

"We set up Footprint Digital because we didn't want to 'keep clients quiet'. We wanted to do good work and to be the best we could be; to be proud of what we do and to push ourselves to grow.

We strive each day to provide the perfect combination of technical expertise and collaborative human relationships to help people achieve things they never thought possible; to deliver exceptional digital marketing services that help people make more money online."

Activity – Refine your why

An exercise that builds on the Simon Sinek concept (see chapter four), and that can help you find the language for this is to write sentences that begin with *"We believe…"*

Write a handful and put these on the wall. Over time you will settle on something that explains your 'why' or purpose.

To take this a step further – Digital Marketing Managers could ask all team members to independently write down why the business exists – this exercise will provide a very quick and eye-opening view of how aligned the organisation is.

For Footprint this looks like the following:

"We believe that there is nothing people can't achieve and that together we can make it happen."

Activity – Articulate the brand's Big Hairy Audacious Goal!

The BHAG or Big Hairy Audacious Goal[45] is an aspirational statement. It explains where you would like to be in your dream of the future, or the change you want to bring about in the world. You are aiming to look beyond the horizon. The output should be aspirational and feel very scary as a target to achieve.

What is the change you want to bring about in the world?

- Is it big and hairy enough?
- Is it clear what it looks like to you?
- How does that make you feel?

Our BHAG feels almost impossible. It is:

"to help every business in the world achieve more."

---

45 Collins, J and Porras, J. (1994) *Built to Last: Successful Habits of Visionary Companies.* New York, HarperBusiness.

Keep your eyes on the prize

In the quest to find their brand's voice, identity, and ultimately its position, it is essential for a Digital Marketing Manager to reconnect with the brand vision and the goals that signpost the way.

What do the good times look like?

Picturing the future and visualising what you would like to achieve can often feel abstract and unrealistic. To make this more accessible, take a look at a model called 'Stages' which was developed by Shirlaws business coaches[46].

It looks at the growth of a business and the feelings of an owner or leadership team at each stage. As the business grows, those involved go through a range of emotions and experiences before the point of 'Good times' and 'Payback' is reached.

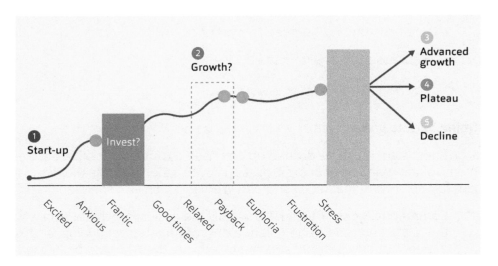

'Good times'[47] is the stage when everything is working well, the energy is good and the business is making good returns. Later, the leadership team

---

46 Rosling, J (2013) *More money More time Less stress.* London, 1Fish 2Fish.
47 Rosling, J (2013) *More money More time Less stress.* London, 1Fish 2Fish.

may get to the point where they look to invest to grow beyond this. Here they may experience stress or frustration before kicking on to advanced growth, plateau or decline.

Activity – What do the 'Good times' look like?

Consider:

- How many people are on your team?
- What products are you selling?
- How do you feel?
- Where are your territories?
- What is your turnover?
- What is your profit?
- What key people exist within the business?
- What products/ services do you offer?
- What are your key marketing channels?
- Major customers/ Sources of revenue
- What assets exist within the business?

Going back to goals

A business's goals can be divided up and used as a focus for different elements of the brand positioning process. They can then become the foundation for the onward marketing strategy. We like to gain an understanding of:

1. **Commercial goals** – these are usually the easiest for the business to articulate and tend to be revenue or profit figures set against a time period. But how a brand sets out to achieve them should be in alignment with its identity.

2. **Non-commercial (or cultural) goals** – these are usually the things that are important to the business, but don't fit neatly within its financial targets. These can be every bit as important as indicators of success to the business. They also tend to be a great starting point when

understanding the brand identity, and very helpful in creating a solid narrative.

3. **Website goals** – these usually play a part in both the commercial and non-commercial goals. A website isn't just a direct sales tool, it has huge value in the benefits it can provide to customers who aren't ready to do business just yet.

Activity – Non-commercial, commercial, and website goals

Define what you are aiming to achieve in each of these areas with the following two exercises.

1. Orbit

The Orbit model is a common business tool that helps define goals over a defined period of time.

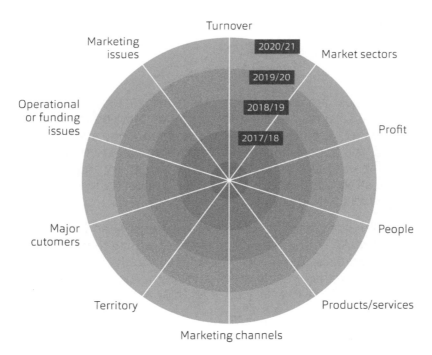

Often developed from a SWOT analysis, the orbit model looks at what you are trying to achieve against each of the following categories:

• Turnover.

- Market sectors.
- Profit.
- People.
- Products/services.
- Marketing channels.
- Territory.
- Major customers.
- Operational or funding issues.
- Marketing issues.
- Assets.
- Culture.

You can use the orbit model to set goals for different areas of your business and map out how these will develop over time. The foundations for this exercise can come from a SWOT analysis of the business.

Activity – Complete an orbit

2. Values

The term 'values' can mean different things to different people, but in a business sense values are the core principles that your business stands for. Often values are lived rather than defined. They are implied rather than stated. You get a feel for the values of the business by observing how people in the business behave. The challenge is to try and find the words for these abstract observations and to try and understand which values the entire organisation believes in.

Earlier, we discussed that a brand needs to be authentic and 'itself', the values are how we make this happen. The benefit of writing them down is that it becomes much easier for potential customers to quickly identify whether this is an organisation they want to do business with. The best way to develop a set of values is to listen to what your team think and go from there.

Values should mean something. They should describe the way that you do business and set standards everyone in the team strives to achieve. At their most simplistic, values can be a series of statements which characterise how and why you do what you do. These shouldn't be 'fluffy' or intimidating – fluffy values are too abstract and intimidating ones will be ignored. The aim is that they are easy to live/work to and generally act as guiding principles.

Going back to Apple, they say its values are:

- Accessibility.
- Education.
- Environment.
- Inclusion and Diversity.
- Privacy.
- Supplier Responsibility.

At Footprint, ours are:

- Believe in people and what they can achieve.
- Value relationships.
- Together we make it happen.
- Be proactive, ask yourself *"what else can I do?"*
- Take responsibility and take action.
- Be open and honest.
- Encourage people.
- Embrace challenges.
- Give a sh*t.

> **Activity – Define your values**
>
> What are the values of the brand you represent?
>
> What makes the brand tick?

Fill your audience with perfect customers

Who does the brand exist to serve? Who is the audience? What are the brand's perfect customers like?

Most businesses, even if they haven't spent time analysing their customers in any detail, will probably know what a good and bad customer looks like. This is beyond 'customers who pay on time' or 'customers who spend the most money'. These are customers who you do the best work for, and those who advocate your brand once you have finished working with them.

To make good use of this information as part of your marketing strategy you will need to have a clearer picture of a good – or even 'perfect' – customer.

With this in mind, you can ask yourself whether your website, marketing activities, and even sales materials might appeal to them.

The perfect customer

The perfect customer exercise will identify the people you need to target, enabling you to develop a position in the market that separates you from your competition and also identifies potential new product opportunities. It should be conducted as a group session that starts with a blank whiteboard or sheet for the group to contribute ideas. This group should represent various members of the team from across the business so that you can incorporate everyone's experiences to understand what really makes the perfect customer.

Start by asking the simple question: *What are the characteristics of your perfect customer?*

To get the best answers to this question ask the attendees to think of their favourite customers from those on your books. More often than not, businesses talk only about the demographic information. Instead, focus on the human characteristics to get a real picture of who these customers are and why the relationship with you is so effective.

Ask:

- What makes them perfect?
- What is it about them that makes you like working with them?

Let the feedback flow and when contributions slow ask the following:

- **Human** – What kind of characteristics do they have? Are they fun / laid back / demanding?
- **Demographics** – What age bracket / gender are they?
- **Spend** – How much value do they bring your company?
- **Geographical** – Where are they located?
- **Qualities** – How would you define their values and what is important to them?
- **Products** – What products do they purchase?
- **Roles** – What kind of job do they work in or household do they come from?

By this point you will have created a list of all of the interesting and detailed characteristics of your customers.

Revisit the list with the group. Which of these characteristics are absolutely essential for the client to work with you? Highlight the minimum requirements for you to be able to work with them. It might be the ability to pay, in the right location or with a certain outlook. Underline these. B customers are those that meet the minimum threshold. Stop working with and disregard all people that do not meet this criteria. We call these C customers.

Now look at the criteria that are left. Which of these characteristics make them perfect? Underline these and this is your list of what an A client is.

How many of your customers have the B characteristics but could become A customers if you supported them with new products? From this create a list of new products that could convert your B's to A's.

How does this categorisation of customers relate to your brand values? Chances are that your perfect customers will be in alignment with your values. This is an important time to remind your organisation that you choose the customers that you work with. Imagine if all of your customers were perfect customers… what would the business look like?

> ### Activity – Undertake a 'perfect customer' workshop
>
> Time to try it yourself, work with others to create a picture of the perfect customer.
>
> Once you think you have the A,B,Cs defined, see how they fit with your current customers.
>
> Are there any obvious things you notice?

How to turn imperfect customers into perfect customers

Go into a supermarket and you will notice that the delicious warm bread is really cheap and is situated at the back of the store. It is sold as a loss leader to get you into the shop. The shop doesn't make money on the bread, but it does when you pick up three other products and a chocolate bar at the till.

A well-crafted product mix will serve to build a funnel of customers that can easily connect with your brand. Choose the products that make it easy for your customers to become loyal.

The product chain

We use the model below, which we call the product chain. We have used Footprint as an example, to show how you can create a funnel of products that develops your customers towards perfection.

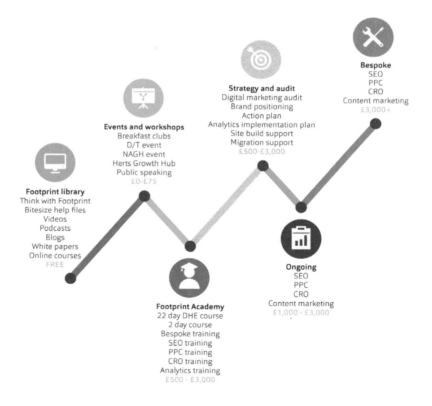

We would love to work with brands that invest £5,000+ per month on bespoke work with us. But when connecting with our vision to *"help every*

business in the world achieve more," we must realise that the chances of every client coming in and signing up for that straight away is slim.

Instead we must create products that allow customers to engage with us in small, bitesize ways. From here we can move them up the product chain to become perfect customers.

This product chain helps us achieve our goal of being able to help every business, but it also helps us to move customers from being imperfect to perfect. It creates a cohesive funnel that graduates customers – with this we can help businesses that aren't in the position to invest £3,000+ per month with us grow to a point where they can!

The amazing thing about the product chain is that it helps you identify and create products that also bring revenue in. Take our example. We would like £3,000pm+ customers, which is a lot to start with, so we created a £1-3,000pm product line that would capture people earlier on and enable them to experience our work. But that is still a large step for some. We realised that those that don't take it often don't have an understanding of the opportunity within digital or a plan to make it successful. So we produced an Audit product and a Strategy product. This helped them progress to the next stage.

Again, this can be a big step for some customers. We realised that those that did not understand digital could not see the benefit of an audit or strategy, so we created education products to upskill them. For those earlier in the chain we created accessible workshops and events. For those not there yet, we have a range of free resources to support people. Each of these products helps move imperfect customers towards becoming perfect customers for us.

Activity – The product chain

What products could you create that would enable people to experience your business in an accessible way?

What products could be introduced to help graduate clients up the chain?

Where, geographically, are your customers?

A clear knowledge of where your customers are shapes the focus of your marketing efforts. The nature of your business will dictate how limited (or not) your marketing efforts will be by target territory. A brand selling digital assets (ebooks, videos, images) may look at a global market, whereas some-one selling haircuts will operate in a small, easily defined local market. It is worth noting that customer needs, fears, and anxieties may be completely different from one territory to another – so what and how you communi-cate with these audiences may be different.

> ### Activity – where are your customers?
>
> Head into your Google Analytics account. Navigate to Audience > Geo > Location to review where your website visitors are coming from.
>
> Do the locations match with your target territories?
>
> Are there any missing? Are there any territories you hadn't expected?
>
> Do you think you should be changing your brand messaging to meet expectations of some audiences?

Great words to make a great brand

As you will have seen throughout this chapter, there are many aspects of your brand, your product, and your customer which you may never have considered before. Investing time to gain a deep and meaningful under-standing of your brand's positioning is crucial to succeed and move on to the next level. Make sure you capture this in your Brand Positioning docu-ment and share it widely with your teams and suppliers.

After we have completed the Brand Positioning document we look at the language that will be used by the brand. We call this the Brand Lexicon and in it we look specifically at the sales messages, calls to action, customer anx-ieties, differentiation or unique selling points, and tone. For each of these topics we have an activity that can help you discover the words you need to use. The output of these activities is shared alongside the brand positioning document. We think language is so important that we have created a whole chapter on it.

Chapter 9: Write your story

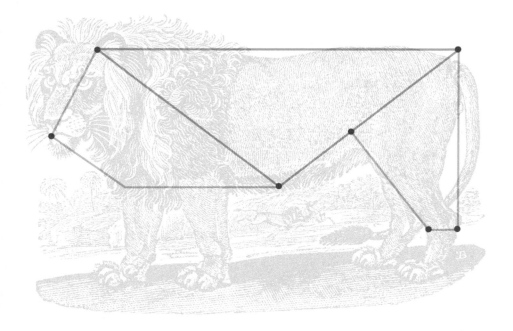

> *"Either write something worth reading or do something worth writing"*
> **BENJAMIN FRANKLIN**

The importance of great writing

The iconic businessman and original 'Mad Man' David Ogilvy valued good writing: *"The better you write, the higher you go in Ogilvy and Mather."* The challenge of distilling complex concepts into an accessible form that moves people to action has been the craft of marketers since marketing began. The world is complex and noisy. When writing for digital media we need to produce compelling, engaging messaging that quickly connects with the reader. The aim of great writing is simplicity. *"Simplicity is the ultimate sophistication"*, as DaVinci put it.

David Ogilvy also stated that: *"People who think well, write well."* So, a chapter on how to write could well be a chapter on how to think. This is a somewhat loftier challenge than simply being adept with spelling, punctuation and grammar. But, the concept of 'thinking well' helps explain our reasons for what we have chosen to include in this chapter.

SHOOT THE HiPPO

In this complex world of noise, cutting through with storytelling is the winning strategy. Our suggestion that Digital Marketing Managers should be great storytellers is often met with a raised eyebrow. But we do believe that the Digital Marketing Manager plays a crucial role in shaping the story that we want the world to hear. It is often down to them to ensure that the brand's voice and message is protected and delivered consistently across a complex matrix of digital platforms. So, while the Digital Marketing Manager may choose to outsource the writing, we think it is very important that they understand how to select the language and the components of effective writing that do justice to the brand. This chapter also operates as a guide for those who simply want to write better.

Luckily, there's a formula that can guide the language you use. In this chapter, we'll:

- Show you how to harness the power of storytelling.
- Equip you with a language toolkit that ensures your content draws attention.
- Deliver some notes on style.
- Share some tools that will help you improve your writing.

Storytelling – the hero's journey

Take some of the world's most recognised stories and you will find a common story arc. In his book *"The Hero With a Thousand Faces"*[48], Joseph Campbell explains the classic plotline known as the hero's journey. He argues that so many of our stories are effectively retelling the same story. *Harry Potter*[49], *Star Wars*[50], *The Hobbit*[51], *Spiderman*[52], *The Lion King*[53] and many, many others all follow the same structure. Here are the plot points that occur in the hero's journey:

1. The story begins with a character who is in a zone of comfort in their ordinary, familiar world.
2. They want something or they experience a call to adventure.
3. They refuse the call.
4. They cross the threshold and enter an unfamiliar situation.
5. They meet a mentor.

48 Campbell, J. (1949) *The Hero With a Thousand Faces*. Princeton, Princeton University Press, N.J.
49 Rowling, J.K. (1997) *Harry Potter and the Philosopher's Stone*. London, Bloomsbury Publishing PLC.
50 Lucas, G et al. (1977) *Star Wars: Episode IV – A New Hope*. 20th Century Fox.
51 Tolkein, J.R.R. (2013 [1937]) *The Hobbit*. New York, HarperCollins Children's Books.
52 Raimi, S et al. (2002) *Spiderman*. Sony Pictures Releasing.
53 Allers, R et al. (1994) *The Lion King*. Walt Disney Studios.

6. They experience trials, failure, tests, allies, and enemies.
7. They adapt to their new world through growth and new skills.
8. They approach the innermost cave where they tackle a deeply held fear.
9. They are faced with death and rebirth.
10. They then experience a revelation.
11. They then change and take the road back.
12. They find atonement or resurrection.
13. A heavy price is paid.
14. They get their reward.
15. Finally, they return to their zone of comfort or familiar situation, having changed.
16. The story ends.

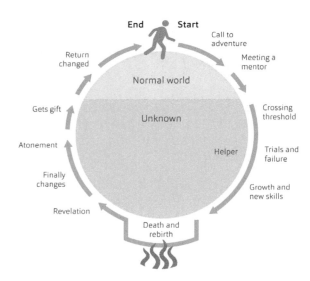

This well-used format is compelling on many levels and, importantly, its structure makes us care about the hero. We root for the hero. We are invested in the hero's trials and tribulations. We want to know what the future holds for our hero. And maybe we recognise ourselves in the hero. You can see this in action in the story of "*The Lion King*" in this example:

Hakuna Matata – Our problem free philosophy

The Lion King tells the story of a young Lion called Simba. He is heir to the throne of a vast kingdom that encompasses "everything the light touches" called the Pride Lands (1 Ordinary World). Soon tragedy strikes and his father the king Mufasa is killed by his brother Scar, who subsequently instructs Simba to leave the Pride Lands (2 The call to adventure). He tricks Simba into believing it was his fault. Scared and alone (3 Refusal of the call) Simba retreats to the desert (4 Crossing the first threshold).

New friends, Timon a meerkat and Pumbaa a warthog, befriend Simba and introduce him to a new life in the jungle (5 Meeting with the mentor). Simba lives with them and learns and embraces their philosophy for life 'hakuna matata', to live with a "problem-free philosophy". In these new surroundings, Simba grows physically and becomes stronger (7 Growth and New skills). Simba is reunited with his childhood friend, a lioness named Nala, and the two fall in love. (6 Trials and Failure. Tests, Allies, and Enemies).

Nala asks Simba to return to the Pride Lands to take the throne from Scar (8 Approach to the innermost cave where they tackle a deeply held fear). Simba must make a choice to save his kingdom or keep living his new life (9 Death and Rebirth). He is visited by a vision of his father's ghost who tells him to return and reclaim the throne (10 Revelation). Simba journeys back to the Pride Lands where he faces Scar (11 Changes and The road back). It is at this point he learns that Scar killed Mufasa.

Simba fights him (12 Atonement/Resurrection) and atones for his father's death by throwing Scar off Pride Rock (13 Pay a heavy price). Simba ascends Pride Rock and reclaims the throne (14 Reward). Simba is now back in the ordinary world having changed himself and the situation (15 returns changed) and the story ends (16 End).

It can be jarring to realise that a story that grabs you at an emotional level is so formulaic. But it is a tried and tested way to structure a story that resonates with an audience. It makes the audience care and keeps them invested in the journey. It helps the audience relate to the characters by allowing them to draw parallels with experiences in their own lives.

This pattern is apparent in a wide range of writing, and it needn't be reserved for books and film scripts. It is every bit as useful to craft a narrative arc for your brand. The audience or customer is the hero of your brand. By creating compelling stories that tell your customer's story, the appeal for them will be much greater. This structure can also be used to write a narrative for blogs, web content, articles, press releases, social media posts and any other form of content marketing that you produce.

Nike – leveraging the power of great storytelling

Nike has long understood the power of great storytelling. They promote products and run campaigns using memorable stories. This creates an understanding, in the eyes of customers, that Nike is about more than just shoes. Take the fictional advert from the film *"What Women Want"*[54] as a great example of this:

> *"This is why I run.*
>
> *You don't stand in front of a mirror before a run...*
> *and wonder what the road will think of your outfit.*
> *You don't have to listen to its jokes and pretend they're funny.*
> *It would not be easier to run if you dressed sexier.*
> *The road doesn't notice if you're not wearing lipstick.*
> *It does not care how old you are.*
> *You do not feel uncomfortable...*
> *Because you make more money than the road.*
> *And you can call on the road whenever you feel like it,*
> *Whether it's been a day... or even a couple of hours since your last date.*
> *The only thing the road cares about...is that you pay it a visit once in a while.*
>
> *Nike.*
> *No games.*
> *Just sports."*

Activity – Create a branded story

How could you, like Nike, create branded stories where your customers are the hero?

In the story, how are you inspiring them, spurring them on, and helping them on their journey?

Components for crafting killer content

> *"Don't wait for the muse. As I've said, he's a hard headed guy who's not susceptible to a lot of creative fluttering. This isn't the Ouija board or the spirit world we're talking about here, but just another job like laying pipe or driving long-haul trucks. Your job is to make sure the*

---

54 Goldsmith, J et al. (2000) *What Women Want.* Paramount Pictures.

> muse knows where you're going to be every day from nine 'til noon. Or seven 'til three. If he does know, I assure you that sooner or later he'll start showing up." **STEPHEN KING**[55]

The next priority for a Digital Marketing Manager is to equip their team with the right language for the brand. But we've all been there... You sit down to pen that masterpiece of creative writing that will engage and inspire the masses to connect with you and your brand, and you find yourself sitting, staring blankly at the screen, devoid of inspiration.

Components of the brand lexicon

Over years of testing, we have found that effective content includes eight components. The best way to avoid writer's block and ensure consistency when writing for your brand is to reflect on each component and write down all the words you can think of for each one. This language 'toolkit' or *brand lexicon* will make it easy to write interesting and compelling content.

The eight components are:

1. **Why** – why your brand exists, beyond what it sells.
2. **Goal** – the goals you can help your customers achieve.
3. **Audience** – who you are writing for.
4. **Keyword** – the keywords that capture your customers' questions.
5. **Anxieties** – your customers' concerns and barriers to buying.
6. **Sales messages** – makes your product or service great and different from other options.
7. **Calls to action** – the phrases that capture what you would like the reader to do.
8. **Tone** – the general character or mood you would like the brand to convey.

Once you've captured all the words you can, against each of these components, you can then begin to string together scintillating sentences that readers love and that bring your brand to life.

The brand lexicon in action

Here is a version of a homepage for Footprint that pulls together the eight components.

---

55 King, S. (2012) *On Writing: A Memoir of the Craft*. London, Hodder.

Key: Why | Goal | Audience | Keyword | Anxieties | Sales messages | Calls to action | Tone

Keyword: Digital Marketing Agency

Meta Title: Digital Marketing Agency In London and Essex – Make More Money Online!

Meta Description:

Header: Make More Money Online

Content:

There is nothing that you can't achieve. With our unique methodology and industry leading digital marketing agency team together we can make it happen.

We help £1-20million turnover SMEs that are itchy, driven, ambitious and frustrated join the dots so you can achieve things you never thought possible.

On average a 2 year engagement with us delivers 144% increase in traffic. Make your marketing more human with specialist data driven marketing services that include Strategy, SEO, PPC, CRO and Content Marketing.

Our proven process and exceptional results have attracted some of the world's biggest brands such as Itsu, Cartoon Network, Huawei and Legal and General, but, more importantly, we will deliver for you.

We're here to help. Contact our friendly team of experts today.

How to create your brand lexicon

To make it easier, we have produced activities for each of these eight components. These activities help tease out the language that truly represents the brand. On completion of the activities, we add the brand language to the brand positioning document. From this, you can then form engaging messages that represent your brand. We also circulate this to all stakeholders involved in marketing your brand.

1. **Why** – an understanding of why your brand exists beyond what it sells.

Hopefully you will have already defined this using activities in the brand positioning chapter. Write your brand's *Why* down and have it front of mind.

2. **Goal** – an understanding of the goal of the content.

Before you jump into the composition, it's time to step back and clarify why this content exists.

- What is the business's objective of the content we are writing?

- What do you ultimately want the user to do?
- What key performance indicators will you use to measure whether or not the content was successful?

3. Audience – an understanding of exactly who you are writing for.

> *"Write to please just one person. If you open a window and make love to the world, so to speak, your story will get pneumonia."*
> **KURT VONNEGUT**

We love this quote from Kurt Vonnegut. Instead of trying to write for a mass of people, think of a specific individual that you are writing for.

- Who are they?
- What do they need?
- Why are they there? What are they looking for?
- Are there any environmental or cultural considerations?
- How can they be the hero in your story?

4. Keyword – an understanding of what keyword you would like to target with the content.

Gone are the days where you need to stuff your content full of keywords. Make sure that your content is written in a natural way and is totally focused on being useful to the person reading it. It is worthwhile considering the keywords that people may be typing to find what they're looking for – and what your content addresses.

- What question do they want an answer to?
- What would they search for to find the answer?
- What are the priority keywords we want to target?

Read more about keyword research in the SEO chapter.

5. Anxieties – an understanding of what the barriers are for individuals.

> *"Marketers and designers need to put themselves into other people's shoes and imagine what they'd want."* **SETH GODIN**

Our experience is that it is not how well you *sell* something: it is how well you *address customer concerns* about buying something. This may sound like a subtle difference, but the implications are huge. For example, we ran a test on a leaflet delivery company's call to action button. The common 'lowest delivery costs around' was soundly beaten by the unassuming 'reliable delivery'. The reason is that, in the leaflet delivery industry, there is anxiety around whether the leaflets get delivered. The 'reliable delivery' message responded to what customers worried about. Gearing your content to address anxieties will yield fantastic results.

Ask yourself:

- What's on your customers' minds?
- Why don't they buy?
- What reasons might they have to not work with you?
- What could have happened in the past that might have given them a bad experience?

One of the best sources of answers to these questions is your own sales team. They spend all of their lives listening to the anxieties of customers. This often becomes such second nature that these gems do not make it through to the marketing copy. Ask them for the most common questions they get asked and their best responses.

Activity – four big questions

To investigate anxieties at a deeper, strategic level, and to develop your position in the market, run a workshop with key members of the team.

Ask them:

- What is wrong with our industry?
- What does the industry need?
- What are our biggest challenges as a business?
- What makes us different?

Another way of helping you understand your customers and how you can answer their anxieties is to take the time to truly understand what they're buying from you. This is about understanding the difference between 'what you sell' and 'what they buy'.

Think about the benefits of your products instead of their features. Armed with this knowledge you will be able to write content that really connects with what matters to your customers. The following examples illustrate the different ways of positioning the same product:

- Saucony Ride running shoes OR a crucial piece of equipment to help you complete the marathon you've just signed up for.
- A 7-seater Nissan OR a safe mode of transport for your new family.
- The latest iPhone OR a symbol of wealth, style, and sophistication.

When we do this with our own services at Footprint, it looks like this:

What do you sell?	What does your client buy?
Digital Marketing Services	Make More Money Online
Digital Marketing Audit	Clarity and direction of what to do next
Paid Search Management	Increased sales with great ROI
SEO Webinar	Loads more customers visiting your site
Content Creation	Engaged clients that buy more

Activity – What you sell versus what your client buys

Make a list of the products you sell and compare what you sell to what the client buys. Think about how you can apply this to your content.

6. Sales messages – an understanding of what makes your product or service great and how you differ.

When we talk about sales messages, we mean the things that a brand says to make it sound attractive. There are sales messages that everyone in an industry uses because they are selling similar products or services. But there are also specific sales messages, called USPs (unique selling points) which define the things that only your organisation can do. These differentiate you from your competition.

Sales messages should be thought about at brand level, but also will be very specific to individual products and services. At this stage, we are trying to find the main general messages that are said about your brand.

For Footprint Digital, we communicate the following messages:

- **Be more human** – We believe that there is nothing that you can't achieve and that together we can make it happen. We use technology to unite. In everything we do we strive to be more human and make technology more human.
- **Join the dots** – We exist to help you see the wood *and* the trees. We understand our part in the whole. We get you results and educate you along the way.
- **On. Your. Terms** – An obsessive 'on it' approach to getting you results. We investigate your business and find answers to help you achieve your goals. Clear contract terms and transparent pricing that make us easy to work with.
- **Approach+able** – Human and processed. Specialist and generalist. Tactical and strategic. Data-led and creative. Exceptional technical knowledge, human relationships, and ruthless execution.

Activity – Elevator Pitch

What would you say to someone that you met in a lift?

What's your succinct and persuasive sales pitch?

Make this about the benefit you provide to the person you are talking to, rather than what you do.

For example, instead of *"I do digital marketing"*, we would say *"I help people make more money online"*.

Activity – Market, Service, Value, Product

This exercise is designed to help you define the characteristics of your Market, Service, Value and Product and capture the language from which you can create impactful messaging.

For each, write down a few points which best describe your brand or your business.

Market – Who do you sell to?

Service – How do you serve them?

Product – What do you do?

Value – Why do you do it?

7. Calls to action – the phrases you could use that state what you would like the reader to do.

You have spent time positioning your product, your brand, and addressing your customers' fears or worries. Now you need them to take action. What language do you use to encourage customers to take the next step?

A Call to Action (CTA) is the rallying cry, the nudge, the next step. It is many things, but its goal is to drive an action. A clear CTA is an essential tool to show customers what they need to do next. It should not only be the desirable action (from the brand's perspective), but also represent a logical step for the user.

A CTA isn't always BUY NOW!!

There are *many* different CTAs you can use, here are some examples:

- Get started
- See pricing
- Contact the experts
- Read more related articles

Some of the best CTAs are abstract but effective. Consider these pre-web examples:

- Dig for victory[56]
- Keep calm and carry on[57]
- Taste the rainbow[58]

Each of these examples demanded action and, in their own way, became a cultural icon. Who knew that something so seemingly 'simple' and so small could be so impactful and iconic?

The creativity and power of a well-formed CTA is hugely underrated. Often businesses don't recognise the power of great writing. What would the value of a well-crafted CTA be to your business? As a Digital Marketing Manager it will be your role to champion investment into it.

---

56 Government campaign to encourage households to grow their own vegetables during WW2.
57 Motivational poster produced in 1939 by the British government ahead of WW2.
58 Tagline for confectionary brand Skittles, designed by New York advertising agency D'Arcy Masius Benton & Bowles.

The context of a CTA is vitally important. Consider, for example, how a call to action will appear depending on whether it is being viewed on a smartphone or a desktop computer. Make sure the words, imagery, and design you use for your call to action are appropriate.

> ### Activity – List your potential CTAs
>
> Think about what your typical customers do on your website.
>
> Write down the simplest calls to action that reflect their likely responses.
>
> Then rewrite each CTA for each of the following audiences:
>
> - A wizened grandparent
> - A competitive entrepreneur
> - A young parent pressed for time
> - A competitive university student
>
> How does the language change for each CTA?
>
> Does this speak to your audience any better or worse than your initial selection?
>
> Remember to measure and test!

8. Voice – the general character or mood you would like the brand to impart.

What is the voice of the brand?

How do you want people to perceive your brand? Cool? Sophisticated? Trustworthy? Knowledgeable? The voice you adopt and present yourself with is key to creating this feeling with your audience. Their perception should relate to your core values and your 'why'. It should tell the hero's story, follow the hero's journey, share the hero's accomplishments. It is, in a way – everything.

Finding a voice which works for you and is achievable can often be a challenge. A voice which isn't realistic or authentic can be spotted a mile off. Most brands are spooked by this and opt not to have a discernible tone or personality beyond 'business formal'. Remember: be yourself!

The real art of defining a voice which works for you is establishing something that is real, is consistent with your values, and something you don't have to work for. Part of the challenge of defining your voice is first to listen. How do you and other team members sound when you're at your best? What words do you use and what kinds of conversations do you have with your stakeholders?

When defining our voice at Footprint Digital, we looked at the traits we wanted our team to have. We hire for them, we train with them in mind, they describe us through and through.

- Approachable.
- Helpful.
- Human.
- Insightful.
- Enthusiastic.

Activity – Establishing your voice

- How would you describe your voice currently?
- What words do you use when communicating with your stakeholders?
- What words don't you use?

Look at the language on your website, your print work, and your social media.

Then:

- How do you want your customers to describe you?
- What words would you like to use?

Ask yourself:

- How do these two lists differ?
- How can you begin to converge the two lists in a way which is achievable?

Notes on style

> *"There are three rules for writing a novel. Unfortunately, no one knows what they are."* **W. SOMERSET MAUGHAM**

There is no fool proof and globally accepted formula for how to write well. Nevertheless, when we write for digital formats we consider the following:

1. **Go in with your knickers down** – state what you want. Don't be subtle, people do not have the time or patience.

2. **Be more human** – make your writing approachable and personal. Gone are the days of the austere 'voice of God' brand. People buy people, and customers understand more than ever that great businesses are made up of great individuals. Embrace it and connect.

3. **Use your voice** – being more human means being yourself. When writing, follow the Stephen King rule and try not to overthink: *"the basic rule of vocabulary is use the first word that comes to your mind"*

4. **Tell a story – paint it so that your reader can see, touch, and feel the experience** – did you ever play rugby at school? I still wake up at night and remember the sting of pressing my frozen fingertips against my red cheeks to try and revive them. Worse still is the vision of the cold, heavy, metal scaffolding structure, wrapped in gym matts, that our PE teacher would tip his head toward as we trudged back in from training. This gesture meant that we were to use the last ebb of energy from our lifeless, hail-stung bodies to shunt this contraption back to the sheds. It looked a bit like the V of a bulldozer. Like a traditional ox plough, it sadistically dug into the ground. To complete this pointless task it was necessary to churn a huge, squelching, muddy channel out of the ground to drive it home. 20 of us would collectively charge, force it back a few inches and go again, and again, and again… and again. Finally, after an eternity, we would be allowed back in to defrost in the mercifully warm shower. I expect it was character building.

   Well… that is what it's like writing a book.

5. **Keep it short** – *"One should use short words, short sentences and short paragraphs"* – David Ogilvy. Get to the point and say it in the least number of words. When your writing is becoming drawn out ask yourself the following: *"what am I trying to say here?"* Then rewrite the sentence using the simple answer to that question.

6. **Keep it simple** – this does not mean that you have to lose depth. There's a difference between dumbing down what you write and simplifying it. Take writers like John Steinbeck, Dr Seuss, and Ernest

Hemingway. Each is known for powerful and evocative writing, but are equally accessible to readers at all ends of the Flesch-Kincaid readability test spectrum.

7. **Remove nothing statements** – to give your writing more confidence and clarity, remove clunky words and phrases that exist for no reason. Here are some examples:

   — 'in order to' – it's just 'to'.

   — 'In terms of' – if you're using this at the start of sentences or clauses, switch your subject and verb. (For example: 'In terms of digital marketing, it's a must in today's retail climate'. Could be changed to: 'In today's retail market, digital marketing is a must'.)

   — 'The fact that' – either don't use it or use 'since'.

   — 'Needless to say' – self-explanatory, don't use it!

   — 'In actual fact', 'basically,' or 'actually' – completely arbitrary, they never need to exist.

   — 'We understand that' – why would you tell me things you don't understand? Demonstrate empathy.

   — 'Tailored to your specific/individual requirements/your unique circumstances' – It's a commodification, be more explicit, or give examples.

   — 'Solution/global solutions' – what makes you different from any other solution? It's a total undersell.

8. **Use bullet points** – bullet points break up information, and when you look at a section of copy, your eyes will naturally be drawn to bullet points first. They act as a focal point and quick conveyor of useful information – just don't plaster your page in them. Here's an example:

   This copy sucks...

   One of the tallest student residences in the world, with spectacular views of the London skyline, Chapter Spitalfields features an on-site gym, as well as a variety of social spaces including a karaoke room, cinema, library, bar/lounge area and communal study spaces.

   This hall of residence offers modern, single bedrooms in 2-bedroom and 4-bedroom apartments, with fully equipped kitchens and bathrooms. Bedding and linen are provided on arrival, but students are advised to bring their own bath towels. Students are responsible for cleaning their apartment and laundering their bed linen.

   Now, not so much...

   One of the tallest student residences in the world, with spectacular views of the London skyline, Chapter Spitalfields features a host of social spaces including:

- An onsite gym.
- Karaoke room.
- Cinema.
- Library.
- A bar/lounge area.
- Communal study spaces.

Rent a bedroom in two or four-bedroomed apartments, with fully equipped kitchens and bathrooms. We provide bedding and linen on arrival, but you need to bring your own bath towels. Cleanliness of the apartment and your bed linen will be your responsibility, but we're always here to help if you've any questions.

9. **Avoid jargon** – there's a difference between jargon and complex language. Just be sure that you are not using words that are intended to bamboozle. And be aware that the words you take for granted may be jargon to everyone else.

10. **Avoid Weeing all over the place** – your customer is the hero. Avoid the excessive use of 'we'.

11. **Write drunk, edit sober** – *"Write drunk, edit sober."* – Ernest Hemingway. Take a space between when you write and when you publish (and drink lots!)

Let's talk tools

Artificial Intelligence is a little way off turning monkeys with typewriters into Shakespearean creators. But there are many tools that can support and enhance your writing. Here are our top picks:

- **Grammarly.** It's so good that everything our content team writes passes through its many algorithms. It makes you rethink all the small bits and bobs, captures your edits, and saves you from looking like a fool – it's a godsend!

- **Hemingway Editor.** While this doesn't cover your basic spellings, it focuses on making your work reader-friendly. It does this by pointing out your complicated sentences, passive language use, and more. A one-off payment required.

- **Each other.** Sometimes there's nothing better than admitting you're not the right choice when it comes to editing your work, because you're far too protective and single-minded, or just too close to the detail. Trust us. Hand it over to another set of eyes and let them do the hard work.

Bringing it all together

There is a lot to consider, we know. But by thinking clearly and creatively, from your customers' perspectives, you will be able to bring together all the learnings from above and craft your own killer content. Keeping storytelling, with your *Brand Lexicon* language toolkit and style guide at the forefront of your thinking. We know you'll succeed.

To the next step

With the Digital Marketing Audit done, the Brand Positioning document nailed, and an understanding of the language of your brand formed into a brand lexicon, it is time to work on the really fun bit – your strategy!

> ### Activity – homepage copy
>
> Complete the brand lexicon exercise and write a new version of your website homepage that includes all of the components of great copy.

Chapter 10: Develop a strategy

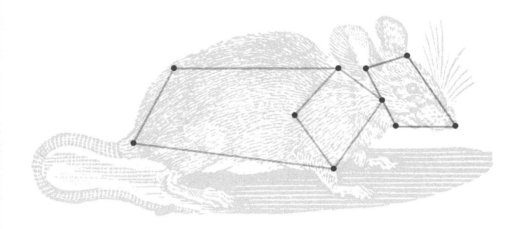

> "A journey of a thousand miles starts with a single step." **LAO TZU**

Who moved my cheese? – Spencer Johnson

The allegory 'Who moved my cheese' by Spencer Johnson[59] tells the story of two mice, Sniff and Scurry, and two little people, Hem and Haw, who live in a maze. One day they arrive at their usually reliable source of cheese, 'Cheese station C,' and realise that the supply is dwindling. The story then follows the different reactions each character takes to this situation. Immediately Sniff and Scurry depart on the hunt for new cheese, while Hem and Haw become angered and annoyed and blame each other for the problem. As Hem and Haw ponder the scenario, fearful of leaving the familiarity of their surroundings, Sniff and Scurry fearlessly tear ahead, taking wrong turns and getting lost, and yet, ultimately, finding a new plentiful source of cheese.

There are many interpretations of this allegory and multiple lessons that can be learned from the story. We learn not to be complacent, to anticipate change, to not fear change, and that the quicker we can adapt to change and explore new territory the more likely we are to prosper. We take these lessons into our approach to strategy.

---

59 Johnson, S. (1998) *Who Moved My Cheese?: An Amazing Way to Deal with Change in Your Work and in Your Life.* New York, Putnam.

Strategy is only real when realised

The strategy is a Digital Marketing Manager's action plan, a roadmap to stay aligned with the vision of the organisation and its goals. It defines exactly what actions are required for your business to succeed online, details who is responsible for each action, and when it is expected that these tasks will be completed.

Strategy is only real when realised – a well crafted plan is meaningless if it only lives on paper. A strategy must therefore be practical.

Strategy needs to be very, very fast

Strategy is direction and provides a focus of energy. Google talks a lot about setting a vision and then working hard to determine how to achieve it. Much like the mice in *"Who Moved My Cheese,"* they focus on action and trying things out. They would sooner 'fail fast' than 'over-plan'. Chairman and CEO of General Electric, Jack Welch, shares this ethos. In his book *'Winning'*[60] Welch refers to strategy as *"a living, breathing, totally dynamic game,"* that *"needs to be very, very fast and always based on learning."*

Strategy, not without thought

Whilst believing that a strategy must be both practical and fast we also believe the military adage, *"Time spent in reconnaissance is rarely wasted"*. This means that a strategy must also be well informed. Ploughing ahead and just 'throwing muck at the wall' is likely to be a slower route to effective results. Success comes faster if supplemented with some time spent strategising.

The one day strategy

The objective of this part of the book is to balance these contradictory forces. We will discuss how to quickly build an informed marketing strategy that you can immediately apply to your business.

---

60 Welch, J; Welch, S. (2005) *Winning*. New York, HarperBusiness.

Our experience is that, regardless of how important planning is, businesses struggle to contribute the time to the process. Conversely, the businesses that do find the time often tend to over-think and under-apply their planning. To keep the energy in the process, we maintain a balance between thinking and applying by limiting the planning process to a single day. We find this keeps us ninja-like and focused on action.

This slimmed down approach means that the resulting plan is not as thorough as it could be. We accept the limitations of this and instead focus on evolving the strategy whilst things are in motion.

The Simple Spreadsheet

Our answer to the challenge of quickly creating a strategy is the Simple Spreadsheet. We call it this because, on the one hand, it is very simple. However, it can become incredibly complex if required. This depends on the depth to which you complete it.

Completing the spreadsheet helps you decide which activities are worth investing in. The process forces you to make disciplined decisions about where you invest time and money. It helps ensure that your budget choices are driven by rational thought rather than by gut feel. It may sound dry, but it more often than not opens up the marketing plan to be more expansive and fun. Done well it will give you and the team the confidence to make bolder decisions.

Through the following process you can work towards creating a Simple Spreadsheet that will serve three purposes. It will:

1. Define the activities that are most likely to deliver results.
2. Become a working Digital Marketing Action Plan.
3. Be the point where results are tracked, reported, and appraised.

The Simple Spreadsheet will also answer the following questions:

- Which activities could we do?
- Which activities do we think have the greatest priority?
- Which messages should we be creating?
- How much will it cost and what will we get back?

The steps we take to create the Simple Spreadsheet are as follows:

1. Set 'global' goals – the overarching goals for your business.
2. Define the key audience personas that you want to target.

3. Define the channels where you will find your audience.
4. Choose which products you aim to sell.
5. Define what type of content you need to create.
6. Define your sales messaging, CTAs, and customer anxieties.
7. Project and prioritise – how much will it cost and what will you get back?
8. Think about KPIs – how will you measure how effective it is?

Here's what is involved at each step...

1. Before starting, revisit the Brand Positioning document

The Brand Positioning document (discussed in chapter eight) helps you develop a top level view of what your brand exists to do in the world, your global goals, and the general language that you want to use. Below, we will expand on a couple of areas that were touched upon in the brand chapter. So, have it in mind throughout the following steps.

2. Define the key audience personas that you want to target

In the Brand Positioning document we set you the challenge to define your 'perfect client'. That exercise focuses your attention on the core market of the business. The next step involves expanding on that work to identify a wider range of target audiences, as well as go deeper into defining each one.

Activity – Audience persona t-shirts

Complete an audience persona t-shirt.

Think about a type of customer that you work with or would like to work with.

Fill in the audience persona t-shirt and make notes on each of the below characteristics.

Repeat this exercise for as many different potential customers that you want to target.

Profile	Descriptive traits
Sex	Personality type
Age	Character archetype
Occupation	Skill levels
Location	Influencers
Income	Likes
Family	Dislikes
Cohort	Brands they trust
Loves	Individual values

Through the process you will find that there are ways in which you categorise your customers. Sometimes all of the characteristics you identify will be the same across customers, apart from a key characteristic that makes one type of customer entirely different to another.

For example, we break our client base into two distinct segments. £1-20million turnover organisations and £20million+ turnover organisations. Each of these groups operate in distinctly different ways.

The main distinction between clients that we work with is in the role the decision maker holds. In £1-20 million turnover organisations the decision maker will either be a Director or Marketing Manager (these organisations tend to have smaller marketing teams). In £20 million plus turnover organisations the decision maker is likely to be a Chief Marketing Officer or they are likely to have someone who is specifically in charge of digital, a Digital Marketing Manager.

Within each of these roles we recognise that some of them have decision making powers and *'can make budget decisions'* and some have to get permission from up the chain, so *'can't make budget decisions'*. This is a key differentiator for us and we pool these people into two separate groups.

So a breakdown of client profiles for us looks like this:

Financial	Role	Characteristic
£1-20 million	Marketing Manager	Can make budget decisions
£1-20 million	Marketing Manager	Can't make budget decisions
£1-20 million	Director	Can make budget decisions
£1-20 million	Director	Can't make budget decisions
£20 million plus	Digital Marketing Manager	Can make budget decisions

Financial	Role	Characteristic
£20 million plus	Digital Marketing Manager	Can't make budget decisions
£20 million plus	CMO	Can make budget decisions
£20 million plus	CMO	Can't make budget decisions

Activity – Segmenting audiences

Think about your own customers and segment them into separate groups based on criteria relevant to your business.

3. Define the channels where you will find your audience

Once you have defined the key audience personas using the t-shirt exercise, we can look into where those people can be found. For each persona you have selected, identify a list of the channels where you think those people spend time.

- Which of the channels are most likely to deliver the best results?
- Will your approach need to cover multiple channels?

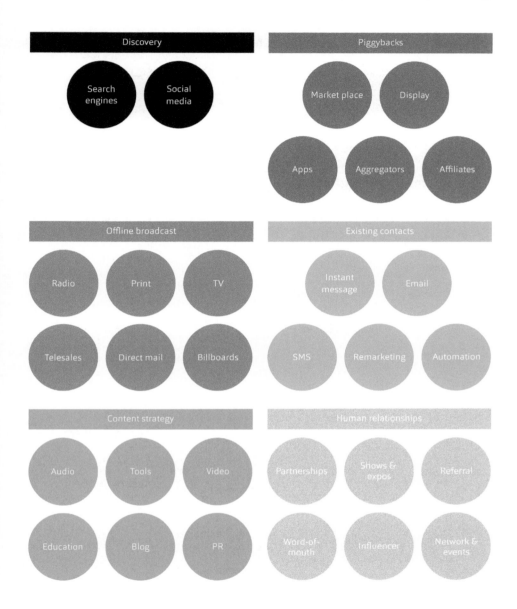

For example we may apply this to one of our key personas, £1-20million turnover Marketing Managers that can make decisions:

Financial	Role	Characteristic	Channel
£1-20 million	Marketing Managers	Can make budget decisions	SEO
£1-20 million	Marketing Managers	Can make budget decisions	PPC
£1-20 million	Marketing Managers	Can make budget decisions	Email
£1-20 million	Marketing Managers	Can make budget decisions	LinkedIn
£1-20 million	Marketing Managers	Can make budget decisions	Facebook
£1-20 million	Marketing Managers	Can make budget decisions	Instagram
£1-20 million	Marketing Managers	Can make budget decisions	Twitter
£1-20 million	Marketing Managers	Can make budget decisions	Word of Mouth
£1-20 million	Marketing Managers	Can make budget decisions	Events
£1-20 million	Marketing Managers	Can make budget decisions	Agency Partner Referrals – PR
£1-20 million	Marketing Managers	Can make budget decisions	Agency Partner Referrals – Accountants
£1-20 million	Marketing Managers	Can make budget decisions	Agency Partner Referrals – Design & Dev
£1-20 million	Marketing Managers	Can make budget decisions	Influencers
£1-20 million	Marketing Managers	Can make budget decisions	Shows & Expos
£1-20 million	Marketing Managers	Can make budget decisions	Workshops
£1-20 million	Marketing Managers	Can make budget decisions	Print
£1-20 million	Marketing Managers	Can make budget decisions	Video

Financial	Role	Characteristic	Channel
£1-20 million	Marketing Managers	Can make budget decisions	SMS
£1-20 million	Marketing Managers	Can make budget decisions	Radio
£1-20 million	Marketing Managers	Can make budget decisions	TV
£1-20 million	Marketing Managers	Can make budget decisions	Billboard

Activity – Choose your channels

Choose the channels that are most likely to deliver the best results

4. Choose which products you aim to sell

Once you have made decisions about the channels that will best reach your audience personas, you can match 'products' that would be most appropriate to them and each channel.

We use the term 'product' in a broad sense. We could ultimately be looking to sell a prospective client a large retainer package with us. You may find that it is far more appropriate to create smaller 'products' that allow potential customers to experience your brand and warm to the idea of working with you. For example a 'product' in this sense might be a 'white paper' that gives someone great value and could be 'purchased' in exchange for their email address. It is likely that there are many new 'products' that you can create that will have a low barrier of entry for new customers and at the same time get them into your buying funnel.

Activity – Match products to channels

Spread out all the audience persona t-shirts you want to focus on.

For each one, identify the channels that are most likely to reach them.

Now match your current products to each persona and channel, or imagine new proxy products that give value to each persona.

5. Define what type of content you need to create

Think of the types of content you can create as 'products'. For each audience persona and channel, which type and format of content would work well? Which would be worth your time and investment to create?

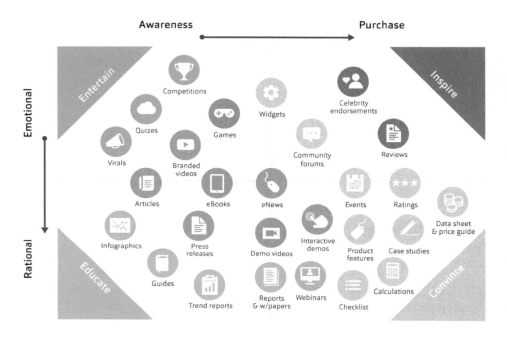

Here's what it looks like when we apply this to selling one of our products – the Digital Marketing Audit:

Financial	Role	Characteristic	Channel	Product	Content
£1-20 million	Marketing Managers	Can make budget decisions	SEO	Digital Marketing Audit	Case Studies
£1-20 million	Marketing Managers	Can make budget decisions	SEO	Digital Marketing Audit	Data Sheet price guide
£1-20 million	Marketing Managers	Can make budget decisions	SEO	Digital Marketing Audit	Calculators
£1-20 million	Marketing Managers	Can make budget decisions	SEO	Digital Marketing Audit	Checklist for picking agency

Financial	Role	Characteristic	Channel	Product	Content
£1-20 million	Marketing Managers	Can make budget decisions	SEO	Digital Marketing Audit	Product Pack
£1-20 million	Marketing Managers	Can make budget decisions	SEO	Digital Marketing Audit	Events Page
£1-20 million	Marketing Managers	Can make budget decisions	SEO	Digital Marketing Audit	Ratings
£1-20 million	Marketing Managers	Can make budget decisions	SEO	Digital Marketing Audit	Webinars
£1-20 million	Marketing Managers	Can make budget decisions	PPC	Digital Marketing Audit	DMA Campaign
£1-20 million	Marketing Managers	Can make budget decisions	PPC	Digital Marketing Audit	Remarketing
£1-20 million	Marketing Managers	Can make budget decisions	PPC	Digital Marketing Audit	Book campaign
£1-20 million	Marketing Managers	Can make budget decisions	PPC	Digital Marketing Audit	Christmas Tree campaign
£1-20 million	Marketing Managers	Can make budget decisions	PPC	Digital Marketing Audit	DMA Campaign
£1-20 million	Marketing Managers	Can make budget decisions	PPC	Digital Marketing Audit	Course Campaign
£1-20 million	Marketing Managers	Can make budget decisions	PPC	Digital Marketing Audit	Recruitment campaign
£1-20 million	Marketing Managers	Can make budget decisions	PPC	Digital Marketing Audit	SEO product campaign
£1-20 million	Marketing Managers	Can make budget decisions	PPC	Digital Marketing Audit	Events

Financial	Role	Characteristic	Channel	Product	Content
£1-20 million	Marketing Managers	Can make budget decisions	Email	Digital Marketing Audit	Infographics
£1-20 million	Marketing Managers	Can make budget decisions	Email	Digital Marketing Audit	White Paper Guides
£1-20 million	Marketing Managers	Can make budget decisions	Email	Digital Marketing Audit	Press Releases
£1-20 million	Marketing Managers	Can make budget decisions	Email	Digital Marketing Audit	Case Studies
£1-20 million	Marketing Managers	Can make budget decisions	Email	Digital Marketing Audit	Events
£1-20 million	Marketing Managers	Can make budget decisions	Email	Digital Marketing Audit	Quiz and Competitions
£1-20 million	Marketing Managers	Can make budget decisions	LinkedIn	Digital Marketing Audit	Posts
£1-20 million	Marketing Managers	Can make budget decisions	LinkedIn	Digital Marketing Audit	30 second videos
£1-20 million	Marketing Managers	Can make budget decisions	LinkedIn	Digital Marketing Audit	Demo Videos
£1-20 million	Marketing Managers	Can make budget decisions	LinkedIn	Digital Marketing Audit	Infographics
£1-20 million	Marketing Managers	Can make budget decisions	Facebook	Digital Marketing Audit	Trend reports
£1-20 million	Marketing Managers	Can make budget decisions	Facebook	Digital Marketing Audit	White Papers
£1-20 million	Marketing Managers	Can make budget decisions	Facebook	Digital Marketing Audit	Demo Videos

Financial	Role	Characteristic	Channel	Product	Content
£1-20 million	Marketing Managers	Can make budget decisions	Facebook	Digital Marketing Audit	Infographics
£1-20 million	Marketing Managers	Can make budget decisions	Instagram	Digital Marketing Audit	Infographics
£1-20 million	Marketing Managers	Can make budget decisions	Instagram	Digital Marketing Audit	Quiz and Competi-tions
£1-20 million	Marketing Managers	Can make budget decisions	Instagram	Digital Marketing Audit	Demo Videos
£1-20 million	Marketing Managers	Can make budget decisions	Twitter	Digital Marketing Audit	Trend reports
£1-20 million	Marketing Managers	Can make budget decisions	Twitter	Digital Marketing Audit	White Papers
£1-20 million	Marketing Managers	Can make budget decisions	Twitter	Digital Marketing Audit	Demo Videos
£1-20 million	Marketing Managers	Can make budget decisions	Twitter	Digital Marketing Audit	Infographics
£1-20 million	Marketing Managers	Can make budget decisions	Word of Mouth	Digital Marketing Audit	Reviews
£1-20 million	Marketing Managers	Can make budget decisions	Word of Mouth	Digital Marketing Audit	Ratings
£1-20 million	Marketing Managers	Can make budget decisions	Word of Mouth	Digital Marketing Audit	Events
£1-20 million	Marketing Managers	Can make budget decisions	Events	Digital Marketing Audit	Interactive demos
£1-20 million	Marketing Managers	Can make budget decisions	Events	Digital Marketing Audit	Trend reports

Financial	Role	Characteristic	Channel	Product	Content
£1-20 million	Marketing Managers	Can make budget decisions	Events	Digital Marketing Audit	Guides
£1-20 million	Marketing Managers	Can make budget decisions	Agency Partner Referrals – PR	Digital Marketing Audit	Partner Pack
£1-20 million	Marketing Managers	Can make budget decisions	Agency Partner Referrals – Accountants	Digital Marketing Audit	Partner Pack
£1-20 million	Marketing Managers	Can make budget decisions	Agency Partner Referrals – Design & Dev	Digital Marketing Audit	Partner Pack
£1-20 million	Marketing Managers	Can make budget decisions	Influencers	Digital Marketing Audit	Testimonial Campaign
£1-20 million	Marketing Managers	Can make budget decisions	Shows & Expos	Digital Marketing Audit	Speaking Attendance
£1-20 million	Marketing Managers	Can make budget decisions	Workshops	Digital Marketing Audit	Presentation
£1-20 million	Marketing Managers	Can make budget decisions	Print	Digital Marketing Audit	Book
£1-20 million	Marketing Managers	Can make budget decisions	Video	Digital Marketing Audit	Online Course
£1-20 million	Marketing Managers	Can make budget decisions	SMS	Digital Marketing Audit	SMS Alerts
£1-20 million	Marketing Managers	Can make budget decisions	Radio	Digital Marketing Audit	Advert
£1-20 million	Marketing Managers	Can make budget decisions	Radio	Digital Marketing Audit	Interview

Financial	Role	Characteristic	Channel	Product	Content
£1-20 million	Marketing Managers	Can make budget decisions	TV	Digital Marketing Audit	Advert
£1-20 million	Marketing Managers	Can make budget decisions	Billboard	Digital Marketing Audit	Advert

> ### Activity – Choose your content
>
> Choose the type of content you will create
>
> You've now created a list of audience personas, channels, and content 'products'.
>
> Can you identify any patterns across this list? Can you reach a number of personas by sharing similar types of content across similar channels?
>
> Is your list becoming a map?

6. Define the messaging, CTAs, and customer anxieties

The next step is to define the messaging that each type of content will convey.

What specific messages, calls to action, unique selling points, and customer anxieties will be appropriate for the types of content you intend to create?

Here are a few examples from our products:

Product	Content	Customer Anxieties	Sales Messages	Calls to Action
Digital Marketing Audit	Case Studies	Can I trust them?	Experienced, Trusted, Proven, Predictable Results	Achieve 44% increase in traffic in year 1. Apply these results to your business

Product	Content	Customer Anxieties	Sales Messages	Calls to Action
Recruit-ment	What it's like to work at Footprint	Is it a good step for my career? What is it like to work there?	Have you got what it takes to work with us? Do you want to work with purpose and have an impact? Do you want to live a life where you are challenged to achieve exceptional things? Do you want a career that is fascinating and ever-changing? Do you want to work in an environment with colleagues that will help build your self confidence and love of life? Do you want to work for a company that values your long term development in life over short term profits? If the answer to the above is yes: Footprint Digital is the place for you.	Learn, Play and Grow. Apply now for a role at Footprint Digital.
Book	Testimonial Campaign	If I put my name to the book will it make me look good?	We really respect you and your status in the industry. Take a look at the manuscript. Some big brands have already contributed. We will print your quote in the book and send you a free copy when it is printed.	Please send us a testimonial before it goes to print.

Product	Content	Customer Anxieties	Sales Messages	Calls to Action
Online Course	Advert	There are a lot of online courses out there what makes this different? If I take the course do I get a recognised qualification? Will it lead to career growth/better pay?	Described by Professor Maged Ali as "the perfect bridge from academia to the real world" this insightful, approachable, helpful, and human course gives you the clarity, confidence, and practical steps to do the best work of your career and achieve the pay rise you've always deserved.	YES! I'm ready to build my career by joining the Shoot The HiPPO online course and start achieving things I never thought possible.

Activity – Define your messaging

Imagine yourself in the shoes of each of your audience personas.

What are their anxieties, needs, and frustrations? What's on their mind?

What messages can you craft to address what's concerning each of your audience personas?

6. Projections and prioritisation – how much will it cost and what will you get back?

By this stage you will have created a long list of goals, target audience personas, content formats, and messaging concepts. The next step is to review this long list and whittle it down to the activities that are most likely to deliver the best returns.

The quick answer is to give each activity a high, medium, or low score against time, cost, and predicted results. This is a quick way of getting there, but can be heavily influenced by what the person scoring it believes will be effective.

A better method is to estimate the frequency, cost, volume, projected conversion rate, average order value, total predicted conversions, predicted revenue, net profit, and ROI. These items seem complicated at first, but, once you have completed this activity for one line of your Simple Spreadsheet you will see how easy it is.

The result will be a more robust prediction of the potential return on investment for each proposed activity. At the end of completing this activity the strategy, that is, the priority list of activities that are really worthwhile for your business, will become self-evident. This will also have the associated benefit of attributing more confidence to investment decisions and making a successful campaign far more likely.

Projections and prioritisation – how much will it cost and what will you get back? In this example we have compared a number of possible activities and their likelihood of success.

Activity	Frequency	Volume	Budget/ Cost	Conv. Rate	AOV	Conv.	Revenue	Net Profit	ROI
Publish daily LinkedIn posts.	Daily	300	£1,875	1 in 300	£18,000	1	£18,000	£3,600	192%
Monthly email campaign to potential customers.	Monthly	12	£3,600	1 in 12	£18,000	1	£18,000	£3,600	100%
Employ team of partnership development managers.	90 meetings per month	1080 meetings	£90,000	1 in 30	£18,000	36	£648,000	£129,600	144%
Produce exceptional case studies.	Once	10	£3,000	1 in 10	£18,000	1	£18,000	£3,600	120%
Update the website.	Once	10	£3,000	1 in 10	£18,000	1	£18,000	£3,600	120%
Establish a paid retargeting campaign.	Monthly	12	£12,000	1 in 4	£18,000	4	£72,000	£14,400	120%
Increase our SEO activity.	Monthly	12	£12,000	1 in 4	£18,000	4	£72,000	£14,400	120%

Activity – Define how likely it is for each activity to bring success

Choose a couple of audience personas, channels, and types of content.

Have a go at estimating the frequency, cost, volume and projected conversion rate for each one.

Now estimate, for each one, the average order value, total predicted conversions, predicted revenue, net profit and ROI.

Get a sense of the value – to you as well as to your audience personas – of each activity.

7. KPIs – how will you measure how effective it is?

Finally, the list of activities that have been deemed worthwhile can now be measured. Using the same spreadsheet we will be able to track over time how effective each activity is. In this example we have chosen to track revenue achieved each month to create a clean and easy to understand report.

Activity	Annual Revenue Target	Revenue achieved in January	Revenue achieved in February	Revenue achieved in March	Revenue achieved in April
Publish daily LinkedIn posts.	£18,000	£0	£0	£18,000	£0
Monthly email campaign to potential customers.	£18,000	£2,000	£0	£0	£6,000
Employ team of partnership development managers.	£648,000	£36,000	£72,000	£18,000	£54,000
Increase our SEO activity.	£72,000	£18,000	£0	£18,000	£18,000
Publish whitepaper PR campaigns through lead generation platforms.	£36,000	£0	£0	£0	£18,000
Establish a paid retargeting campaign.	£72,000	£0	£18,000	£18,000	£18,000

Activity – Define how you will measure and track performance

Keep a detailed note of the marketing activities you carry out.

Capture the frequency and volume of your activities and the costs you incur.

Track your conversion rates, order values, revenues, profits, and ROI.

How accurate were your expectations? Which marketing activities pay off over time?

Bringing it all together

You will have seen by now how this process can expand into a huge piece of work. Throughout the process make decisions about what will evidently be worth the effort, and what won't. This should leave you with a short list of actions that you have a high confidence will succeed. When completed, the Simple Spreadsheet will look like something like the following.

You will notice that we have removed everything that does not have a positive ROI. This leaves a simple and manageable range of activities. We anticipate an investment of £175,000 to return £1,167,000 at a net profit of £245,400.

Activity	Frequency	Volume	Budget/Cost	Conv. Rate	AOV		Conv.	Revenue	Net Profit	ROI
Publish daily LinkedIn posts.	Daily	300	£1,875	1 in 300	£18,000	1		£18,000	£3,600	192%
Publish daily Facebook posts.	Daily	300	£1,875	1 in 300	£18,000	1		£18,000	£3,600	192%
Publish daily Instagram posts.	Daily	300	£1,875	1 in 300	£18,000	1		£18,000	£3,600	192%
Publish daily Twitter posts.	Daily	300	£1,875	1 in 300	£18,000	1		£18,000	£3,600	192%
Monthly email campaign to partners	Monthly	12	£3,600	1 in 12	£18,000	1		£18,000	£3,600	100%
Monthly email campaign to potential customers.	Monthly	12	£3,600	1 in 12	£18,000	1		£18,000	£3,600	100%
Employ team of partnership development managers.	90 meetings per month	1080 meetings	£90,000	1 in 30	£18,000	36		£648,000	£129,600	144%
Produce exceptional case studies.	Once	10	£3,000	1 in 10	£18,000	1		£18,000	£3,600	120%
Update the website.	Once	10	£3,000	1 in 10	£18,000	1		£18,000	£3,600	120%
Establish a paid retargeting campaign.	Monthly	12	£12,000	1 in 4	£18,000	4		£72,000	£14,400	120%
Increase our SEO activity.	Monthly	12	£12,000	1 in 4	£18,000	4		£72,000	£14,400	120%
Perform a Customer Journey Mapping exercise and create marketing literature that nurtures people through the sales funnel.	Once	1	£4,000	2 in 1	£18,000	2		£36,000	£7,200	180%

Activity	Frequency	Volume	Budget/Cost	Conv. Rate	AOV	Conv.	Revenue	Net Profit	ROI
Publish our book.	Once	1	£5,000	2 in 1	£18,000	2	£36,000	£7,200	144%
Film our digital marketing course and produce an online learning management system.	Once	1	£8,000	50 in 1	£300	50	£15,000	£15,000	187.5%
Publish whitepaper PR campaigns through lead generation platforms.	Once	100	£5,000	1 in 50	£18,000	2	£36,000	£7,200	144%
Establish a paid search campaign.	Monthly	12	£18,000	1 in 2	£18,000	6	£108,000	£21,600	120%
Total			£175,000				£1,167,000	£245,400	

Don't get it right, get it going

Our approach to strategy strikes a balance between moving fast and thought. The Simple Spreadsheet can help you build a roadmap (in one day) that brings together your goals, target personas, locations, and what you sell so that you can produce content and messaging that is effective. Through projections and KPIs you can also reduce the risks of decisions not being effective and ensure that success is monitored so you can adapt en route. Whilst thorough, no plan can be perfect. So follow the words of our business coach Mark Constable: *"don't get it right, get it going!"*

Activity – Complete a Simple Spreadsheet for your business.

Chapter 11: Create compelling reports

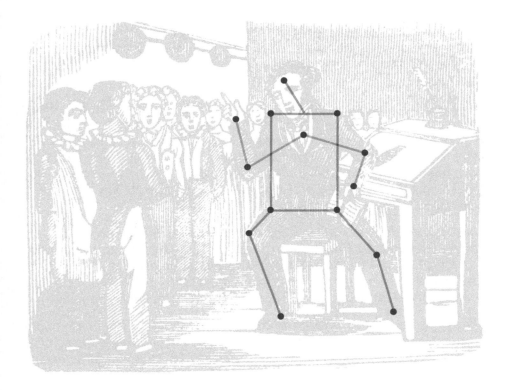

"The world cannot be understood without numbers. But the world cannot be understood with numbers alone." **HANS ROSLING**

Moneyball and the art of sabermetrics

The 2011 film "Moneyball" starring Brad Pitt, based on the book "Moneyball: The Art of Winning an Unfair Game"[61] tells the story of Billy Beane, the general manager of baseball team the Oakland As, whose epiphany is that baseball's conventional wisdom is all wrong. Faced with a tight budget, Beane must reinvent his team by outsmarting the richer baseball clubs.

---

61 Lewis, M. (2004) *Moneyball: The Art Of Winning An Unfair Game.* New York, W.W.Norton.

Billy Beane meets Peter Brand, a quiet Yale Economics graduate, who developed a data driven method of assessing players using their historic stats (this is known as sabermetrics – a statistical analysis that can predict player performance). Typically, scouts in the game rely on their own judgement and human view of players, which often leads them to pick players based on their charisma, a pleasing technique, or on their reputation; overlooking unfashionable, cheaper players who may have better performance stats. Brand's approach is vastly different.

Equipped with the data from this alternative method of assessment, Peter Brand and Billy Beane set about building their team. As an example, they acquire former catcher Scott Hatteberg, whose career is seen as over by all other teams due to an elbow injury that doesn't allow him to throw. Although not a hitter, they choose him for his ability to "get on base" in whatever way required (usually by walks), and plan to teach him how to play first base, a generally non-throwing position.

These moves don't sit well with the A's scouting team and sports analysts. The A's Manager, Art Howe, doesn't agree with or understand the strategy, and refuses to listen to Billy about how best to manage the team as assembled. Billy knows that his and Peter's jobs are on the line if they don't deliver, which he realises means nothing less than winning the World Series.

The team subsequently starts an amazing winning streak. Billy Beane famously does not watch games, but when they tie the American League record of 19 consecutive wins, his daughter persuades him to attend the next game, against the Kansas City Royals. Oakland is leading when Beane arrives in the fourth inning, only to watch the Royals even the score. Thanks to a walk-off home run by Hatteberg, the A's achieve a record-breaking 20th consecutive win.

The success of the Oakland As with a budget the fraction of the size of other teams in the league demonstrates the power of data insights. It is a great example of the application of data to make better, more informed decisions and to achieve better results. It is such a simple idea, yet how many organisations do you know that make their decisions this way? How many employ data scientists on their team?

More data at our fingertips than God

The sabermetrics approach delivered industry breaking results for the Oakland As. Having the right data to hand allows you to make informed decisions. You can reduce risks and gain huge competitive advantages. The Digital Marketing Manager is utterly spoilt by the amount of data they can access. Digital Measurement evangelist Avinash Kaushik put it best when he said: *"We have more data at our fingertips than God"*. Yet we continue to make poor decisions as a result of not using data.

If only they would listen

The wealth of data inherent in digital marketing means that the Digital Marketing Manager often holds some of the most crucial information for the business. If senior management paid more attention to their digital teams, their organisations would likely grow quicker. This chapter looks at why this great information so often falls on deaf ears and how we can harness the wealth of data that is available and use it to drive decision making in the organisation. The key to this is compelling reporting.

Drive action and change

The outcome of a great report should be measured against the action that is taken as a consequence. We want the organisations we support to make bold decisions that allow them to move fast and win, so the report we deliver should drive action and change. If a decision is made as a result of the report you have given, then your report was effective. If nothing changes, the chances are you have not delivered an effective report.

Where it often goes wrong

If you feel like senior management is not making decisions off the back of the reports you provide, there is a strong chance you are guilty of one (or all) of the following:

- You wrongly expect that your audience is as interested in the detail as you are.
- You often mistake metrics for KPIs – just because you can measure it, it doesn't mean it's a key indicator of the performance that senior management is interested in.
- You feel like more data equals more value.
- You (or a project stakeholder) assumes a report has to provide all the answers.

- You are not confident of the data and what it's telling you.

How to create compelling reports

The key to overcoming these common issues and creating compelling reports that drive action and change is knowing the answers to the following questions:

1. Why am I reporting?
2. Who am I reporting to?
3. What data am I reporting on?
4. What insights have I found?
5. How am I going to tell that story in an engaging way?

1. Why am I reporting?

> *"Half the money I spend on advertising is wasted; the trouble is I don't know which half."* **JOHN WANAMAKER (1838-1922)**

This is not a new problem. Despite being over 100 years old, John Wanamaker's quote is still relevant today. The primary function of your reporting is to drive action and change, and this is done through effective resourcing and budgeting decisions. To create an effective report you must therefore understand the overarching goals of the business.

Report objectives

The vast majority of the tension around reporting can be solved by correctly identifying and communicating its purpose. For example, a report request could require you to:

- Plot the website's performance against the business goals.
- Measure the return on investment from Paid Search activities.
- Identify content on the website that drives most value into the business.
- Track the success of email campaigns.

Notice that these are quite specific queries and relatable to specific marketing campaigns or activities. A report which starts with the question *"how is the website doing?"* risks producing a long and unhelpful document. There are thousands of things you can report on to answer this question, 99.9% of which won't be wanted.

Activity – Reports

Think back to the last report you sent or received. Can you succinctly describe its purpose?

Now, be as honest as you can be – does the report deliver on the objectives?

2. Who am I reporting to?

"People don't know what they want until you show them." **STEVE JOBS**

Understanding your audience is a theme that we talk a lot about throughout this book in the context of marketing to the wider world. The same principles apply within your organisation. You are looking to deliver the right message to the right person at the right time. Understanding the audience, their needs and requirements and their communication style is essential to pitching the information in an effective way.

The right information relevant to their role

As reporting is about decision making, it is helpful to think about your audience's level of seniority and ability to act. Ask yourself the following:

- What role or roles does your audience have?
- What level of influence do they have to action your recommendations?
- What do they need to know?
- What is their level of understanding?
- What is the value of the data to them?
- What communication style do they have? (read the section on Think/ Feel/Know in the *Communication Skills for Digital* chapter)
- How can you make it fun for them?

This isn't an exact science, but to guide your approach think of which level of seniority you're reporting to:

Reporting level	Interest	General metrics (examples)
Business Owner/ C-level/ Director	Impact to the business/division – high level KPIs framed against the goals set. How effective is the marketing spend at growing the business?	Revenue, ROI, Cost.
Head of Marketing or similar	Performance of individual campaigns against their target. Which channel should we invest more in?	Conversion Rate, ROI/ROAS.
Marketer / Practitioner (typically you, the Digital Marketing Manager)	Tactical elements relating to relevant channels within campaigns.	Conversion Rate, Cost per Acquisition, Cost per Click, Quality Score, Landing Pages, Keyword rankings, Email open rate, etc.

There may be business owners who want to get stuck into quality scores in Google Ads or a Head of Marketing who only wants to see revenue against target. But these are often the exception to the rule.

Once you have judged the objective against the audience, you can then move on to the construction of the report itself.

3. What data am I reporting on?

> *"The root cause of failure in most digital marketing campaigns is not the lack of creativity in the banner ad or TV spot or the sexiness of the website. It is not even (often) the people involved. It is quite simply the lack of structured thinking about what the real purpose of the campaign is and a lack of an objective set of measures with which to identify success or failure.* **AVINASH KAUSHIK**[62]

Ensuring you are reporting on the *right* data is critical. Knowing what you need to start tracking, or who you need to ask for your critical marketing data, is key to this process.

---

62 Kaushik, A. (2020) *Occam's Razor by Avinash Kaushik* [online] available at: https://www.kaushik.net/avinash/digital-marketing-and-measurement-model/

Many assume that tracking is an inherently 'technical' task and quite often someone else's problem. This can often blind people to what is achievable with relative ease.

The great news is that web analytics packages are easy to install on your website and, even without any setup, can provide a substantial amount of detail on who your visitors are and what they are doing on your website. Google Analytics is the *de facto* standard and is, most likely, the software you will start with. Setting up 'goals' to measure things like contact form sends or purchases is relatively straightforward – it is something you may be able to do yourself or ask your developers to do quickly and easily.

Your search for the right data shouldn't end there! Accounting software holds much of the data that you need, you just need to understand whose job it is to administer it – or who built it – and discuss with them what you are looking to achieve and what data you need.

Most businesses have some record of their customers and the orders they place. Whether this is in a CRM (Customer Relationship Management software) or in a spreadsheet, you should at least have detail of a) who purchases and b) how often. As these often overlap with the sales operation, you also should have access to where that customer came from.

There is little-to-no reason why any website cannot have a degree of that tracking enabled. If it is not technically possible, you need to understand why and start formulating steps to address this – otherwise you will struggle to understand the value of your marketing efforts on the business.

4. What insights have I found?

> *"He who would search for pearls must dive below."* **JOHN DRYDEN**

Data for data's sake is pointless. It is your role as a Digital Marketing Manager to derive insights from the data you have to hand. It is very easy when faced with a heap of data to suffer 'analysis paralysis'. We follow a very simple method developed by Google Analytics evangelist Avinash Kaushik known as *See, Think, Do, Care*. This method for investigating data should keep the focus and prevent you getting lost in a rabbit hole of information.

For each report that you review ask:

• What can you **see**?
• What do you **think** is the problem?

- What will you **do**?
- How will you make someone else **care**?

The outcomes are the most important thing. If there are no outcomes or ideas or suggestions as a result of the review of the data, then it is a good sign that the analysis has not been effective. Look again.

5. How am I going to tell that story in an engaging way?

> *"I want people, when they realise they have been wrong about the world, to feel not embarrassment, but that childlike sense of wonder, inspiration, and curiosity that I remember from the circus"*
> **HANS ROSLING**

Understanding your audience and their profiles is the foundation to winning their hearts and minds. It is important to remember that, in spite of having access to great data, humans make emotional decisions – so do not discount the value of making your reports emotive and fun. Take a look at talks by the brilliant Hans Rosling to see how to deliver incredible data in the most compelling ways.

Make it human through storytelling

In the chapter on writing your story we discussed the hero's journey. This shows us how to bring data to life with a narrative. The trick in telling the reporting story well is not to be afraid of giving bad news, but to remember that *how* you tell it is critical.

If your report message is:, *"We're down 20% against target"* – and that's it – the report is really missing a massive opportunity. A better approach could be: *"We're down 20% against our target **because** the bank holiday fell on a different weekend this year."* This isn't perfect, but it is a rational explanation for the shortfall, which is more insightful and useful.

An even better way would be to say:

- What happened.
- Why it happened.
- What the solution is going to be.

*"We're down 20%, **because** the bank holiday fell on a different weekend this year. With a 10% increase in spend over the next two weeks, **we believe we can make up the shortfall.**"*

What happened, why it happened and a possible solution to it – the whole picture in one sentence. This is equally as prudent for providing positive news as for negative. *"Cost Per Acquisition is down 10% [because we're awesome]"* is quite self indulgent and not that helpful.

Remember: What do you see? What do you think has happened? What will you do about it?

*"CPA (cost per acquisition) is down **because** of the negative keywords we added at campaign level – **we're now going** to roll this out across the rest of the account".*

Make it beautiful with data visualisation

Visualising data is something we have a lot of control over, perhaps more than you would expect. This can be both great and terrible in the same measure. The decisions we make on what we can do with the data is key to telling the right story.

There are many charts and graphs available that enable us to visualise data, most of which you're likely to be familiar with. The appropriateness of a chart can vary – all reports will need to look and feel different – but the elements a successful report needs to contain will seldom change.

- Report title – a few words that capture the question the report addresses.
- Report scope – a brief description of the goals of the report.
- Primary KPIs against their targets.
- 3-5 metrics which feed each KPI*.
- Observations*.
- Actions or next steps.

The two steps marked with an asterix (*) depend on whether your report needs to 'stand-alone' or is reported in person or over a call and is sensitive to who is in the room. Only add additional metrics if they're needed to help tell the story or give context to the primary KPIs.

Always finish a report with actions and next steps – the *"...so what?"* A report without clear actions will struggle to add value and, in time, will only lead to apathy and indifference.

Activity – time to bring it all together

Imagine you are preparing a board report for the owner of the company (or one of the directors).

Using PowerPoint or a similar tool, select the data and charts which most accurately describe the following:

- A campaign's performance over the last three months.

- The campaign effectiveness.

- Recommendations for the next quarter based on your observations.

During the board report you have only been given 15 minutes to present your data, so focus specifically on making arguments that are easy to understand, substantiated by data, and actionable.

Activity – what are your core marketing measurements?

Monitoring and analysing your marketing campaign's performance is vital, but it can be a daunting task. The following calculations allow you greater insight into the successes and failures of your campaigns. Use them in combination with information from **Google Analytics** to tweak your strategy, by emphasising more successful campaigns or adjusting any that are underperforming.

We use five measurement methods to calculate the success of an advertising campaign. Calculate each of these measurements for a campaign that you have run.

1. **Conversion Rate** – the percentage of visitors to your site that make a conversion

$$Conversion\ Rate\ (\%) = \left(\frac{Conversions}{Visits}\right) \times 100$$

2. **Cost per Acquisition (CPA)** – how much you are spending for each person who makes a conversion

$$Cost\ Per\ Acquisition\ (£) = \left(\frac{Total\ Ad\ Spend}{Number\ of\ Acquisitions}\right)$$

Preliminary CPA: If you haven't yet started a campaign and don't have access to all of this information, you can work out a preliminary cost per acquisition if you know the average revenue of each conversion and the percentage of that revenue you are willing to spend on marketing.

$$Acquisition\ Cost\ (£) = Average\ Acquisition\ Revenue\ \times\ \left(\frac{Marketing\ Budget\ (Revenue\ \%)}{100}\right)$$

3. **Return on Investment (ROI)** – a percentage measure of how much revenue you are making compared to your total outgoings (marketing and costs)

$$Return\ on\ Investment\ (\%) = \left(\frac{Net\ Profit\ per\ Order}{Total\ Outgoings}\right) \times 100$$

4. **Return on Marketing (Marketing ROI)** – the return you are receiving from your total marketing spend as a percentage

$$Return\ on\ Marketing\ (\%) = \left(\frac{Net\ Profit\ per\ Order}{Marketing\ Spend}\right) \times 100$$

5. **Return on Ad Spend (ROAS)** – how much return you are receiving from a specific marketing campaign

$$Return\ on\ Ad\ Spend\ Rate\ (\%) = \left(\frac{Revenue\ From\ Ad\ Campaign}{Cost\ Of\ Ad\ Campaign}\right) \times 100$$

Chapter 12: Communication for Digital

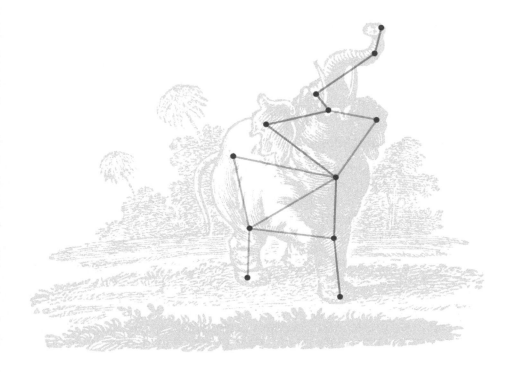

> "The single biggest problem in communication is the illusion that it has taken place." **GEORGE BERNARD SHAW**

Mokusatsu

On 6th August 1945 the US Army dropped the first atomic bomb 'Little Boy' on the Japanese city of Hiroshima. This was followed three days later with the second atomic bomb 'Fat Man' on the Japanese city of Nagasaki. "The two bombings killed between 129,000 and 226,000 people". On 15th August, 1945 Japan surrendered, effectively ending World War Two.

On 26th July 1945, just a few days before the bombs fell, UK Prime Minister Winston Churchill, Chairman of China Chiang Kai-shek, and US President Harry S. Truman issued The Potsdam Declaration. This called for the "unconditional surrender" of all Japanese armed forces or they would face "utter destruction" The official response from the Empire of Japan was the phrase "黙殺," mokusatsu.[63]

The issue arises in the complex range of interpretations for this word when translated into English. Literally the word translates to "silence killing" or 'killing with silence'. The phrase can also mean "withholding comment". The interpretation received by the Allied leaders was "rejection by ignoring".

Could the devastation caused by these two atomic bombs be attributed to a mistake in translation?

Communication breakdown

Communication is wrought with subtlety and nuance. It works on so many different levels that it is no wonder we often find ourselves misunderstood and facing conflict rather than connection. This is made worse by our total lack of formal education around the topic. School may have taught us how to compose a letter, spell properly and interpret poetry. But who was taught how to give feedback without wanting to curl up and die, or how to stand up and talk persuasively to a group of people without wanting to be swallowed up by the ground beneath you? This chapter aims to help.

They call them 'soft skills', yet they are the hardest to master and the most powerful when mastered. If you want to get anything done, then the ability to communicate effectively is vital. After all, lives may depend on it...

Communication in digital

Communication is integral to everything. In this chapter we share some of the communication skills we find are helpful in the day to day role of a Digital Marketing Manager. Often called 'soft skills' we think these are hard to master. But those who can do these things well will be the ones who deliver exceptional results and have a long and enduring career.

---

63 Kawai, K. (1950) *Mokusatsu, Japan's Response to the Potsdam Declaration.* Pacific Historical Review. Volume 19, Issue 4.

Too important to make a guess

Being obsessed with data we have, in collaboration with communications guru Nick Looby, developed a survey that can help diagnose how well you and your organisation communicate. From this we determine a priority plan for the organisation as well as a priority plan for an individual. The survey explores the following aspects of communication:

- Cultivating empathy.
- How to hold a meeting.
- Networking.
- Presenting.
- Assertiveness.
- Authenticity.
- Crucial conversations.
- Story telling.
- Voice.
- Active listening.
- Body language.
- Psychological safety.
- Creating connection.
- Written skills.
- Systems.

The survey helps you appraise how confident you feel in each area and develop a plan to work on areas where you feel less confident. We have provided guidance for many of these themes throughout this chapter.

1. Cultivating empathy

Effective communication is not just about rules and goals, it is also about understanding. A useful tool that helps us understand one another is the Think/Feel/Know model. Think/Feel/Know[64] was designed by business coaches Shirlaws to increase our understanding of how we and others communicate.

Through self–analysis, we can profile the way that people think as a blend of three factors: think, feel, and know. Some people are more inclined towards

---

64 Rosling, J (2013) *More money More time Less stress.* London, 1Fish 2Fish.

one of the three, while others are in balance. The particular blend that you have determines the style of communication which you prefer. None of the blends or styles are 'better' than any other, simply different.

To find out whether you are a thinker, feeler, or knower, look through the following descriptions and decide what percentage each factor would be to you:

- **Think** – Analytical and detail orientated, thinkers revel in data and like to make choices only when fully informed on the subject.
- **Feel** – Emotionally perceptive and based on metaphor and narrative. Feelers make decisions based on the energy of the situation.
- **Know** – Based on 'gut' and instinct. Knowers are decisive, preferring concise summary rather than a detailed analysis.

Activity – Think/ Feel/ Know

What is your communication style?

What are your colleagues' communication styles?

How might you use the knowledge of someone's communication style to adapt your communication?

2. How to hold a meeting

Effective communication follows a good structure, but feels fluid and intuitive. So much of a Digital Marketing Manager's performance can come down to how well they hold meetings. Meetings should be focused and efficient and everyone should leave them feeling excited. At the same time they should not feel rushed. Take your time, let everybody share their ideas, and encourage contributions.

Clear Communication Framework – 7 steps to a great meeting

The Clear Communication Framework ensures that you communicate effectively and walk out of a meeting or conversation with everyone feeling good and excited about the next steps. A version of this was originally shared with us by Equip Business Coach Mark Constable which stems from concepts developed by Shirlaws. We have subsequently added our own twist. It covers both the commercial side of a conversation but also with the cultural benefit of building stronger more meaningful relationships. It is perfect for both meetings and for phone calls. Become a master of the Clear Communication Framework and you will go far.

The start of your meeting is the opportunity to lay the foundations. The first three steps help you do this well. These can be delivered and discussed in any order and should feel natural to everyone involved.

Step 1. Fact find and feel find

This section enables you to understand how your fellow meeting attendees are feeling and what is on their mind.

'Feel find' can be as straightforward as asking *"How are you?"*, *"How's things?"*, *"How are you feeling?"*. It will enable you to adapt everything hereafter to their needs and allow you to be more empathic and connect with everyone in the room or on the call.

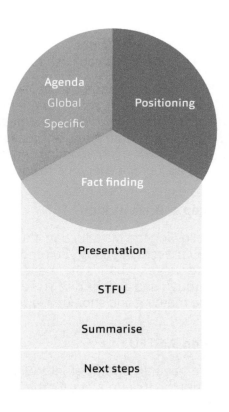

'Fact find'. This is where you investigate the more practical things that are going on. For example questions like *"How's business?"*, *"What's new with you?"* This is always really illuminating and will enable you to gauge what is important to those you're meeting with.

Step 2. Positioning

'Positioning' is making sure that everyone is on the same page for the meeting. For example this could be things such as, *"How long have we got?"*. It is also the time to address things that might affect the meeting such as, *"I'm expecting short a call that I will need to take during the meeting but I will re-join as soon as it's finished"*, *"please forgive the noise on the line it sometimes cuts out but I will soon re-join if it does"* etc.

Step 3. Global and specific agenda

There are two parts to agreeing on an agenda. Covering both is important because it frames everything, allowing everyone to start from the same point.

The global agenda is the answer to the question: why are we having this meeting?. Think 'global' to start with, outline the topic of the meeting and the general goals you wish to accomplish.

The specific agenda can be reached by asking questions such as: *"What would you like to get from our time today?", "If you had a magic wand and we could resolve anything in this meeting, what would that be?".* Your 'specific' agenda is a more granular breakdown of the specific thoughts, introducing the structure of the meeting and the areas you wish to cover. Take your time and encourage everyone to contribute to this.

Step 4. Presentation

Following the introduction, this is the body of your meeting. This is where you present anything you prepared in advance: statistics, ideas, questions, and suggestions. It's the 'meat' of the meeting, where decisions are thought through and actions discussed. This is obviously a hugely important part of the meeting and should take up the vast majority of the time.

Step 5. STFU

We have an unofficial interlude after step four that we unsubtly call the 'Shut the f*ck up' stage (or the 'count to 10 method'). If you are pitching in a sales meeting it is the most vital of all stages. He who speaks first loses. This is the pause that follows the delivery of the content in which your colleague, manager, or client is allowed the head space to draw their own conclusions. Wait and count to 10 once the presentation stage is completed.

Step 6. Summary

Towards the end of your meeting, after the presentation, is the time to sum-marise what was covered in the meeting. Quickly run through what took place during your time together, then return to the specific agenda list you prepared earlier. For each question on the list, ask the room whether they think the specific agenda item was adequately covered. Put a tick (✓) if it has been covered adequately, a dash (-) if it has been partially covered, and a cross (x) if it has been left unanswered.

For each of the dashes and crosses, offer either an explanation or other further information. Answer the dashes and some of the crosses if you can. Don't leave anything unanswered – if something is not covered by what you have said, offer advice on where to find out the information. Or, check with others whether they still feel that item is important.

This is also an opportunity to invite everyone in the meeting to write down three things that they got from the meeting. This really helps people reflect on their experience and see the positive outcomes of the meeting.

Step 7. Next steps

The final stage is to define the next steps. Ask *"What are the next steps?"*. This is the point where you capture the action points and agree who is responsible for completing what and by when.

3. How to connect to your clients and colleagues

"Assumptions are the termites of relationships." **HENRY WINKLE**

To create a culture of collaboration and human connection with customers, suppliers, and colleagues we propose a radical method: talk more! Think about how much of your time is spent with your head in a device or hiding behind emails and written messages. Take the time to put down your devices and talk more.

We accept that sometimes you will need to check the latest cat pictures on Facebook, or Instagram your lunch. But please be mindful of the time you are spending staring at your screen and how this might impact your relationships with your colleagues.

Informal chats can be a great time to:

- Get feedback on a new idea.
- Build rapport within the team.
- Learn more about your colleagues.
- Discuss ways of improving how we work.
- Find out how someone likes their tea.
- Discuss cat pictures.

Creating a space where you can have more informal chats is hard in the video call world. Those moments where people just hang out and have a coffee do not happen naturally. We therefore need to try to consciously manufacture these moments. Time before and after video calls is an opportunity to connect and setting up group Facebook or WhatsApp groups can be good spaces for fun conversations.

4. How to win friends and influence people

The advice from the famous book by Dale Carnegie[65] is surprisingly simple. If you would like to make people feel happy (and win them over) make a concerted effort to do the following. Your teams will appreciate it.

- Become genuinely interested in other people.
- Give positive eye contact and smile.
- Remember that a person's name is, to that person, the sweetest and most important sound in any language.
- Be a good and active listener.
- Talk about the other person's interests.
- Make the other person feel important – and do it sincerely.

5. Create a powerful first impression

First impressions are everything. It's easy to take for granted your posture, clothing, setting, and tone. We encourage you to arrive on time for your meetings and make sure that you are prepared to give the best impression of yourself from the outset. Take a moment to be conscious of the following things so that you are prepared to make a good first impression.

- Give excellent eye contact and smile.
- Stand tall in a powerful position to enhance your self-confidence or getting your posture right on video calls.
- Give a big strong handshake or a strong confidence "Hello" and smile.
- Be the person to start the conversation. We encourage our team to be the leader in the conversation rather than a passive person as this will inspire confidence in the people you are talking with.
- Avoid openers about the weather or traffic conditions if at all possible. Try opening conversations with thoughtful and interesting questions:
  - *"How's business?"*
  - *"How's the project coming along?"*

---

65 Carnegie, D. (2006). *How To Win Friends and Influence People.* London, Vermilion.

- *"How is your month going?"*
- *"How are you and how are the kids?"*
- *"Are you having some incredible adventures?"*

- Listen. Really listen. And observe the initial body language signals between you.
- Communicate chin to chin – imagine an invisible piece of string between your chins which will keep you both 'connected' during your interaction.

If you consistently turn up prepared to make a good first impression it will take you a long way.

6. Learn to listen, not just to hear

Here is another lesson from the brilliant Nick Looby. Are you listening or waiting to respond? It can be so easy to go into a conversation with your head full of the things you want to say. Compared to the physical act of hearing, Active Listening is an incredibly powerful way to build understanding, empathy and rapport. People will reveal more than you first imagined.

Deep, all-in, distraction-free listening is hard, it takes real concentration and requires focus. Listen with your eyes and your ears and work hard to absorb the entire message. Do not focus on what you are going to say – you cannot listen to someone else while you are holding your own response in your head.

Listen for and observe the following:

- Tone.
- How words are being used.
- Paralanguage – the pace, loudness, and quality of the speaker's voice.
- The meaning behind their words.
- Body language.
- The emotion expressed through their words.

> ### Activity – Active listening
>
> Actively listen during your next conversation and make a mental note of the following:
>
> - What emotions are being expressed?
>
> - What are you learning about the other person from their tone of voice and delivery?

- Are they using words in an interesting or unusual way?

- Could you repeat or paraphrase what has just been said?

- Are you struggling to concentrate because you are focused on what you're going to say?

Practice all-in focus and dedicated listening and see your conversations blossom.

How to show your interest in a meeting

There is nothing worse than feeling that someone in a meeting is not interested. We all intuitively sense when people appear disinterested and mark them off as rude or, far worse, feel rejected by them. Don't make the mistake of appearing disinterested. Instead follow these steps:

- Be in the room.
- Down with devices.
- Smile.
- Lean forward and mirror others' gestures appropriately.
- Open body position.
- Palms up and active hand gestures.
- Eye contact and empathic facial gestures.
- Really listen.
- Nod.
- Take notes.

General guidelines for emails

So much of working life takes place through email. Make your emails effective by:

- Being mindful that some clients love emails, some hate them. Ask the client their preference. Remember the difference between Think, Feel, and Know clients.
- Keeping emails short and using bullet points to make things clear.
- Making it clear what the client needs to do. If you are just sharing information say *"I am just sharing observations – no action is required from you"*.
- Always opening with a friendly statement like *"I hope you are well and business is good"*.

- Signing off with *"Many thanks"*.
- Being careful not to cc in team members if their attention is not required. If you're not sure, just ask.

Much of this advice is common sense. But the devil is in the detail. If you consistently write really polite, welcoming, direct emails that are nice and clear to people you will get much better responses.

Tips for networking

Networking is a great opportunity to start a new relationship. But networking can be hard work. It is very easy to shy away from these interactions and for them to not result in positive outcomes. For effective networking, we offer the following lessons learnt from the communication guru Nick Looby.

Have a plan

- Who do you want to talk to? Remember networking is often about finding people who can introduce you to the right people. So therefore the 'target' of the networking is likely to be the potential introducer rather than the end customer or lead. Who in the room can introduce you to leads?
- Be clear about what you will say and practice this until it feels natural.
- Set yourself networking targets or goals based on the actions you can control, e.g. the number of strangers you can talk to.

In the room

- When approaching people who are having a conversation, ask *"may I join you?"* With people on their own, introducing yourself will start the conversation rolling well.
- When asked "what do you do?" focus the answer on the outcome of the thing you do. For example, instead of saying *"Digital Marketing"* say *"I help people make more money online."* Chances are the response will be *"oh, that sounds interesting, do tell me more"*. Clarify the importance of what you do with an example or appropriate anecdote.
- Ask *"who are you looking to meet?"*
- To exit from a conversation, *"it's been really great talking to you"* means it's time for me to talk to someone else. The past tense psychologically tells the other person that the conversation is coming to a close

One-to-one calls versus conference calls

One-to-one calls are more intimate than conference calls. It can be easier to build a closer rapport and structure your call – according to any of the guidelines above – to make the other person feel happy, show interest, position the agenda and goals, etc. Conference calls need a bit more structure and guidance so everyone feels that their time and effort has been well spent. But it is still important to make people feel happy and important, and to build on all the relationships involved. Use the Clear Communication Framework to ensure your calls are effective.

Outbound phone calls

It should never be the Digital Marketing Manager's role to hit the phones with sales in mind. Alas, we know sometimes people in the role are asked to help. The tips below are also as relevant to making outbound calls to potential new suppliers. Here are some thoughts around making phone calls:

1. If you are making sales calls ensure discipline by setting yourself a target number of calls for the day. e.g. 20.
2. Don't hesitate. It is easy to overthink a phone call. Be prepared to just pick up the phone and start talking!
3. Check previous notes to see updates from previous conversations.
4. Double check contact name and number.
5. What does the person you are talking to care about? For example if they are a business development manager they may be most interested in what new leads you could bring or how co-pitching could win them more work.
6. Have a clear goal for the call.
7. Be clear and positive. Consider standing up.
8. Introduce yourself. "I am Raffaele, Partnership Manager at Footprint Digital.
9. Ask, "Is now a good time?".
10. Say why you are calling "We've not met before, but I am calling to help strengthen our partnership."
11. Show interest with open ended questions. "How's business?" "How are you finding things?"
12. Share your genuine thoughts/challenges. "Yes I have found working from home challenging too, but I am finding my rhythm now and it's great to be able to talk." or "Yes, we also decided to furlough a few team members but we are all back now and raring to go." or "We have

also left the office open for now with just a few people popping in from time to time".

13. Say, "We can definitely help you with that". For example, "Things have been a bit quiet in terms of new business": "We can definitely help you with that." "It's been weird working remotely": "We can definitely help you with that".

14. State why you called. "I wanted to book in some time for a video call to get a fresh understanding of the clients and type of work you guys are looking for."

15. Ask them when they're free. Say yes and send an invite. "Yes, I can be available then. I will send a calendar invite now".

16. Say, I really look forward to chatting more.

17. Say, if anything crops up in the meantime don't hesitate to call me.

18. Say, "Thank you".

19. After your call send an email with a quick summary. If you discussed a follow up meeting then send a calendar invite and say how excited you are to "meet" again.

20. Update your CRM or records with a quick summary so you can remember in the future.

Presenting to an audience

Use this Nick Looby list of guidelines when preparing a talk:

- Consider your goals – what do you want to achieve for you and for your audience?
- Who is your audience? Tailor your presentation to them, ideally informed by their specific needs.
- If you are presenting to win business, know some names where appropriate and ask questions where relevant.
- Start strong. Hook your audience with something that wakes up the ears. Build rapport as early as you can.
- Consider which stories you will tell to illustrate your key messages – real, interesting and enjoyable stories will add huge value for your audience.
- Use visuals that illuminate your message. Think 'signposts' not 'wallpaper'.
- Remove as many bullet points as you can from your slides – text will slow down your delivery and tire your audience.
- Be human. Be authentic. Remember your story.

- Enable a healthy Q and A *before* you summarise your talk – don't have Q and A right at the end of your presentation.
- Finish incredibly strong. A detailed and specific call to action is required. What will your audience be doing differently tomorrow because of what you have shared today?
- Review. Did you achieve your goals? If so – great talk. If not, where can you improve?

Ideas to keep the energy in a meeting

Maintaining high energy during meetings and lengthy interactions can be hard. The foundation of a meeting that is full of vibrant energy is getting the positioning right. That is to know exactly what the other people in the meeting want to get from your time together and how long they have with you to discuss it. If you've really understood how long people have got and what they want to get from the meeting then you'll be sharing information that is relevant to what the attendees want to know and they will therefore be interested and engaged. The worst scenario is when you spout off a lot of stuff that people are not interested in. So make sure that you don't plough straight into the content of the meeting without asking what people what to get from the meeting. Then be led by the questions that are raised.

It is important that when the energy has gone flat that you do something. Consider the following options to provide additional vitality:

- Try and observe the energy of the room. Listen as much, if not more, than you talk and make sure you have a 'feel' of the room so you can adapt when needed.
- Take a break. Stopping the meeting and taking a tea and toilet break can be very effective in re-energising the meeting.
- Move. Get up, move, change position. In some meetings we encourage attendees to switch ends for the second half and physically move to a different seat. Much like in a football game.
- Take a verbal break. If you have delivered a lot of the content of the meeting then asking a question can be a great way of taking a verbal break.
- Take a break from the topic. Be confident in introducing a new topic not related to the current subject.
- Change your environment. Change the scenery. Open a window.
- Be mindful of everyone in the room. Take turns and involve different people. Make sure that people that have been quiet in the meeting are included in a safe and interested way.

Ask and get what you want

Digital Marketing Managers regularly need help from a wide range of people. Asking for what you want can be intimidating. We hope this short guide will help:

- **Have a plan** – know what you want to ask for.
- **Check your timing** – is now the best time to ask?
- **Be clear and don't rely on mind reading** – don't assume.
- **Understand others' priorities** – what you care about may be different to others.
- **Use the power of silence** – ask and then STFU.
- Make it easy for the other person to say yes.
- Provide options. Make it convenient. Compromise if appropriate.

How to say *"No"*

As a Digital Marketing Manager you will be used to receiving a deluge of requests from colleagues. You cannot say yes to them all and remain effective. But how on earth do you find the words to say no?

This all sits under the philosophy of psychological safety. Ideally we would be working in an environment where you can be open, honest, and fair and say what you think without the other person being offended.

Here are some ideas from Nick Looby:

- Just say no. *"No"* can be a complete sentence.
- Don't make it personal – say no to the situation, not the person.
- Add a caveat (or two) – *"No, unless you can... x,y,z"*.
- Make the other person jump through hoops – *"Send me x,y,z before I consider"*.
- Bait and switch – *"No. But, what I can do is..."*.
- Pass the buck – *"No, but my colleague Trevor can..."*.
- To say *"No"* to entire categories of request, use the phrase *"I don't..."* rather than the (negotiable) *"I can't..."*

How to give feedback

Candid feedback[66] is the key to helping one another grow. But giving open, honest feedback in a way that empowers the recipient is a tough skill to master. Here are some simple steps for delivering feedback in a way that won't make you want to crawl under a rock. Or make people think you are a Digital Marketing Manager with issues.

1. Introduce the conversation.
2. Empathise with the other person – show you are interested in them and their experience.
3. Describe the behaviour, *"I have noticed..."*
4. State the impact or consequence of this behaviour.
5. Ask the other person for their perception of the situation.
6. Make a suggestion, not a request.
7. Build an agreement about next steps.
8. Say thank you.

Go into a feedback session in the belief that by telling someone the truth you do them a favour. Have an objective to either reinforce or change behaviour – anything else is likely to just be passing judgement.

----

66 Harley, S. (2013) *How to Say Anything to Anyone: A Guide to Building Business Relationships That Really Work.* Texas, Greenleaf Book Group Press.

Chapter 13: Project management for Digital

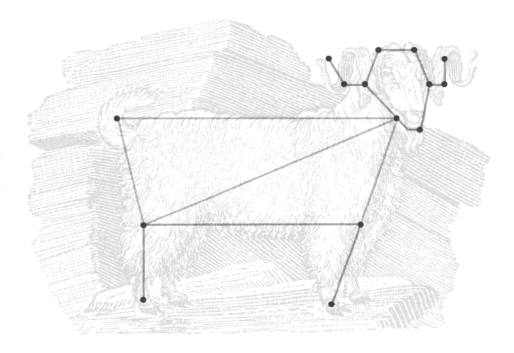

"Slow is smooth. Smooth is fast." **NAVY SEAL SAYING**

Q: Why do people climb Everest?

At 8,848 metres high Mount Everest is the highest mountain in the world. The area above an altitude of 8,000 metres is known as the "death zone". There is so little oxygen that the human body starts to die. Climbers' brains and lungs do not function properly and the risk of heart attacks and strokes is increased. Most of the 200+ climbers who have died on Mount Everest have died in the death zone. 6.5% of all Everest climbers die. Climbers have to pass the dead bodies as they ascend. It costs in the region of $45,000 to climb Everest.

A: Because it's there

The question is, when faced with such a risk to life and financial cost, why do people climb Everest? "Because it's there" was George Mallory's response. It is *a matter of hot debate whether he, with his climbing partner Andrew Irvine, was the first to summit Everest in June 1924. The reason for the ambiguity is that he was found dead on the mountain 75 years later. No one knows if he died on the way up or on the descent, having reached the summit.*

In spite of the risks and the ever increasing death toll, the summit attempts continue. The human desire remains strong.

Activity – Mount Everest case study

Read the following case study, then answer the subsequent questions.

On 10th May 1996, 47 people in three teams set out to climb the 8,848 metre high Mount Everest. Eight of them would not come back.

The three teams climbing to the summit were the following. A New Zealand team, Adventure Consultants, was made up of eight clients and four Sherpas, led by the experienced 36 year old Rob Hall. Rob had led groups to summit Everest five times and had a reputation for being a serious, methodical, and steady guide. The second team, Mountain Madness, was from the US. Led by Scott Fischer, the team consisted of eight clients and five Sherpas including two experienced guides, Anatoli Boukreev and Neal Beidleman. The final Taiwanese team was led by Ming Ho Gau and included ten climbers and three Sherpas. All of the teams had spent six weeks on the mountain preparing for the summit day which included altitude acclimatisation, team building, and safety procedures.

To avoid congestion on the summit the teams staggered their departure times. This was important for waypoints on the climb known as the Balcony and the Hillary Step. These points required fixed lines to be set which could only accommodate one climber at a time and the teams wanted to avoid a bottleneck. On 9th May, these three teams collectively agreed that Adventure Consultants would leave shortly before midnight and Mountain Madness shortly after midnight. The Taiwanese team agreed to postpone their ascent to another day.

Prior to embarking on a climb, teams agree on a time to turn around. This prevents the temptation to push on 'in the moment' and reduces risks. During one of the practice ascents, when facing deteriorating weather conditions, Rob Hall had ordered his team to turn around at a predetermined time. This had built client trust in his decision making.

A climb from camp four to the summit takes approximately 12 hours. Summit expeditions leave camp four at 12am so they should reach the summit by 12pm. The fading light and risk of poor weather on the return make it risky to start descent after 2pm. At 11.35pm on 9th May, Rob Hall's Adventure Consultants left camp. They were followed shortly after by Mountain Madness. Gau's Taiwanese team departed camp at 1am on the 10th which broke the agreement the teams had made. Fischer had to return to camp with a client who was suffering from altitude sickness and began his re-ascent even later.

The fixed lines that needed to be set at the Balcony and Hillary Step had not been set up so climbers had to wait for over an hour at each. Realising that the traffic jam would cause them to miss their turnaround time many of the climbers aborted their attempt. The first successful climbers were from the Mountain Madness team and they reached the summit between 1pm and 2.30pm. They waited for their leader Fischer for over 70 minutes before deciding to *"get the hell out of there".*

When subjected to the altitude and with oxygen at 20% of what is found at sea level the human body suffers significant stress. As well as affecting physiological performance many climbers experience an altered sense of reality and cognitive ability. This is exacerbated by the strenuous physical activity, dehydration, and lack of sleep. Hall's wife, who had been an expedition doctor with four previous groups, said that you *"don't make decisions at high altitude... the decision-making is already set in place".*

At around 3pm one of the Adventure Consultants climbers was found unresponsive by a Sherpa at the Hillary Step. Hall took over the climber's care, offered him oxygen from his own canister and instructed all Sherpas and climbers to descend. Around the same time the leaders of the other two groups, Gau and Fischer, reached the summit. This was 90 minutes later than their predetermined turnaround time.

The weather soon changed and a surprise storm hit at around 4pm. A blizzard made it hard to see and windchill reached -75°C. Most climbers couldn't descend in these conditions and had to tough it out, knowing that their oxygen tanks were only equipped for 18 hours.

Fischer and Gau managed to descend but couldn't see their team members. The Taiwanese team was not equipped with radios. Beidleman assumed leadership of a mixed group of eight climbers from the Mountain Madness and Adventure Consultant teams and started on the route down at 5.20pm. Climbers began to collapse.

Those that had aborted their summit attempt arrived back at camp at 5pm. They avoided the most savage weather conditions yet were still knocked off their feet by the 110km/h winds and blinded by the whiteout.

At around 8pm Beidleman's group huddled together unsure in which direction to go. Unknown to them, they were just a few hundred metres from camp. As conditions improved they made it back to camp. Many were unable to move but a few of the climbers went on rescue missions. Boukreev left two climbers he found assuming them to be dead and managed to successfully rescue two more.

Hall was alive but stranded near the peak. Equipped with a radio he maintained communication with base camp for the next 12 hours. They even managed to patch through a call to his wife in New Zealand where he said his last words to her, *"Sleep well my sweetheart; please don't worry about me too much"*.

The following morning three teams of Sherpas headed out to see if they could rescue any more climbers. Fischer could not be saved but they rescued Gau and two others who had been assumed dead. Within 36 hours of starting the summit ascent eight climbers had died.

Discussion questions

Where did it all go wrong?

How could we categorise the failures?

Here are some example answers:

Where did it all go wrong?	Categories:
Too many people	Human
Not enough support	Leadership
Lack of experience	Preparation
Not following the original plan	Plan
Not adapting the plan on route	Environment
Unexpected weather conditions	Training
Fisher was late	
Lack of preparation	
Blind commitment	
Personal Attachment	
Poor nutrition/ dehydration/ sleep deprivation	
Arrogance (they'd done it before)	

This mountaineering example may seem a heavy analogy to use. However, it illustrates how a wide range of factors can influence the ultimate success or failure of a project. There are numerous factors involved in a digital project so, like the Everest example, they are all (somewhat) destined to fail. The skill lies in planning ahead and doing everything you can to mitigate, in advance, all of the risks that the project faces. Once this is done, you must implement constant review points and reassessments to keep the project on track.

Project planning

There are so many moving parts and different stakeholders in a digital project. It is no wonder that projects often fail. At Footprint Digital we create a project plan for every project we run. The intention is to ensure that all projects have a clear goal, risks of failure are reduced, adequate resources are provided, a communication framework is developed, change management processes for adaptation are thought about, and waste is minimised.

The extent to which you plan is up to you. However, it can often take too long and eat into time when you should be *running* the project. We want to maintain momentum in the overall process, so we opt to make this process fast (it should take no more than a few hours). The short amount of time involved in conceiving the plan is well worth the investment.

To demonstrate what a simple digital marketing project plan might look like we have included an example below. What follows is a series of examples that show – section by section – a real digital marketing project plan for Footprint Digital. There are exercises along the way to enable you to apply these methodologies to your own project plan.

1. The purpose of this project plan and ground rules

This part of the project plan:

- Introduces the project and explains why the plan exists.
- Defines some of the shared ground rules for the project.
- Provides guidance on how to report issues that arise during the project, and how to escalate unresolved issues.

It should be easy for anyone that receives a copy of this document to understand. For example:

This is intended to be a real plan and not a document produced 'just because'.

The function of the plan is to reflect the journey that gets the project to the agreed completion date. The most important dates are the Start and Finish.

This plan exists to help make sure that everyone involved is on the same page. It is to be shared with all priority stakeholders and to include contributions from all relevant stakeholders.

Please read this plan and raise suggestions for improvements or further things to consider with the project manager at the earliest possible point.

Those involved in the project are encouraged to reflect on the benefits that come from a well run project.

What is a project? "A temporary endeavour undertaken to create a unique product, service or result. A project is temporary in that it has a defined beginning and end in time, and therefore defined scope and resources."[67]

What is a process? "A set of interrelated actions and activities performed to create a pre-specified product, service or result."[68]

---

67 Brook, Q. (2017) *Lean Six Sigma and Minitab (5th Edition): The Complete Toolbox Guide for Business Improvement.* Winchester, OPEX Resources Ltd.
68 Brook, Q. (2017) *Lean Six Sigma and Minitab (5th Edition): The Complete Toolbox Guide for Business Improvement.* Winchester, OPEX Resources Ltd.

The project will run to the principles of Agile DSDM model[69]. Time, cost, and quality will remain fixed with the only variable being the features of the project.

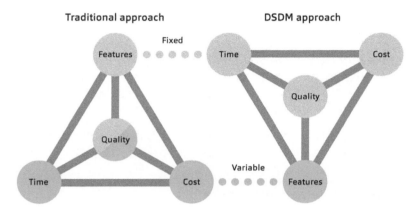

Those involved in the project should consider the concepts of:

Lean = stripping back waste to improve efficiency.

6 Sigma = "Lean Six Sigma is a methodology that relies on a collaborative team effort to improve performance by systematically removing waste and reducing variation".

This visual from the 6 sigma methodology shows the impact of being 99% Good to 99.9% Good:

99% Good (3.8 Sigma)	99.99966% Good (6 Sigma)
20,000 lost articles of mail per hour	7 lost articles of mail per hour
Unsafe drinking water for almost 15 minutes per day	One unsafe minute every seven months
5,000 incorrect surgical operations per week	1.7 incorrect surgical operations per week
200,000 wrong drug prescriptions each year	68 wrong drug prescriptions each year
No electricity for almost 7 hours each month	1 hour without electricity every 34 years

It is a requirement of this project that everyone involved works in a psychologically safe environment where it is encouraged to share mistakes and discuss ways of

---

69 Agile Business Consortium (2014) *The DSDM Agile Project Framework, 2014 Onwards.* DSDM Consortium.

doing things better. Mistakes themselves are not a problem, but, the failure to report any mistakes or observations that could jeopardise the project is an issue.

Regular reporting and structured communication will ensure that everyone is kept up to date.

The project manager is the first point of contact for all issues related to the project. Should anyone have concerns about anything that is happening on the project these are to be raised quickly and directly with the project manager and then reported through email for our records.

Root cause analysis will be performed for every challenge faced with a view to resolving the core cause of any issue that arises.

Activity – Statement of purpose

Define the purpose of the project plan and the ground rules for the project.

2. The Customer

The project should be focused on a customer need. This section defines who the customer for the project is. It ensures that their needs are understood and provides evidence of these needs.

Footprint Digital is a digital marketing agency with offices in Colchester and London. Offering digital marketing services with a focus on performance marketing. Its main product lines are SEO (Search Engine Optimisation), PPC (Paid Media Management), Site Build Support & Migration with additional products such as Outsourced Digital Marketing Manager, Digital Marketing Audit and CRO (Conversion Rate Optimisation).

Operating for the last seven years the company has grown to 16 employees and a turnover of £700,000. Footprint Digital specialises in supporting £1-20 million turnover organisations. Has worked with or is working with brands such as Huawei, Safestore, Itsu, Legal and General.

- *80% of business comes through Partnerships with web design, accountants, etc.*
- *10% through the website*
- *5% through education events in partnership with New Anglia Growth Hub, Department of International Trade etc.*
- *5% of business comes through client referrals/ upsales*

Footprint Digital has a two year objective to reach £1.25million turnover by the end of 2021/2022 (June year end). Throughout this time the directors would like to be removed from the day to day business development roles in the business.

As well as increasing the revenue and profit to the business, Footprint Digital has the objective to build asset in the business. That is to improve all of its processes, systems, literature and documentation throughout the business. This is with the intention to make the business less reliant on any individuals and increase the value of the business.

Activity – Define the customer

- Is it clear who the customer for the project is?
- Are the customer's needs understood?
- Is this supported by any evidence?

Now ask the same three questions about your own project.

3. Goals statement, problem statement, and project scope

In this part of the document we briefly define what the project is. We use data to explain why the project is needed and define the project's scope. We aim to do this using simple, clear language.

This part of the process looks straightforward, but it is the hardest part. Expect to spend a little time scratching your head. But, it is also the most important part of the process. Once defined everything that follows is easier.

Problem statement

The problem statement clearly states the problem – the reason why the project is necessary. It describes how frequently the problem occurs and its impact.

Problem statement

During the last two financial years the business achieved £700,000 of sales generating profits of 15%. This has hindered the business's ability to reinvest into staffing and marketing. This means that the growth of the business is constricted and it is over reliant on key team members in each department. A turnover of £1.25 million would enable the business to hire across each department so that there is no single point of weakness, invest £150,000 per year into marketing, and achieve a greater profit margin of 25%.

Goal statement

The goal statement is the response to the problem. It should clearly define the targets of the project.

Goal statement

To achieve £1.25 turnover by end June 2022 we must increase new business revenue 75% from £400,000 per year to £700,000 per year.

Maintaining our current 1 in 3 lead to sale conversion rate we must increase the volume of new business leads from 160 per year to 250 per year.

Project scope

In this section we define the scope of the project. We define what we are going to do to respond to the problem and achieve the goal. This is the place to list the specific outcomes of the project.

Project Scope

Led by the marketing department, this project will utilise a £175,000 budget to mobilise a range of digital marketing resources to achieve the project goal within the current financial year.

> **Activity – Write a problem statement, goal statement and project scope for your own project.**
>
> - Is the problem clear?
> - Are the goals of the project clear?
> - Is the project focused on a customer requirement?
> - Does the project have a clear business case?
> - Has the potential business benefit been estimated in cash?
>
> Keep it brief, avoid technical language, quantify the problem, explain the costs of the problem, define the scope.
>
> Be SMART[70]. Make sure the statement is Specific, Measurable, Achievable, Relevant, and Time Bound.

---

70 Doran, G. T. (1981) *There's a S.M.A.R.T. way to write management's goals and objectives.* Management Review. Volume 70, Issue 11, Pp 35–36.

4. Project team

In this section you identify who is part of the project delivery team and define who is responsible for what in the project.

This project delivery team is made up of the following.

- *Marketing Manager – Footprint Digital*
- *Project Manager – Footprint Digital*
- *Director – Footprint Digital*
- *Head of Marketing Innovation – Footprint Digital*
- *Head of Content – Footprint Digital*
- *Head of Paid Search – Footprint Digital*
- *Head of SEO – Footprint Digital*
- *Technical SEO – Footprint Digital*
- *Graphic Designer – Outsourced*
- *Web Developer – Outsourced*
- *Videographer & editor – Outsourced*
- *Publisher – Outsourced*
- *Web Designer – Outsourced*

Activity – Project team

Identify who is part of the project team and who is responsible for what.

5. Stakeholders, Stakeholder engagement, and progress reports

Who are the Stakeholders? Stakeholders include everyone involved and affected by the project – directly and indirectly. We define and recognise them by using an affinity diagram[71]. This allows us to brainstorm and start to arrange stakeholders according to what they have in common.

We then list the stakeholders and their role in the project. Each stakeholder is likely to have different core goals and may view success differently. For example, the project manager may view completing the project on time and on budget as the most important indicator of success, whereas a designer may think that the creation of a fantastic experience is more important than

---

71 Devised by Jiro Kawakita in the 1960s and sometimes referred to as the KJ Method.

finishing it on time. Consequently, different stakeholder goals have to be weighed up and prioritised.

Market	Business	Authorities	Resources
Partners	Director	Advertising Standards	Web developer
Education Partners	Marketing Manager	Google Compliance	Graphic designer
Clients	Director/ Partnership Development Manager	Web standards	Videographer
Potential clients	Partnership Team	GDPR	Web designer
Competitors	New Business Development Team		Print designer
Digital Marketing Managers	Footprint digital wider team		Publisher
University students			
Business owners			
Chief Marketing Officers			
Lecturers			

Activity – Identify the stakeholders

Identify your stakeholders using an affinity diagram.

Include a description of each in the document alongside an explanation of the role in the project.

Stakeholder engagement

To define this, categorise each stakeholder based on their power and their interest. This makes clear the level of communication and involvement each stakeholder needs throughout the project.

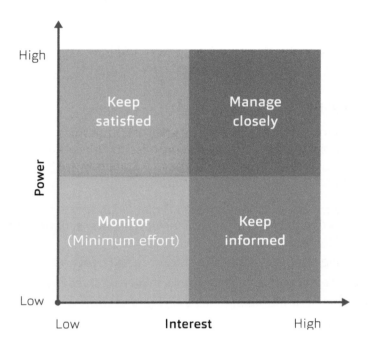

Keep Satisfied (High Power, Low Interest)	Manage Closely (High Power, High Interest)
Partners	Director
Education Partners	Marketing Manager
Clients	Project Manager
Potential clients	
Digital Marketing Managers	
University students	
Lecturers	
Monitor (minimum effort) (Low Power, Low Interest)	**Keep Informed (High Interest, Low Power)**
Competitors	Director/ Partnership Development
Advertising Standards	Manager
Chartered Institute of Marketing	Partnership Development Team
	Sales Team
	Head Client Services
	Footprint digital wider team
	Developer
	Graphic designer
	Videographer
	Publisher

> ### Activity – Stakeholder prioritisation
>
> Group the stakeholders by their power and interest.

Progress reports

This is a statement that addresses the level of communication expected for the project. It details the updates you promise to deliver and your expectations for those involved in the team. You can state how frequently reporting will happen and the nature of these reports:

- *A weekly progress catch up between Project Manager and Director for 30 minutes on Google Meet. (This will include results, actions for that week, signing off things).*
- *Informal five minute update summary in weekly delivery team meeting.*
- *Informal five minute update summary in weekly sales meeting.*
- *Monthly one hour Marketing Focus Group sessions.*
- *Formal update in the quarterly review. (This will include: results, sales figures, key campaign information, requests for support).*
- *Results to be reported in the sales data file spreadsheet.*
- *Send all outsource partners our Brand Positioning Document/ handbook/ future brand guidelines.*
- *Annual marketing plan sharing session with outsource partners. (This will include a video call in which the brand positioning document, marketing plan and project plan is shared with ample opportunity for questions and answers).*
- *Partners, Education Partners, Clients, Potential clients, Digital Marketing Managers, University students, Lecturers need to see the outcomes of the work, but do not need to be kept in the loop about the specifics.*
- *No updates for Competitors, Advertising Standards, Chartered Institute of Marketing etc.*

> ### Activity – Progress Reports
>
> Identify the types of communication and reporting that will be followed through the project.
>
> Identify your communication and reporting priorities and schedule accordingly.

6. Specifications

This is the part of the document where you list the specifications of the project.

In order to increase the volume of new business leads from 160 per year to 250 per year and achieve a 75% increase in new business revenue from £400,000 per year to £700,000 per year we could:

- Publish daily social media posts.
- Email campaigns to partners and potential customers.
- Publish whitepaper PR campaigns through lead generation platforms.
- Establish a paid search campaign.
- Increase our SEO activity.
- Employ team of partnership development managers.
- Employ a lead generation telesales introducer company.
- Publish our book.
- Film our digital marketing course.
- Produce exceptional case studies.
- Establish a paid retargeting campaign.
- Perform a Customer Journey Mapping exercise and create marketing literature that nurtures people through the sales funnel.
- Run an influencer marketing campaign.
- Update the website.
- Perform competitor research.

7. Prioritised Requirements List – MoScoW

Once you have defined the specifications we can use the MoScoW methodology[72] to prioritise the tasks. This is a prioritisation technique that helps project managers, project teams, and stakeholders understand the importance of the requirements of the project plan. It identifies which tasks are 'must have', 'should have', 'could have', or 'won't have for now'.

Must have

- Publish daily social media posts.
- Email campaigns to partners and potential customers.

---

72 Clegg, D; Barker, R (1994). *Case Method Fast-Track: A RAD Approach*. Boston, Addison-Wesley.

- Employ team of partnership development managers.
- Produce exceptional case studies.
- Update the website.

Should have

- Establish a paid retargeting campaign.
- Increase our SEO activity.
- Perform a Customer Journey Mapping exercise and create marketing literature that nurtures people through the sales funnel.

Could have

- Publish our book.
- Film our digital marketing course and produce an online learning management system.
- Publish whitepaper PR campaigns through lead generation platforms.
- Establish a paid search campaign.

- ### Won't have for now
- Establish a paid social campaign.
- Run an influencer marketing campaign.
- Employ a lead generation telesales introducer company.

> **Activity – Perform a MoSCoW prioritisation for your project.**
>
> Think carefully about which aspects of the project are 'must have', 'should have', 'could have', or 'won't have for now'.
>
> Discuss these priorities within the project team.
>
> Can you reach an agreement on what's important?

8. Budget

Here we define the budget. These are ranked in priority order with the 'must have' in green, 'should have' in orange, and 'could have' in red. The 'won't have for now's' have been removed.

Activity	Budget
Publish daily social media posts.	£7,500
Email campaigns to partners and potential customers.	£7,500
Employ team of partnership development managers.	£90,000
Produce exceptional case studies.	£3,000
Update the website.	£3,000
Establish a paid retargeting campaign.	£12,000
Increase our SEO activity.	£12,000
Perform a Customer Journey Mapping exercise and create marketing literature that nurtures people through the sales funnel.	£4,000
Publish our book.	£5,000
Film our digital marketing course and produce an online learning management system.	£8,000
Publish whitepaper PR campaigns through lead generation platforms.	£5,000
Total	£157,000

Activity – Define the budget of your project

9. Schedule

At this point we define the project start and end dates. We can also define key 'milestone' dates – deadlines for activities within the project that will support completion within the overall timeline.

We have set a firm project start date of 1st January. At this point we shall procure the relevant resources and materials. The project will come to a close on the 30th June at which time a new project plan will be launched.

- *January: Perform a Customer Journey Mapping exercise and create marketing literature that nurtures people through the sales funnel.*
- *January: Employ team of partnership development managers.*
- *January & February: Film our digital marketing course and produce an online learning management system.*
- *February: Produce exceptional case studies.*
- *February, March April, May June: Publish daily social media posts.*

- *February, March April, May June: Email campaigns to partners and potential customers.*
- *February, March April, May June: Increase our SEO activity.*
- *February: Establish a paid retargeting campaign.*
- *February: Publish our book.*
- *March: Update the website.*
- *March: Establish a paid search campaign.*
- *April: Publish whitepaper PR campaigns through lead generation platforms.*

We have laid out into a Gantt style chart to show the schedule of tasks over time. This is to demonstrate which tasks need to be completed in sequence and which can be performed concurrently.

Activity	January	February	March	April	May	June
Perform a Customer Journey Mapping exercise and create marketing literature that nurtures people through the sales funnel.	▓					
Employ team of partnership development managers.	▓					
Film our digital marketing course and produce an online learning management system.	▓	▓				
Produce exceptional case studies.		▓				
Publish daily social media posts.		▓	▓	▓	▓	▓
Email campaigns to partners and potential customers.		▓	▓	▓	▓	▓
Increase our SEO activity.		▓	▓	▓	▓	▓
Establish a paid retargeting campaign.		▓				
Publish our book.		▓				
Update the website.			▓			
Establish a paid search campaign.			▓			
Publish whitepaper PR campaigns through lead generation platforms.				▓		

There are many online tools which can help you plan and track your project, these include Microsoft Planner, Monday.com, and Accelo.

Activity – Define the schedule for your project

Set realistic start and end dates.

Identify 'milestones' between the two to keep the project on track.

Think about the consequences of missing a milestone, or missing the end date. Are there any activities that require the completion of another activity before they can start?

Define the concurrent work that will occur throughout your project.

Can you identify any activities that require the same resources to achieve completion?

Conclusion

It is easy to have moments where a project feels insurmountable, especially when there are so many variables and individuals involved. But if you follow these project management steps it will help make a difficult challenge manageable. It will enable you to scale your Everest.

As we move on and look at the range and complexity of digital marketing channels in the following chapters you will fully appreciate the benefits of having created a project plan.

Activity – Complete a project plan for your project and share it with the stakeholders.

Chapter 14: Turn visitors into customers with Conversion Rate Optimisation (CRO)

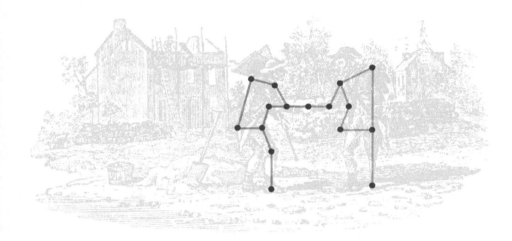

> *"If you want a great site, you've got to test. After you've worked on a site for even a few weeks, you can't see it freshly anymore. You know too much. The only way to find out if it really works is to test it."* **STEVE KRUG**[73]

Which test won? – Quiz

We've tested thousands of websites. The results are always fascinating, surprising and often downright weird. As well as being a lot of fun, Conversion Rate Optimisation (CRO) is also the discipline through which we achieve the fastest and most radical results. Yet it is the least utilised weapon in a marketer's armoury.

We'd like to share some of the results of tests that we have run on clients' websites. When we do this with a live audience we ask everyone to stand up and answer multiple choice questions about website content and design. If they pick the option that has the highest conversion rate, they stay in. The last person standing wins a prize. We have presented this quiz to thousands

---

73 Krug, S. (2014) *Don't Make Me Think, Revisited: A Common Sense Approach to Web Usability.* San Fransisco, New Riders

of people over the years. There have only been a handful of people that have ever got all of the answers right.

Note that each test was run with live traffic to the site. Those taking the test did not know they were part of the test. Each test was then measured against the commercial impact on the business. Try and avoid the temptation to look at the results. Before you look at the answers below, pick which one you think will win. Compare your guesses with the ultimate winner. Chances are some of these will surprise you!

Question 1: Which resulted in more enquiries?

Leaflet delivery company: Call to action button

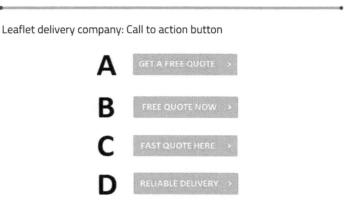

Question 2: Which webpage sold more products?

Question 3: Which ad resulted in the most bookings?

Oasis Overland: Promoting holidays in Paid Search.

A - Price

Africa Expeditions
Great Value Africa Overland Trip,
Africa Expeditions 19 days to 39 weeks.
OasisOverland.co.uk/Africa-Expeditions

B - Encouragement

Africa Expeditions
Change Your Life Now. See Africa,
Africa Expeditions 19 days to 39 weeks.
OasisOverland.co.uk/Africa-Expeditions

C - Descriptive

Africa Expeditions
Worry Free Organised Overland Trips,
Africa Expeditions 19 days to 39 weeks.
OasisOverland.co.uk/Africa-Expeditions

FOOTPRINT
DIGITAL

Question 4: Which homepage resulted in more enquiries?

Question 5: Which form produced the most submissions?

Contact forms: Field design

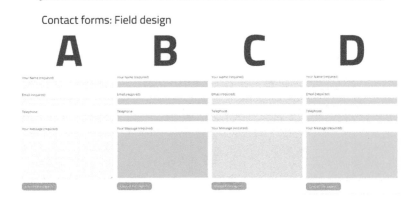

195

Quiz answers

1. *D – this CTA button received 28% more conversions than the original*
2. *A – this webpage received 22% more sales*
3. *B – this ad got 12% more bookings than the next best ad*
4. *C – this webpage got 268% more website enquiries than the original*
5. *C – this contact form received 31% more enquiries than the original white form*

Which test won? – Lessons learned

We've learned a lot from years of testing websites. The main lesson is that the more we test the less confident we are in expert opinions. Tests often throw up surprise results and website visitors often respond to things that are surprising.

The tests we shared above taught us some lessons for CRO:

Lesson 1: It's not about how well you sell something, it's about how well you address user concerns and customer anxieties.

Lesson 2: Don't make assumptions. You only know if you test it!

Lesson 3: Different people respond to different messages. Find a good message that appeals to as many people as possible.

Lesson 4: Design isn't always about aesthetic. It's about engagement.

Lesson 5: Value your checkouts and contact forms.

The main lesson is that to be successful you can throw out the rulebook. Take Amazon as an example. If a web designer came in with that site as the culmination of their expertise and presented it to the Board, they would be booted out of the room. Yet, the Amazon website is one of the most effective sites on the internet.

Be more human

The Google Analytics video 'In Real Life – Online Checkout'[74] does a beautiful job of demonstrating the absurdity of a poor online user experience. Highlights include the checkout assistant presenting a customer with an

---

74 Google Analytics (2011). *Google Analytics In Real Life – Online Checkout.* *[online] available at:* https://www.youtube.com/watch?v=3Sk7cOqB9Dk [accessed 26 April 2020]

incomprehensible CAPTCHA (the thing that tries to ascertain whether you are human), a moment where hidden delivery charges are revealed, and the assistant 'timing out' and starting the frustrating process over again. Absurd as the video is, it is a reality that websites consistently deliver poor customer experiences.

The gap between technology and human intuition is a long way from being bridged.

What is CRO?

> *"Conversion Rate Optimisation (CRO) is the art and science of getting people to act once they arrive on your website."* **TIM ASH**[75]

CRO: The art and science of finding out what's wrong, then fixing it

Conversion Rate Optimisation is the process of learning why visitors to your website aren't doing the things you want them to and then improving your website to ensure that they do. It is the *process* of improving your website to maximise the number of people who turn from views into sales. The most important thing to remember is that CRO is a *process*. There is no quick fix or easy method for CRO.

The power of applying the process is that you guarantee improvements. Good CRO is data driven, systematic and intelligent. This well organised approach will mean that you will never make results worse. You either stick where you are or you win.

What is conversion rate?

> *"The conversion rate reflects the interaction between a website and its consumers' purchase choices and is defined as the percentage of users purchasing a product out of the total unique visitors entering a website".* **MCDOWELL ET AL**[76]

---

75 Ash, T. (2012) *Landing Page Optimization: The Definitive Guide to Testing and Tuning for Conversions.* Sybex.
76 McDowell et al. (2016) An examination of retail website design and conversion rate. *Journal of Business Research*, Volume 69, Issue 11, Pp 4837-4842.

Who needs CRO?

Imagine the worst website you have ever seen.

It's old. It's slow. It's probably got flashing images that distract you and links that don't work. It might receive a million views a day and sell brilliant products – but no one would ever buy something from it.

It needs Conversion Rate Optimisation (CRO).

Now imagine the best website you have ever seen.

It's fun, it's exciting, it's an integral part of your life and you often buy things from it. Are there improvements that could make it even more fantastic? Chances are that because this website is so great it will also be very popular. As a result, the benefit of even a tiny improvement to conversion rate will have a big difference.

It needs Conversion Rate Optimisation (CRO).

No website is perfect, and that means that every website would benefit from the CRO process.

CRO helps businesses to:

- Increase sales, revenues, and profits.
- Increase revenue per visitor.
- Acquire new customers.
- Permanently improve conversion rates.

What did CRO ever do for us?

Good CRO can make a massive difference to your business. With a more streamlined, user-focused website, conversion rates are likely to go up, and that means more customers, more conversions and more revenue.

Let's take a look at the impact an increase in conversion rate can have:

Traffic	Cost of Traffic	Conversion Rate	Conversions	Average order value	Revenue
1000	£500	1%	10	£50	£500
1000	£500	2%	20	£50	£1000
1000	£500	3%	30	£50	£1500
1000	£500	4%	40	£50	£2000

An improved conversion rate improves the performance of everything that you do.

Benefits of increased conversion

The impact of an increased conversion rate is an improvement to your online asset that will deliver a long-term payback beyond your initial investment and effort. To understand what you might gain over an extended period of time, take a look at the principles of compound interest.

Also consider the impact of increased conversion rates on the business. Consider how a better website benefits the brand and contributes to the increased value of the asset.

Why is CRO not more widely adopted?

So if everyone can benefit from CRO, and it guarantees results, why is it not applied more often?

The truth is that many of the tools we use in our everyday lives often fail to live up to their promise. When things are not intuitive to use they become very frustrating and, as a result, it becomes very hard to realise their full benefit.

Why is this? Why is technology not easier to use? More intuitive?

The answer is a combination of the following:

- The organisations that win big do apply it (Amazon, for example).
- It requires the buy in of the organisation to invest the time, money, and effort.
- It requires the psychological safety needed to notice what's wrong, fix it, test it, and repeat.
- It requires the complex task of bringing various data sources together.
- It requires a champion to put their neck on the line.
- It requires a fundamentally different approach to budgeting.
- HiPPOs.

Much of the list above goes back to environment and culture – the two key aspects of a business that a Digital Marketing Manager has the power to influence! Here's a five phase approach to help you persuade your organisation to adopt a CRO project.

5 phases to a successful CRO project

Phase 1 – Creating the environment.

Phase 2 – Business case and goal setting.

Phase 3 – Research.

Phase 4 – Design.

Phase 5 – Test, Measure, Repeat.

Phase 1 – Creating the environment for an effective CRO campaign

- **Organisational buy in** – Organisations that win big apply the principles of CRO in everything that they do.
- **Brave individual champions** – You will need to be brave and willing to try things. Do not be afraid to make mistakes – you will learn from them.
- **Psychological safety** – Teams in which ideas are encouraged. The intention is to find out what's wrong, fix it, test it and repeat.
- **Real-world budgeting** – Resourcing that is reactive to successes rather than set in stone.
- **Fast processes** – It is important that you don't dwell in research. The majority of the time is used to test your hypotheses in the real world.

Phase 2 – Business case and goal setting

Use the principles of Six Sigma[77] to define the business case and set a goal for the project.

Keep it brief	Specific
Avoid technical language	Measurable
Quantify the problem	Achievable
Explain the costs of the problem	Relevant
Define the scope	Time Bound

Problem statement

During the last 12 months Footprint Digital had a website 'visit to ultimate sale' conversion rate of 0.2%. This resulted in £330,00 of revenue and profit

---

77 Six Sigma is registered as a Motorola trademark (on December 28, 1993)

of £50,000 for an investment of £15,000. Low customer satisfaction and lost revenue.

Goal statement

Increasing the website conversion rate from 0.2% to 0.3% over the next 3 months would deliver an additional £115,000 of annual revenue and profit of £25,000 for an investment of £3,000.

Potential impact of a conversion rate improvement

Then it is worthwhile to consider the potential impact of an improvement in conversion rate, calculating the impact of changes into the future using the concept of compound interest.

Phase 3 – Research

How do we make a HIPPO listen? With data. And how do we get data? By using tools to learn about users. What follows is a list of tools that a CRO specialist turns to in the research stage. Remember that as a Digital Marketing Manager your role is to be strategic – it is great for you to know what needs to be done, but your digital marketing strategy will yield far better results if you leave the actual doing to a CRO expert, or team of experts. Get the technical aspects outsourced!

A CRO expert's top tools for shooting HiPPOs

Below are some tools that Digital Marketing Managers might find helpful for completing the CRO process.

- **Surveys** – you could set up an internal survey using something like SurveyMonkey, Google Forms, or Informizely to ask your sales team or customer services team about the interactions they have with customers. They probably know a lot about what your customers want that would be very valuable for a CRO exercise.

- **Google Analytics** – You can use Google Analytics during your research phase to track what people are searching for on your website, and find out which pages are most important to them (as well as the ones they bounce off from or spend least time on). Once you have got your webpage tests designed and developed, you can also use Google Analytics to run the A/B tests for free. Use annotations in Google Analytics to track specific events including when you start the test and when you finish it. Note which test won and whether you have chosen to make the new test design live.

- **Live chat** – a great way to compile a list of customer anxieties and common questions is through live chat. Some live chat platforms include Snapengage and Olark, but there are lots out there to choose from. The problem with live chat is that it needs to be done really well in order to be useful. There needs to be someone (or a team of people) constantly managing it otherwise it's likely to annoy potential customers instead of help them.

- **Phone tracking** – It's important to use phone tracking to get a comprehensive view of your traffic. Examples of phone tracking providers include TTNC, MediaHawk, and ResponseTap. By using something like this you'll be able to measure how many people are converting through phone calls.

- **User testing** – a key part of conversion rate optimisation is seeing how people, who have never been to your website before, navigate and use your site. Fresh eyes often pick up on things that you simply can't see because you've gotten used to how your site is organised. You can set up user tests on a number of platforms such as UserTesting, Userlytics, and TryMyUI. Tests vary in cost, but are usually around £30-£50. You'll be able to choose your parameters (e.g. age, gender, location) and the questions you ask. We recommend being *very* careful with how you word your questions, so that they are not open to interpretation or misunderstanding. Bad questions are a costly mistake!

- **Click or heat maps** – click maps allow you to track where users click on your website, either on desktop or mobile devices. You can use this data to work out which buttons they are engaging with, how far down the page they are scrolling, and much more. They are really useful for understanding which of your CTAs are underperforming, and then testing out new CTAs to see if your conversion rate increases. Examples of click map providers include Hotjar, ClickTale, and Crazy Egg.

- **Customer feedback software** – creating a way for website users to give you direct feedback on your site can be a very useful way to improve your website and make it more customer focused. Platforms like Qualaroo offer inbuilt website surveys and Usabilla provides a way for your customers to rate your emails and your website.

- **Copy and paste tracker** – if your website is a knowledge hub, then it's likely that people will be copying and pasting, or sharing your content. It might be helpful for you to understand which bits of content they are sharing the most, in order for you to create more content like that. Tools like the Tynt Measure Copy and Paste will tell you just this.

Activity – Gather the information needed for the research phase

- Research briefing questions

- Brand guidelines

- Any historical marketing literature, branding information, and any supporting documentation

- The last 50 emails or live chat qualitative messages from people who have engaged with the site

- Access to Google Analytics and any other reporting or testing tools

- Developer info and insights

- Calls to action, sales messages, anxieties, differentiation or unique selling points

- A list of five main online competitors

- A list of common questions that the sales team receive during the sales process

- Any other sources of relevant information

CRO – Applying the theory

The objective is to find out why people are not converting and then fix any problem areas in the website to encourage them to start converting into customers. The Digital Marketing Manager must be well informed with data, but not overwhelmed. Try to use multiple sources of data, but make sure that the process is fast and do not get bogged down in the wealth of potential data. As a rule of thumb at Footprint we do not like to spend more than a week pulling together the information from which to make our recommendations. In real terms, this process may take a total of eight hours.

This can be done in several ways and draw from a huge range of sources. Our method is not exhaustive of everything you can do, but it does give a reasonable range of useful information quickly.

Research outcomes

Once you have collected all this data, you should be able to clearly see the problems that people are having with your site. Create a bullet point list of all of the outcomes from the research. Also write lists of the calls to action, sales messages and potential customer anxieties. You can then start to create some new designs that incorporate better messaging and design.

Footprint produce the following reports:

1. Tracking check

You can't achieve anything if the data from which you are making decisions is incorrect. Make sure Google Analytics is installed and tracking. You must analyse and ensure that all goals are tracked and work correctly. This includes adding the code required to run the testing platform you wish to use.

2. Google Analytics analysis

This report focuses on an in-depth look at a large amount of existing data using Google Analytics (or another web analytics service). These services can provide crucial information about where people are 'bouncing' your site (where they're leaving from after just arriving), or about specific pages that are not engaging users adequately. Google Analytics can also be set up to track your goals. The most important outcomes are to find which pages to focus your work on as it is unwise to perform CRO across your whole website all at once. This can be found through using a comparison of bounce rate against sessions on the landing page report tab. Of course there are other ways, but this gives a fast and simple view.

3. Existing documentation report

Here, you need to analyse all digital and non-digital information for USPs, CTAs, customer anxieties, and important sales messages. The goal is to ensure that your website accurately reflects your marketing literature and vice versa.

4. Sales and client services team insights

The best form of data is qualitative human feedback. This really helps to get under the skin of your customers. Your sales team probably talks to prospective clients all day, every day. They are used to all of the questions that people ask. Often these are so common that the sales team are able to instinctively give an answer. There will be many things that your sales team say that have not yet made it to your website in FAQ pages or even on product or service pages.

5. Competitor analysis

This is a view of how you compare with your competition. We typically carry out a comparison with five competitors on a variety of dimensions. Look at methods your competitors are using, and repurpose it as inspiration to produce even better design and usability. Compare what they are doing well with any problems your website may have. Don't plagiarise – you are unique and beautiful!

6. Customer feedback analysis

Analyse feedback from your customers to see what they say about your website. This can often be done through reading the last 50 contact forms that were sent through your site as well as from questions that customers have emailed in. Remove any identifying information, such as email address or name, then sift through your stored customer emails and tally up the most common queries. If people have to email you to ask, then it means they haven't been able to find the information they need on your site which is a major barrier to conversion.

7. User Testing video analysis

It's very hard to think objectively about your own website, and almost impossible to see it with fresh eyes. That's why watching somebody else use your website for the first time can offer really useful information about why people aren't converting. We typically run three user tests using a third party for these kinds of insights. Websites like User Testing are set up for this purpose, and you can set up your own test choosing:

- How many users you want to test your website.
- Demographics of the users.
- Questions the users will have to answer whilst navigating your website.

Once you have received the videos of people using your website and answering your chosen questions you can analyse them and make a list of areas which may need improving. Some key areas that users may have problems with include:

- Understanding what your business does.
- Navigating around your website.
- Understanding what and who your website is for.
- Completing the product purchase journey.

8. Qualitative feedback

This involves questioning impartial users to gather their perspectives on your site performance. Ask users to complete a short questionnaire with relevant questions, such as *"What can you tell about the company from the homepage?"* or *"How would you find more information about this product?"* Fresh perspectives on the design or usability of your site can be invaluable.

Phase 4 – Creating your hypothesis: Eight steps

Now that you know the problems with your site, it's time for the fun to begin – fixing it! We usually think of this in eight steps:

1. Start with the end in mind. What is the primary objective of the website? Focus on this and work backwards.
2. Usability or persuasion? Are users failing to convert because the website is difficult to use, or because they are not being persuaded by your messaging? Use your research to find out which it is. This will help shape your CRO process.
3. What is the purpose of each page on your website? Seek clarity. Get deep into the specifics to figure out exactly which parts of each page are working towards this purpose, and more importantly which parts are not.
4. Remove everything that does not fit in. Be ruthless, because any 'fluff' leftover might mitigate the success of your CRO. You may be left with a blank page, but don't panic – this is all part of the process!
5. Flip the focus to the customer. A lot of businesses can get so excited about their products that they focus their entire site on what they want to sell. Good CRO will always focus the website onto the user, streamlining their experience.
6. Use your research! Your customer questions, user test analysis, and competitor analysis can provide crucial insight into what users want and how you can deliver it. Make lists of questions that came up during your research.
7. Hypothesise. Find creative and interesting ways to answer the questions you found, while keeping one eye on the design aesthetic of your site. Answering everything in detail can be useless if you make your site horrible to use!
8. Sketch out your designs and **stand back**. Fresh eyes and new ideas can help to refresh your concepts and improve them even further.

Having completed these steps, you should be left with a fresh and focused website design. But is it better? Time to put it to the test.

CRO in action – the anatomy of the perfect contact form

Contact forms are amongst the most important pages on your entire website. But, more often than not, they are treated like an afterthought. Think about a visit to your local supermarket. Think about the range of different ways you can make the final purchase. You can go to a checkout, you can scan as you shop, you can click and collect, and you can go to a self-serve checkout. There is a reason that supermarkets invest so much at this stage. This is where you hand over your money.

At Footprint Digital, we are self-confessed contact form nerds. We have been able to work on many contact forms for a huge range of different websites. The performance of a contact page can have a huge impact on the performance of everything else. It is common that we see conversion rates go from 2-10%. Imagine what five times more business through the site would mean to you.

Here are 13 elements that contribute to the anatomy of the perfect contact form:

1. **Progress bar** – show people where they are in the process and how many more steps there are until the process ends.
2. **Clear heading** –
   a. Include a call to action – 'fill out the form below'.
   b. Include a reference to it being easy – 'simple'.
   c. Be approachable and polite – 'please'.
   d. State what will happen when the form is sent – 'our team will call you back'.
3. **Reassure your visitors** – explain why you need the information and state that you will never share it.
4. **Use oversize, colour form fields** with field descriptions in the fields.
5. **Use inline errors** – or rather inline congratulations! Reward with a lovely tick for each success.
6. **Terms and Conditions** – if you have to have terms and conditions make them easy to tick.
7. **Security logos** – demonstrate that the page or information is secure.
8. **Oversize your buttons** – not only does this make your button easy to click, using an oversize button also means you can describe what

happens when the form is completed. Use this opportunity to remind people that you are great – 'to the experts'.

9. **Share the next steps** – explain when people should expect a response and how they will receive it.

10. **Remind them what they're buying** – add an image or description about the product or service that the person is enquiring about to remind them that they are in the right place.

11. **Testimonial** – present a testimonial or review on the contact page to remind people that other people think you and your products are great.

12. **State your services** – this helps to remind people that they are filling out the correct form.

13. **Show your physical address** – this demonstrates that you are real and reputable!

Most importantly, regularly test your contact forms on multiple devices. You might find bugs or glitches that are making it difficult for people to convert.

Activity – contact forms

Get your website's contact form up on mobile and on desktop. Think of yourself as a potential customer and fill in the form. Ask yourself:

- Is the process quick and easy?

- Are there any red flags or reasons why you might stop inputting information?

- Are there any bugs e.g. broken buttons?

- Is all the necessary information on the page?

- Do you receive confirmation once you have pressed submit, and what does this confirmation look like?

- Could you improve your contact form?

Phase 5 – Measure it, test it – rinse and repeat

Potentially the most crucial part of the whole process, testing is when your ideas are exposed to the cruel scrutiny of real use.

The most common type of testing for CRO is known as split A/B testing. This is a direct comparison, with a random 50% of users being sent to your new site and the other half to your old site.

Using Google Analytics, you can set this up automatically and collect the relevant data on goal conversion. This allows you to contrast the performance of the two sites, and see if the changes made any difference!

Remember, this is run on live traffic and people do not know they are part of a test.

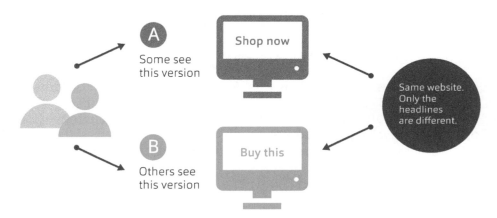

If this testing shows an improvement for the new design over the old one, then well done! You have successfully optimised your website and you can make your test page the live version for everybody.

At least for the moment. Remember, CRO is an ongoing process, and your site may need more tweaking in the future!

Some tools CRO experts use for A/B testing

Google Optimise

- Free!
- Offers A/B and multivariate testing.
- Lets you test and tailor different versions of your website.
- Integrated with Google Analytics.
- Has both visual and code editors.

Optimizely/ Visual Website Optimiser/ Convert/ Unbounce

- Focused on web experimentation and personalisation.

- Easy to use A/B and multi page experimentation tool.
- Supports experiments across different platforms (web, mobile, iOS, etc).
- User friendly presentation of statistics – although quite basic.
- Targets your experiment variations based on ad campaign, geography, cookies and other factors.
- But not cheap...

The big CRO secret

CRO looks easy, but only when it is done really well. Optimised websites can look very simple, with clean interfaces and effortless interaction. Sometimes it can be easy to discount these types of design as minimalist, chosen more for aesthetic rather than purpose.

Of course, the exact opposite is true. All the information on a Conversion Rate Optimised website is carefully chosen for a single purpose and the design comes afterwards. Some sites may require more content, while others can be very sparse. Whatever choice is made, it is the result of careful consideration of what *needs* to be on the website.

Chapter 15: Generate more business through Search Engine Optimisation (SEO)

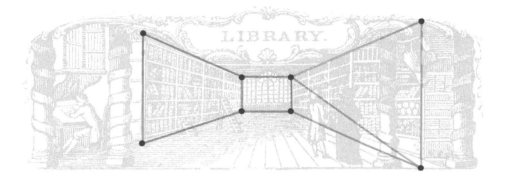

> "The 21st century will be dominated by algorithms. Algorithm is arguably the single most important concept in our world. If we want to understand our life and our future we should make every effort to understand what an algorithm is and how algorithms are connected with emotions." **YUVAL NOAH HARARI**[78]

People need Google. Google needs people. And SEO is the magic that makes it work!

The web is an endless source of knowledge – an Aladdin's cave of everything you could possibly want to know, learn, and explore. The only problem is, how do you find it?

As we learned in the chapter *How the web works*, the web has brought content to the masses. Search engines have enabled people to find it. Without the likes of Google, Bing, or the search engines that came before them, the internet would be an inaccessible mess. Not only would it be very difficult for a person to find a website without an exact address, it would be near impossible for a business to gain traction online.

---

78 Harari, N.Y. (2016) *Homo Deus: A Brief History of Tomorrow*. London, Harvill Secker.

Why is it all about Google?

Google delivers the best results, so people prefer to use their search engine to find something online. Google alone now handles almost 70% of all searches, equalling over two trillion searches a year, 5.5 billion a day, or 63,000 a second[79].

This makes Google a BIG deal.

What does Google want?

According to Larry Page, one of the founders of Google, the goal is to create *"The perfect search engine [that] understands exactly what you mean and gives you back exactly what you want."*

But what does Google *really* want? Hint – to make lots of money.

By helping consumers search accurately for what they need, they keep people coming back. This means that they can then sell ads to companies who want to target these searches. Ads like these make Google **billions** of dollars a year[80].

Let us not forget, Google is a business, its job is to protect this ecosystem at all costs.

How do search engines work?

In the simplest terms…

- Search engines 'crawl' the web using software called 'spiders'.
- Spiders find content by following the links found on other web pages.
- Each found page is then crawled, analysed, and processed.
- Provided the page is considered of value, it is then saved by the search engine in their 'index'.
- The index is the search engine's database of all the pages on the web.

---

79 Search Engine Journal. (nd) *60+ Mind-Blowing Search Engine Optimization Stats. [online] available at:* https://www.searchenginejournal.com/seo-101/seo-statistics/ [accessed 18 April 2020]

80 Trefis. (nd) *Alphabet's Revenues: How Does Alphabet Make Money?* [online] available at: https://dashboards.trefis.com/no-login-required/HMtQjcWW/Alphabet-s-Revenues-How-Does-Alphabet-Make-Money-?fromforbesandarticle=goog191224 [accessed 2 August 2020]

- When someone puts a word or phrase into a search bar, the search engine goes through these indexed pages again – using complex algorithms to determine which pages hold the information most relevant to the user's particular query.
- Sites are then ranked, with the most relevant at the top.

To rank your site higher, you need to ensure your content is found, indexed, and relevant to the queries you wish to rank for.

How does Google pick which site to rank?

Google does share general guidelines on how to make a website rank well. But to stop people gaming their algorithm they do not reveal the details of their secret recipe with anyone.

Experienced SEO practitioners believe that Google looks at hundreds of factors to determine which websites rank highest. Google also constantly tries to improve the results it delivers. It is reported that 500 to 600 changes to its algorithm are made each year. This means achieving a good ranking is a moving target.

Google's main advice is to *"focus on the end user and all else will follow"*[81]. Although this guidance is very vague, it is also a good thing to keep in mind. Google's revenue comes from people using their search engine. They want the people who use it to have a fantastic experience. So the better you can make your website, the more likely it is to rank well.

What is Search Engine Optimisation (SEO)?

SEO is the process of changing your website to rank higher in 'organic' search results. The aim of SEO is not to trick Google, but rather to help it decide that your website is the most relevant and useful to a search that someone has made.

A Red Queen contest

There's a moment in Lewis Carroll's *"Through the Looking Glass"* when the Red Queen explains to Alice, *"Now, here, you see, it takes all the running you*

---

81 https://research.google/pubs/pub34422/

can do, to keep in the same place."[82] SEO is a Red Queen contest in which SEO practitioners have to work really hard just to stand still.

> *"The Red Queen evolutionary hypothesis proposes that organisms must constantly adapt, evolve, and proliferate in order to survive while pitted against ever-evolving opposing organisms in a constantly changing environment"* **WIKIPEDIA**[83]

SEO is generational. As search engines update their algorithms, we modify and update our methodologies. In response to our modified and updated methodologies, search engines update their algorithms.

Staying on the right side

'Black Hat' SEO is a term for SEO work that attempts to cheat the system, using techniques that trick search engines into thinking that a website is more relevant than it is. When search engine algorithms were simpler, 'Black Hat' techniques were much more common and easier to implement. The danger these days is that people can use these techniques unintentionally or based on outdated advice.

Some basic techniques that can be considered 'Black Hat' include keyword stuffing (content full of keywords with no regard for whether it reads naturally), hidden content (text that is hidden from the user, but may be full of keywords) or creating manipulative backlinks.

Effective SEO is generally a 'slow burn', so the desire for a quicker solution is naturally an attractive one. While 'Black Hat' techniques may seem like an enticing alternative to compliant SEO efforts, if you're after longevity they should be avoided at all costs.

Unethical SEO practices may work briefly but, if you are building a real brand online, you cannot afford to risk bad practice. Google enforces penalties that can damage your site's performance for years to come.

---

82 Carroll, L. (1991) [1871]. *2: The Garden of Live Flowers. Through the Looking-Glass* (The Millennium Fulcrum Edition 1.7 ed.). Project Gutenberg. Retrieved 26 September 2017.

83 Wikipedia, the free encyclopedia. (nd) *Red Queen Hypothesis*. [online] available at: https://en.wikipedia.org/wiki/Red_Queen_hypothesis [accessed 28 April 2020]

The SEO Pyramid

While it may be impossible to figure out Google's exact recipe – and predict how this might change – fear not, there are some constants in the way SEO operates.

Over the years, despite all the changes and updates, the following pyramid remains relevant and illustrates four critical steps to SEO success.

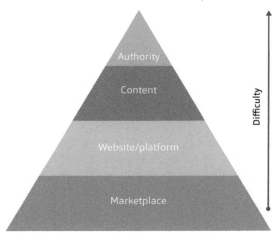

Let's start at the bottom, with the first step, and work our way up.

1. Marketplace: Understanding your audience and what they're looking for

Gaining a true understanding of your audience is the foundation of any SEO strategy. Get this wrong and you'll find yourself ranking – and getting traffic – based on queries that do nothing for your business. Months and years could be wasted. Do not be tempted by shortcuts, do not assume you know what your customers are thinking about.

Ask yourself these questions: Who is your audience? How do they use search engines? What are they searching for? What are their intent and needs? What types of search results are being returned? How much competition is there? Are we a relevant option? What content can we provide to help our audience? What type of content do we need to write to be the best?

2. Website: Building a solid platform

Make sure your website is optimised for search engines and real people. A site that runs smoothly and efficiently for all users is a key aspect of SEO. This pillar includes all the technical aspects of your site: markup, server configurations, speed, mobile compatibility, and much more. Good SEO in this area means that your site will be fast, easy to use, without technical problems, and coded in a way that is easy for 'spiders' to explore, find, and process.

3. Content: Answering questions well

Content is everything your audience sees and interacts with. Make sure it is of exceptional quality, highly relevant, and answers the questions they're asking.

If your website offers original, query, or keyword focused content, it will be deemed more relevant by Google and will therefore rank higher. To rank for a key phrase, you need to make sure you have a page that is relevant to that specific topic, your audience's needs, and the intent that will drive their decisions and actions.

4. Authority: sending out the right signals

Your online reputation is precious and can have a huge effect on the ranking of your website. It builds over time, based on what the rest of the web says about your brand, content, and website. Search engines rate your reputation using various 'signals' such as links, reviews, mentions, authority, trust, and engagement.

Google's original success was built on one critical element – the quality of its results. In 1996, whilst studying at Stanford University, Larry Page and Sergey Brin developed a new algorithm that drastically changed the way in which web content could be ranked, this they called 'PageRank'[84]. The idea was simple, that the importance of a webpage could be determined by the number and quality of other pages linking to it.

Since then, the links and signals that your website or content receive from the rest of the web has been a cornerstone of SEO. They are the endorsements of your content and represent the authority of your brand in a particular area.

----

84 Wikipedia, the free encyclopaedia. (nd) *PageRank*. [online] available at: https://en.wikipedia.org/wiki/PageRank [accessed 28 April 2020]

But be warned, it's not a volume game – relevance and quality are everything.

5. The anatomy of a Google search results page

Search Engine Results Pages (SERPS) come in many different flavours. By understanding what your audience is searching for, and the types of search results that are displayed in response to the words and phrases they use, you can develop your SEO strategy and create and optimise your content.

To do this, simply start by writing a list of the search queries you want to rank for. Type them into Google to see what is returned in the search results. Are there images, maps listings, videos, answer boxes? By establishing what Google is returning for your queries, you can start to build a clearer understanding of what you are going to need to rank.

But does your list of search queries relate to the words and phrases your audience is searching with?

Keyword research

What words and phrases are your audience using to find what they are looking for? Keyword research is fundamental to the success of SEO. So knowing the types of searches your audience make, and what type of action they want to do as a result of their search, is vitally important. Here is what you need to know.

There are three types of search queries:

1. **Navigational GO queries** – e.g. *"Footprint Digital"*. Building brand awareness will ultimately drive navigational queries to your website. This can be achieved through both online and offline activity.
2. **Informational KNOW queries** – e.g. *"what is SEO?"*. As a general rule, KNOW queries produce the highest volume of traffic on the web, but have the lowest chance of conversion. These are a 'top funnel' activity, carried out by people who want to learn something and who are likely to link to and share content. Your responses to know queries are great for building brand awareness.
3. **Transactional DO queries** – e.g. *"SEO company near me"*. These are the money makers with the highest chance of conversion.

While DO queries are the obvious choice for SEO focus, they are usually the most competitive because they are the most likely to result in a conversion.

Protect your GO and grow your KNOW queries. In return, you will build your DO over the longer term.

Long-tail keywords provide different results to short-tail keywords

When selecting keywords, the natural inclination is to go with those that have the most searches. However, this generally isn't the best strategy, particularly when first starting out. Remember to get inside your audience's head: what kinds of words, phrases, or questions are they searching with?

Some will be using single words. We call these 'short-tail keywords'. Others will be typing in whole phrases or 'long-tail keywords'. It is important to understand the benefits and drawbacks of long-tail and short-tail keywords.

- **Short-tail keywords** – like *"shoes"* – generate a high volume of search results. They have lots of competition and therefore require more effort to achieve. As they have a broad meaning they have a lower probability of visitors finding the content directly relevant to what they want and converting.
- **Long-tail keywords** – like *"vintage wedding shoes in Colchester"* – generate a lower volume of search results. They have less competition so are easier to achieve. As they have a more specific meaning there is a higher probability of visitors being in the right place and converting.

The trick is to find balance between the two. To find keywords that are both highly relevant and also have a good volume of searches.

When determining your keywords:

- Be cautious of using words or phrases that are too generic.
- Be cautious of words or phrases that will flush out too much competition.
- Look for areas – products, services, topics, and themes – where you already have visibility.
- Avoid words or phrases that will reveal low levels of traffic, unless your business is ultra niche.
- Consider the intent of the searcher and whether the keyword is likely to convert them.
- Avoid putting all your bets on a handful of keywords.

When choosing keywords you should think about casting a wide net first with long-tail keywords and to look at more generic, short-tail phrases for your longer term strategy. You need both. The short-tail keyword will help drive traffic and raise brand awareness, but the long-tail keyword will drive greater relevance and likelihood of conversion.

Steps to performing effective keyword research as a Digital Marketing Manager

Answering the following questions can help you identify the right keywords:

- What would you search to find your product or service?
- What is my audience searching for?
- What words are you already using on your website?
- What words are you already ranking for?
- What words are your competitors using?
- What variants could you use?
- Are there non-industry phrases or terms – the 'lay' words that my audience use?
- What are the regional variants? e.g. 'flat' versus 'apartment'?

With an initial list established, an SEO specialist will then go on to research the viability of targeting each keyword. They'll understand the potential number of searches for each query, spot trends in user intent, and identify any missed keyword opportunities.

They'll also dig deeper, exploring the importance and potential value of each keyword, using the following approaches:

- SERP analysis.
- Competition analysis.
- Google Search Console.
- Google Trends.
- PPC Campaign Insights.
- Google Keyword Planner.
- Current ranking.

On-page SEO

With a deeper understanding of how search engines work, and what your audience is looking for, you can ensure that your website content contains all the elements that will help inform the 'spiders' as they crawl your site. You can optimise your content and work towards solid 'on-page' SEO. Here are the steps that will help you achieve this:

Step 1: Agreeing the goal of your content

Before you jump into the optimisation of a web page, it's time to step back and clarify why this page exists – both for the business and the user. These questions will help reveal what is required from the content to be produced.

User focus:

- What are the user's needs, emotions, and intent?
- Why are they there? What are they looking for?
- What would they search for to find this?
- Are there any environmental considerations?
- What part of their journey – or your sales funnel – are they in?
- Most importantly, what are the priority keywords you want to target?

Business focus:

- What is the business objective for this page?
- What USPs or ideals do we wish to communicate to the user?
- What do we ultimately want the user to do?
- What 'call to action' will encourage them to do it?
- What KPIs can you measure to indicate the success or failure of the page?

Step 2: Writing titles and meta descriptions

Page titles and meta descriptions should be present on every page of your website. Although they are never shown on the page, they are used by search engines and make up the **Blue Link** and **Description** you see in the search results.

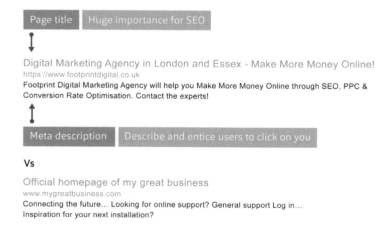

The **page title** is considered the most influential on-page optimisation area. If there is only one thing you can do, get this optimised first.

The **meta description** is not a Google ranking factor, but it is critical in engaging and enticing users to click your result. Think of this as your opportunity to pitch your page against all the other listings in the search results. You have to be relevant and compelling. Give them a reason to click.

Which would you be more likely to click?

Digital Marketing Agency in London and Essex - Make More Money Online!
https://www.footprintdigital.co.uk
Footprint Digital Marketing Agency will help you Make More Money Online through SEO, PPC & Conversion Rate Optimisation. Contact the experts!

Versus

Official homepage of my great business
www.mygreatbusiness.com
Connecting the future... Looking for online support? General support Log in... Inspiration for your next installation?

Craft your page titles and meta descriptions carefully. Use keywords to improve their relevance, and be descriptive and appealing!

A well optimised page title should ideally take the following format:

- Aim for titles between 50-60 characters (governed by a maximum of 512 pixels).
- Lead with the most important keywords or phrase.
- Include a relevant call to action (where feasible).
- Reference your branding (where feasible).
- Avoid duplication across pages.
- Avoid keyword repetition.

A well optimised meta description should ideally take the following format:

- Aim for an optimal length of 155 characters.
- Reference the name of the service, category or product (for relevance).
- Include a call to action or incentive to entice the user to click through to your website.
- Reference your branding (where feasible).
- Avoid duplication across pages.
- Avoid keyword repetition.

Activity – Page titles and meta descriptions

Practice writing a new, keyword optimised page title and meta description for your homepage.

Step 3: Creating a document outline and heading structure

Using headings on your web page not only improves its readability, it also helps theme your page and give a clearer description of its content to search engines.

The image below outlines the heading structure of two different web pages. How easy is it for you to establish what each page is about?

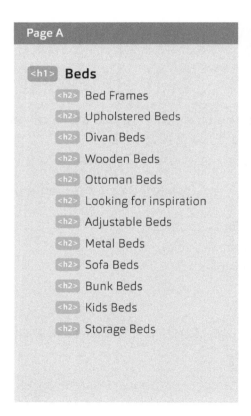
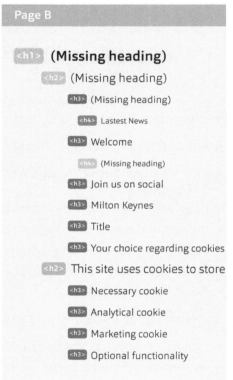

When writing content, think carefully about how you can use heading to theme and structure your content. And, where possible, use keywords to optimise and build relevance around your goal and target topic for each page.

Activity – View your heading structures

Use Chris Pederick's[85] Web Developer browser extension to view your page's heading structure.

Download the tool here: https://chrispederick.com/work/web-developer/

Get your website's homepage up then open the tool and go to: Information > View Document Outline.

You will see the heading structure for your homepage. If this was all you could see, would you understand what your homepage was about?

Step 4: Creating unique content

Every page on your website must have high quality, relevant content. Most importantly, this content must be unique to a specific page. If content is duplicated, copied or very similar to content on another site or page it is unlikely to be indexed and, in extreme cases, at risk of being penalised by Google. View Google as the ultimate plagiarism detector!

What is really not cool in SEO?

- **Pages with little or no content** – say more!
- **Pages with low value content** – say something useful!
- **Pages with plagiarised content** – don't copy what someone else is saying!

All of the above must be avoided to increase the likelihood of ranking. If these points are ignored, it could lead to exclusion from the index and even affect the rest of your website's performance. One way to check whether your website is plagiarising someone else's is to use a tool like Copyscape which searches the web for duplicated content.

---

85 Pederick, C. (nd) *Web Developer*. [online] available at: https://chrispederick.com/work/web-developer/ [accessed 28 April 2020]

Step 5: Editing your content

How many words should you write? And how many keywords should you include?

There is no magic word count, just as there isn't a magic number of times a keyword should be mentioned on a page. This common belief is dated and counterproductive.

Numerous studies have been performed over the years, all suggesting that there is a correlation between the number of words on a page and its ranking. i.e. the more words you have, the higher the likelihood of a page ranking well. But there are a few issues with taking these findings at face value:

- The type of content will influence the amount of text content you wish to use. A research blog post might require thousands of words, but this volume of content would not necessarily suit a homepage or a category page.
- Writing words for the sake of it will result in poorly written content. This is unlikely to rank well and, even if it does, it will not engage the reader and be effective long term.
- On the flip side, creating pages with just a few words on them is unlikely to excite a search engine.

Your users' needs come first – use the right number of words to provide them with the best possible resource or answer to their question. Here's our advice on deciding how much content to include:

- Remember, thin pages (i.e. pages with little text content) are unlikely to perform well.
- Don't stuff words in for the sake of it – it reads badly and is ineffective.
- Look at the web pages that are already ranking for the search query and take your guidance on content length from those.

Ultimately, your benchmark is what already ranks top. Your job is to create something better than that. Better doesn't necessarily mean longer:

- Include the phrase or keyword as early in the content as you can.
- Reference keywords and phrases naturally within the content.
- Enhance the relevance of the page by using similar and related words that are themed around the topic.
- Do not write to meet a target keyword density. Be warned – spamming your pages with keywords can be a negative signal to search engines and it will frustrate your readers!

If your content doesn't read well and you're putting search engines before your audience, you're doing it wrong.

Step 6: Including internal links

Links are a BIG deal when it comes to SEO.

From a search engine's perspective, the more a web page is linked to from the other web pages, the higher its importance.

If you have target pages that you want to promote, link to them from elsewhere within the site.

Wikipedia is a great example of this in action. Every page of content is linked to other pages, or other sections, that covers related content. It helps the reader follow their train of thought, explore new questions and find out more. And including internal links on your website helps you to:

• Guide your audience from one piece of content to another.
• Boost your website's usability, discovery value and usefulness.
• Build the authority and prominence of your pages through increased referencing.

Step 7: Optimising images for search engines

Images can help break up text content, enhance your audience's experience and communicate whatever it is you are trying to convey to the user. A picture is worth a thousand words, right?

Although we might be able to glance at an image and understand its content and meaning, it is much more complex for a search engine to do this. Thankfully, there is an incredibly simple way we can help search engines with this challenge, by writing a descriptive label for each image.

Using the HTML IMG ALT attribute you can explain what the image shows. This attribute is an HTML standard that allows for a text-based description to be included with the image.

Not only does this benefit search engines, it also provides an accessibility benefit for users who are visually impaired as this description can be read by screen readers.

When working with images on your site, consider the following:

• Use Alt tags for all images.

- Give an image a descriptive file name. Such as Man Walking Dog.jpg rather than image_1.jpg
- Include a keyword that relates to the theme of the page, but also a description that is true to what the image displays.
- Think of an Alt as a caption for an image that can support those who are visually impaired.
- Use appropriate size and formatting to balance quality and file size.

Step 8: Test it, measure it!

The job isn't done when you hit publish! As with anything a Digital Marketing Manager does, every change should be tested and measured for effectiveness. **Test it, measure it** is a top tip! You can't expect to get it 100% right the first time, so this is about testing, learning, and then refining what you have created.

Step 9: Reviewing and refining

After a short period of time (1-2 weeks) it's time to take a look at what how your website is doing:

1. Check your ranking. How has your ranking changed since launching the new page or content?
2. Check organic traffic and performance changes. Have you seen any changes in organic traffic to this page? Any change to the overall performance and KPI metrics? Does the data suggest you are fulfilling your audience's needs?
3. What else has changed? How else can you improve things?
4. Review Google Search Console to identify any new keywords that you are now ranking for. Are they of value? Are they mentioned on the page? Are they relevant to that page or is there the opportunity to create a new page targeting this query?
5. Update the page to improve optimisation and include new long-tail search opportunities.
6. Consider opportunities to improve internal and external links to your content and resources.
7. Repeat every couple of weeks until you're satisfied with overall performance.

Technical SEO

Right back in Chapter Two, *Head Chef Syndrome,* we stated that the core function of the role of Digital Marketing Manager is to be strategic. Continue to monitor your rankings and be aware of new content that comes and takes your place. People are always going to try and out rank you, the secret is to continually improve your content so that it is the best resource on the web for your audience. While the optimisation of your content is key, there are many other factors that can limit a website's organic search performance. Specialised, highly technical tasks that address these should be outsourced – your digital marketing strategy will yield far better results with the technical support of an SEO expert, or team of experts!

What follows are some aspects of SEO that are fundamental to success online – things a Digital Marketing Manager should be aware of when analysing the bigger picture of online performance, but shouldn't really be expected to carry out as part of their job.

In addition to being *au fait* with the more technical side of SEO, we advise that a Digital Marketing Manager stay up to date with any changes Google makes to the way pages are indexed and ranked. There are as many as 600 algorithmic advancements per year, each of which could affect performance in organic search. So, keep a finger on the pulse and regularly review traffic and performance.

Below are some critical technical SEO elements that would be beneficial for you to have an understanding of. Unless you're an SEO prodigy in the making, do not be too focused on committing these to memory. Even if you do not end up running your SEO strategy yourself, a knowledge of these elements will set you up for success.

1. Multiple domain names.
2. www versus non-www.
3. Secure versus insecure.
4. Optimising URLs.
5. HREFLang tags.
6. Crawl budget.
7. Robots.txt and Sitemap.xml.
8. NOINDEX.
9. Canonical tags.
10. Faceted (or layered) navigation.
11. Server response codes and redirects.

12. Schemas, rich snippets, and cards.
13. Inaccessible content.
14. Site integrity.
15. Site and page speed.
16. Mobile SEO.
17. PageRank.
18. Link building best practices.
19. How NOT to build links.
20. Understanding anchor text.
21. Understanding rel="nofollow".
22. So how do you build links?
23. Creating content with link potential.
24. Influence-targeted content.
25. Social signals.
26. User engagement as a ranking factor.
27. Local SEO – For businesses that service a local area.
    a. Building Local Citation.
    b. Building Local Reviews.
28. Rebuilding your website.

1. Multiple domain names

More often than not, an organisation will have a number of domains in their possession. This might be to protect the brand, or to use in the future, but often these are set up so that they all point to the same website.

example.co.uk
example.com
theofficalexample.com

What happens here is that search engines find each of these sites and then index them independently under the different domains. This causes duplication and indexing issues, as well as potential tracking problems.

To avoid such a situation, decide on the preferred domain and set up 301 redirects to link all the other domains to this chosen location.

2. www versus non-www

To make matters worse, servers are often configured to serve the website under both www and non-www versions of the domain. Using the previous example, this would result in six versions of the site being indexed.

example.co.uk	www.example.co.uk
example.com	www.example.com
theofficalexample.com	www.theofficalexample.com

Add HTTPS and HTTP into the equation and we now have 12 complete versions of the same site in Google's index.

http://example.co.uk	http://www.example.co.uk
https://example.co.uk	https://www.example.co.uk
http://example.com	http://www.example.com
https://example.com	https://www.example.com
http://theofficalexample.com	http://www.theofficalexample.com
https://theofficalexample.com	https://www.theofficalexample.com

As previously stated, this can be resolved simply. Choose a single version of the domain (e.g. https://www.example.com/) and 301 redirect all alternative domains to the relative location under the chosen domain.

3. Secure versus insecure

Ever noticed a little padlock near the URL of a site you're on? This means that the site you are viewing is using HTTPS, and that the data being transferred between your browser and the server is secure. HTTPS is encrypted using an SSL certificate which means that anyone who intercepts it would be unable to decipher it without a private key.

HTTPS is advantageous for users and for businesses, not just because it is a more secure means of communication, but also because Google favours it. So much so that they introduced it as a search ranking factor.

Google is on a mission to make the web more secure, to the extent that they now call out websites that do not use the protocol. Over time it is likely to become even more of a focus, so ensuring your site is secure and safe should be a high priority.

4. Optimising URLs

The URL structure of your website can be used to optimise for search and to improve usability.

Consider the following URLs:

```
https://www.example.com/cid=2535
https://www.example.com/shoes/trainers/
```

Both of these are valid options, but the second shows clearly what that page and its content are about.

By using logical and descriptive URLs on your website, you can help both users and search engines understand your site and its content.

When considering your URLs, ask yourself the following questions:

- Are they of a reasonable length?
- Do they make good use of keywords?
- Is there a consistent structure and format throughout the website?
- Does the folder structure support usability and navigation?
- Do they avoid using problematic characters?

Do not change URLs without first setting up redirects! (see 'Server response codes and redirects' below).

5. HREFLang tags

Any business worth their salt will create pages specific to the audience that they want to serve. Multilingual websites have multiple versions of the same page, each targeting a specific language or region. Traditionally, search engines have had a hard time working out which of these pages to show to which users, particularly where multiple pages in the same language are intended for different regions, for example UK, US, Canada, Australia, Ireland, etc.

What happens here is that visitors from the UK end up landing on content for the US, or visa versa.

HREFlang tags can solve this problem by indicating alternative variants of pages that are in different languages or places. For example, they can be set up to tell search engines that there is a US or French version of this page that should be used for users searching from this location or in this language.

Using this approach not only helps deliver the right content to the right user, but it can also improve the bounce rate and conversion rate of your site and provide a smoother experience for the user.

6. Crawl budget

As amazing as Google is, it still has limited resources. The web is a BIG thing to crawl and deciding how frequently to check for changes is a challenge.

Google deals with this by effectively setting a limit to the number of pages Googlebot crawls and indexes over a period of time. This is known as 'crawl budget'. It could be the case that if your site has exceeded its crawl budget that there are pages on your site that Google don't index.

As search engine spiders just follow and index the links they find, they often discover URLs that we don't expect or want them to find. This can lead to wasted crawl budget and getting low quality pages in the index. An SEO professional deploys their website's crawl budget to ensure the priority pages are crawled and indexed first.

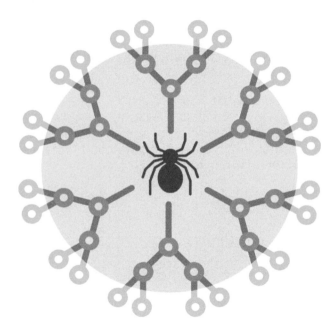

How much crawl budget does a website get?

There is no known answer to this, but we do know the following areas will influence this:

- The authority of the website.
- The size of the website.
- The frequency of content change.

- The degree of site-wide change.
- The response status of the page.

One of the most common challenges of a technical SEO is ensuring that search engines are spending their time looking at the important areas of the site.

7. Robots.txt and Sitemap.xml

To maximise crawl budget, you need to make sure that your site is well organised and easy for search engines to crawl and index. Pages that cannot be crawled will never get indexed and will therefore not show up on search results, meaning that all your SEO hard work on that page is useless.

Robots.txt is text file located in the root directory of your website: https://www.example.com/robots.txt

This file is one of the first things a search engine spider looks for when crawling a website, as it directs them on what they should and should not crawl.

Below is an example of what a robots.txt file looks like. In this example, full access has been given to all crawlers, but disallows have been made to an entire folder, a specific html page and all ("*") pdf files. In addition, a reference to a sitemap.xml file has been provided to help search engines find the pages (more on this in the next section).

```
User-agent: *
Allow: /
Disallow: /dont-crawl/
Disallow: /dont-crawl-this.html
Disallow: /*.pdf
Sitemap: http://www.example.com/sitemap.xml
```

Robots.txt is an extremely valuable way to utilise crawl budget and limited indexing. However be extremely careful, as getting this wrong can easily lead to blocking areas of the site and stopping them from being indexed altogether.

Note, the robots.txt will only be obeyed by ethical bots and crawlers, so do not use this as a means to restrict spambots or crawlers as it will be ignored. This is a publicly visible file, so do not disclose hidden or sensitive areas of the website!

Be very careful when editing the robots.txt file as it can have drastic effects if not properly configured. Use Google Search Console's robots testing tool to verify and test your robots.txt file

https://www.google.com/webmasters/tools/robots-testing-tool

XML sitemaps are structured, machine-friendly files that tell search engines which pages are on a website. They aren't intended for humans, but provide software and search engines with a list of resources that you want to be crawled and indexed. This can include pages, images, videos, and local or mobile variants of your site.

Below is a simplified example of a web page sitemap containing just two URLs.

For each of these URLs you will see a location or resource – 'loc' – and additional attributes such as the last modified date, the frequency in which the resource is expected to change, and its perceived priority (a value between 0-10). Note these are optional.

```
<?xml version="1.0" encoding="UTF-8"?>
<urlset xmlns="http://www.sitemaps.org/schemas/sitemap/0.9">
 <url>
  <loc>http://www.example.com/</loc>
  <lastmod>2020-01-01</lastmod>
  <changefreq>monthly</changefreq>
  <priority>1</priority>
 </url>
 <url>
  <loc>http://www.example.com/blog/</loc>
  <lastmod>2020-01-01</lastmod>
  <changefreq>hourly</changefreq>
   <priority>0.8</priority>
 </url>
</urlset>
```

Creating sitemaps, uploading them to your website, and submitting these to search engines is a great way to guide which pages and resources they should prioritise and crawl.

Many content management systems generate sitemap files automatically, so be sure to check if this is already the case. Alternatively, plugins (e.g. Yoast for WordPress) and software (e.g. Screaming Frog) can be used to generate the files.

Include sitemap references in your robots.txt and use Google Search Console to submit your sitemaps directly to Google. For more information on sitemaps, please visit https://www.sitemaps.org/ or search Google's Search Console Help.

8. NOINDEX

If you have pages on your website that you do not want Google or other search engines to index, you may consider using the NOINDEX tag.

```
<meta name="robots" content="noindex">
```

This is a simple HTML tag that, when included in a page's <HEAD>, instructs search engines not to keep a copy of the page in their index. As a result, the page will never be returned in any search results.

9. Canonical Tags

Search engines see each different URL as a unique page. This can be problematic for modern websites, because CMS platforms and dynamic sites may add parameters or create multiple paths to a page. Some websites may have thousands of pages of duplicate content, simply because of different currency, language, or location options. As a consequence, this can often lead to indexing of multiple versions causing duplication problems.

```
https://example.com/my-page/
http://example.com/my-page/
https://www.example.com/my-page/
https://example.com/my-page/?sort=
```

One way to solve this problem is to use a canonical tag in the <head> of the page to indicate to search engines the original or 'master' page.

```
<link rel="canonical" href="https://example.com/my-page/" />
```

Including a canonical tag on each of these pages will tell search engines to ignore the URL they are looking at and associate the content with its true location. This will define the true identity of the page, resolve indexing issues, and consolidate the value of that page to its true location.

Implement canonical tags on all the pages of your website to ensure that there is only one true location or identity. Search engines will then spend their time crawling and ranking the right location, rather than the duplicates.

10. Faceted (or layered) navigation

Faceted navigation or search is a method used by many e-commerce sites to allow users to filter or sort search results by different attributes. For example, on a website selling laptops you are often able to filter products by screen size, amount of memory, price, etc.

This is great for users, but can be problematic for search engines. Each time a new filter is added to a search, it often creates a new URL for that specific search. On websites with lots of filters, this can create hundreds or thousands of results – each only slightly different or even completely identical.

These duplicate or very similar results can cause signal dilution or indexing problems, but they can be solved. To handle faceted navigation properly, you have three methods:

- **Restrict redundant filters** – reduce the number of variations.
- **Use the canonical tag for identical pages** – let search engines know what's going on.
- **Use a better implementation** – one that users can use but search engines won't get lost in.

11. Server response codes and redirects

When your browser inputs a request to a server, the server responds with a code that corresponds to the status of that resource.

These response codes tend to represent four groups:

- 200 – OK/SUCCESS – the resource was found.
- 30x – REDIRECTION (e.g. 301) – the resource has moved.
- 40x – CLIENT ERROR (e.g. 404) – the resource was not found.
- 50x – SERVER ERROR – something went wrong at the server.

You want as many of your pages to respond with a 200, but in the real world it doesn't always work like that. Things break or get removed, and the role of an SEO professional is to be vigilant and perform regular health checks and good housekeeping.

If a search engine can't follow a link because the page has been moved or changed, this causes problems with the page indexing and search rankings. Google is not going to send one of its users to a page that is broken, so any rankings that page may have had in the past are going to disappear really fast. In addition, any links to that page are going to result in lost traffic and link equity.

Setting up redirects helps to smooth this out by sending both users and the spiders crawling your site to the new location of the page.

There are two main types of 30x redirects:

- **301 Redirect – a permanent redirect**. This informs the search engine that the URL will not be coming back. Its new location is permanent, and therefore passes all historic value on to this new location.
- **302 Redirect – a temporary redirect**. This will not necessarily pass on all its power to the new location. The old URL is also not guaranteed to be dropped from the index.

Redirects are vital, especially during a site build or migration. If a webpage moves, use a 301 response and redirect it to its new location!

12. Schemas, rich snippets, and cards

HTML is great at defining what content on the page needs to be displayed as a heading, paragraph, link, list, image, etc. But it is also incredibly limited. There is no standard way to tell which part of the content is an address, postcode, price, name, rating, recipe etc. This is where a schema comes in.

A schema is an additional markup you can include in your HTML, adding structure and meaning to the way your site's content is read by search engines.

There are hundreds of schema types that can be used including:

- Product
- Address
- Person
- Business
- Review
- Recipe

- Webpage
- Event
- Film
- Comment
- Place
- Offer

This can have many uses – a shop could bring in more local business by giving clearer direction on its address, or a product page could use a review tag to show off its good ratings. Help search engines understand your content with schema markup.

Rich snippets and cards give your organic search result extra detail, including any of the information included in your schema. You may see these snippets or cards on the top or side of search results. These cards catch the eye, improve your search rankings and click through rate, and increase the number of high-value visitors to your site.

13. Inaccessible content

There are some webpage elements and technologies that are delivered in a way that search engines can struggle to understand. These include images, flash, ajax, and video.

Using the latest technologies and methods are great, but is the content delivered in a way that search engines can see it?

Use Google Search Console to fetch and render pages to see exactly what Google sees.

14. Site integrity

For a site to be considered credible, it needs to be reliable and quick. To be considered reliable, you need to make sure that your site is structurally sound, with little downtime or broken links.

Use tools like Uptime Robots and Pingdom to monitor your website uptime 24/7. Tools like Google Search Console and ScreamingFrog can find the broken links on your website and, most importantly, where they are linked from.

15. Site and page speed

When ranking a website, Google takes into account the time it takes for pages to load, meaning that a slower site will be ranked lower than a faster equivalent. Make sure that your website runs quickly and smoothly on mobile and desktop, without long loading times.

Activity – Page loading speed

See how fast your site loads on desktop and mobile using a tool such as Google's Page Speed Insights, GT-Metrix or Pingdom.

These tools also offer tips for how to improve the speed of your site so you can start to build a list of what to do to improve your speed.

16. Mobile SEO

Sometime in 2014, the number of Google searches from mobile devices finally overtook those made on desktop computers. In 2018, Google made the big decision to move over to a 'Mobile First' index and in 2020 they announced they would be switching to Mobile First indexing for all websites[86]. This essentially replaced the previous desktop priority and adapted this to the growing demand for and use of mobile search.

Mobile websites generally come in one of three flavours, each with their own advantages and drawbacks:

- **Responsive websites** – This solution works under a single website that delivers the same content to both mobile and desktop. When a mobile user clicks on the website, the site can fluidly readjust itself and display the content in a way that complements the screen being used. The advantages of this are the ease of use and maintenance, as there is no chance of accidental duplication or redirect errors. Responsive design is the standard for most sites and generally the most highly recommended for SEO.

- **Dynamic serving sites** – This approach allows you to have a single website that delivers different content depending on the device you are viewing it on – one for mobile and one for desktop. The advantage of this is that users can have a highly tailored user experience on both mobile and desktop. However there is the risk of content difference – the wrong content being delivered to the wrong device. Dynamic serving sites are also difficult to set up and maintain and can be difficult to optimise for search engines.

- **Separate site for mobile** – This setup will generally have a separate domain for both mobile and desktop. The mobile version will be something like http://m.example.com. When a user accesses the site from a mobile device or desktop device they are redirected to the appropriate version of the website. This option makes it easy to create a tailored mobile experience and is easy to set up. But you have two versions of the site to maintain, with content that can differ and duplication errors that can be easy to miss.

Here are some helpful tips for how to make sure your site looks and works great on mobile:

---

86 Google (2020) *Announcing mobile first indexing for the whole web. [online] available at:* https://webmasters.googleblog.com/2020/03/announcing-mobile-first-indexing-for.html [accessed 30 April 2020]

- Adopt a responsive design – one that adapts to the device you are viewing it on.
- Be careful of hiding or removing content on mobile devices. With the new Mobile Index, if it isn't seen on the mobile version, then the content might be ignored.
- Audit your website on your mobile, not just your desktop!
- Deliver exceptional mobile experience and UX.
- Do everything you can to improve speed.

Google's Mobile Friendly Test tool and Google Search Console are a great way to start accessing the mobile performance of your website.

17. FUN FACT BREAK: PageRank

Did you know, Google's PageRank algorithm is named after Larry Page, not web pages?

In 1996 Larry Page (co-founder of Google) went to work on creating a better way of ranking web content.

By analysing all the links to and from web pages, Google came up with a way to define the credibility of each page. A link to a web page acts as a vote or an endorsement. By analysing the vast connections between web pages across the web, Google is able to derive a score for each page. This is called its 'PageRank'.

PageRank was the breakthrough ranking algorithm that distinguished Google from other search engines. This one algorithm was arguably the source of Google's original success – the accuracy of its results – but it was more than this. It fundamentally changed the search industry.

A lot has changed since then, there are many new signals and algorithms, but the concept is still the same. To succeed in organic search and become a true authority in your field, your website needs to have on-topic, relevant signals from a range of sources on the rest of the web.

And rather than being a name to reference the ranking of a page PageRank is named after the genius that inspired it: Larry Page.

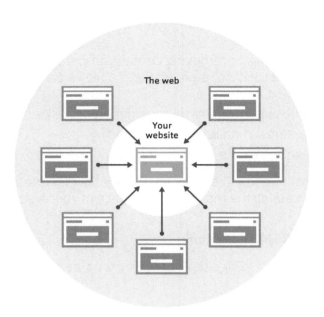

18. Link building best practices

Link building is the process of gaining links from other websites to your own, in an effort to build your authority (PageRank) and improve your visibility in organic search.

Because SEO professionals knew that links were an important part of ranking in Google, this got abused by 'Black Hatters'. Early link building techniques were about getting any link possible, regardless of where it came from and how legitimate and relevant it was. The approaches were unnatural and at times, spammy. This worked really well, for a while. But then it didn't.

Numerous algorithm updates from Google have had catastrophic consequences on the effectiveness of such techniques and have even led to huge penalties, in some cases literally destroying a website's organic traffic overnight.

This isn't to say that link building is no longer relevant or effective as a search strategy. On the contrary, research suggests that links are still one of the most influential factors in search ranking – the rules have just changed and the process has to be done right, focusing on:

- Quality of links NOT quantity.
- Relevancy to your website.

- Online authority of the link's source.
- Whether the link adds value and enhances the content and user experience.
- Building genuine relationships.

This is not a volume game. It is about getting links from sources that are **trustworthy** and **relevant**.

19. How NOT to build links

Google is quite clear on its guidance when it comes to link building:

> *"Any links intended to manipulate PageRank or a site's ranking in Google search results may be considered part of a link scheme and a violation of Google's Webmaster Guidelines."* **GOOGLE**

Put simply, don't build links just to improve your site's ranking.

But let's face it, this is unrealistic for an SEO professional. There are benefits to be gained from a link beyond ranking improvements that warrant this a worthwhile activity (referral traffic, reputation, etc).

Having addressed the elephant in the room, let's look at some techniques you definitely want to steer well away from. To stay in Google's good books avoid:

- Buying links.
- Link exchanges.
- Over optimised anchor text.
- Automated link building.
- Forced links.
- Comment spam.
- Large-scale article marketing or guest posting.
- Text adverts that pass PageRank.
- Low-quality directories.
- Forum links.

There are also a number of other areas that can make your links appear unnatural or even suspicious:

Natural	Unnatural
Links are acquired over time	Links are created all at once
Links are from relevant sources	Links are from anywhere and every-where
A broad range of types of links	Links are all of the same type or resource
Brand or natural anchor text	Heavy 'money term' anchor text
A mix of 'follow' and 'no follow' links	Only 'follow' links
The destinations of the links vary	Links all go to the 'money term' internal page
Location link on the source page changes	Location of the link is always the same (e.g. footer)
Content surrounding the link is different	Content surrounding the link is the same
IP addresses of the linking websites differ	IP addresses are the same or class C (network)
The WHOIS of the linking domains are different	The WHOIS of the linking domains all belong to the same organisation or person

2. Understanding anchor text

The anchor text is the clickable text of a link. Looking at the raw HTML of a link, this would look something like this:

<a href="https://www.example.com">*Anchor Text*</a>

Historically, the anchor text has been a hugely influential part of link building. For example, if I link to a page with the anchor text *"Tasty Burgers"*, you (and search engines) can assume that the page being linked to is going to be about tasty burgers.

This led to website owners and webmasters building as many links to their website using their 'money term' as the anchor text.

Although it is widely regarded that anchor text is still significantly influential, it has become an easy way for Google to detect manipulative practices. Today, overuse of anchor text can lead to more harm than good and, in some cases, to penalties.

If you are trying to optimise your anchor text, consider the following tips:

• Keep it natural.

- Keep it relevant.
- Include keywords but don't be repetitive – diversify.
- Use your brand name.
- Use the website URL.
- Use keywords in the surrounding text as these will also be looked at when establishing context and relevance.
- Link to the most relevant page.
- If the link is an image, optimise the alt text.

21. Understanding rel="nofollow"

Another important thing to be aware of is that not all links pass the test on PageRank or value.

Back in 2005, the web was awash with comment spam. With the rise of popular blogging platforms such as WordPress and Blogger, spammers had found a new and easy way to drive traffic by posting comments that included links back to their website.

To combat this growing trend and abuse of the new technologies, leading search engines decided to introduce a new attribute for links called rel="nofollow".

<a href="https://www.example.com" rel="nofollow">*Anchor Text*</a>

This attribute essentially tells search engines that a link to an external resource is not endorsed by the website linking to it. As a result, the links exist but no value is passed to the destination page.

As a digital marketer, it is essential to understand this to know which links are passing 'value' and which aren't.

When qualifying your own outbound links, it is worth consulting Google's guidelines on rel="nofollow" as well as rel="sponsored" and rel="ugc". These will bring clarity in what is being endorsed, sponsored, or user generated.

22. So how do you build links?

In a perfect world you shouldn't need to build links. The amazing content you publish and the incredible brand you are building would naturally accrue them of their own accord. That said, everyone can do with a leg up, and the competition doesn't always play by the rules. So here are some tips:

- **Internal links** – As described earlier, internal links are the easiest ways to build links to the important sections within your website. Although this may not be an external endorsement, you have control and, as a result, they should be your quick wins.
- **Look in your own backyard** – This is often the best place to start. Look at the contacts and relationships you already have and identify relevant sources that you might be able to approach to link back to you.
- **Look at your existing link profile** – Google Search Console is a great place to start looking into what links you already have. But if you want to dig deeper we recommend using tools such as Majestic, Ahrefs, Moz or SEMrush. These tools will help you understand who is linking to you and who isn't, the quality of those links, and the content you are creating that is naturally acquiring links.
- **Analyse your competitors' link profiles** – Performing the exact same research on your competition will provide great insight and highlight the opportunities you are missing.
- **Academic and governing bodies** – Governing bodies are naturally high sources of authority, so if you have connections or relationships in these bodies, these can be a powerful source of links.
- **Guest posts** – Write and publish content for other websites in your industry or niche. This is an area that has lost popularity and respect over the years, but this is only because the sites people are publishing guest content on are not always of high enough calibre. If you can find credible websites in your sector – ones that will allow you to post thought leadership or other engaging pieces of content that demonstrate expertise, value and insight – this can be a great way to build high quality links and referral traffic.
- **Trusted business directories** – Directory building is one of the oldest methods of link building and, as a result, has been abused in the past. This is not about submitting your website to every directory on the web. It's about being selective and choosing only the most trusted sources, e.g. Yellow pages, Best of the web, Hotfrog, Yelp, etc.
- **Find industry specific directories** – Look for online directories that are specific to your niche or industry and submit your site to those that look credible and have the potential for referral traffic.
- **Testimonials** – If you have relationships with suppliers or others in the industry who you would endorse, offer a testimonial with a link back to your website.
- **Reverse image search** – Tools such as Tineye can be a great way to find websites that are using your images. You can also set up alerts to notify

you when they are found. Approach these sites and request that they link back and credit your site or page.

- **Broken link building** – Find relevant websites that link out to external resources that are now 404. Publish a resource or your own piece of content to take its place, reach out to the website and inform them about the broken link. Suggest they might want to update it with your resource.
- **Earn your links** – This is the most important of all. Create and promote high value content that will acquire links of its own accord. The main emphasis here is on the word 'promote'. To gain the greatest traction, for both traffic and links, you have to actively promote.

23. Creating content with link potential

Content is a huge and varied area, with numerous approaches and techniques available. Broadly speaking though, there are ten types of content appropriate for SEO that may also prove beneficial from a linking perspective:

1. Thought leadership and blog posts (with regular updates or republished on a regular basis).
2. Short-form evergreen content and articles.
3. Long-form articles.
4. Photo and visual galleries.
5. Detailed and information-rich lists of information.
6. Interactive tools and content.
7. Comprehensive category landers.
8. How tos and guides.
9. Data or complex information that is visualised.
10. Video, YouTube or embedded video on a particular page.

Working out what type of content is right for your site can be difficult. Instead of asking *"What type of content is right for our site?"* ask *"What is the user's intent? What are they trying to achieve?"* Take a look at what you filled in on the Simple Spreadsheet from the Strategy chapter to help with this.

The presentation of your content is hugely important, but it is not everything. Read on to find out more about content creation and what you can do to improve your SEO.

24. Influencer-targeted content

To gain rankings and grow domain authority, SEO campaigns need to get links from three types of sites and pages:

1. **High domain authority sites** – links from huge sites such as the BBC will add some of their domains authority to yours, boosting your entire site.
2. **High-value keyword-targeted pages** – links from webpages that target similar keywords to your own page will add to their credibility and boost the rankings of individual URLs.
3. **Sector or niche** – links from other sites in your own sector or niche will tell search engines exactly what your site is for and about, giving you extra topical authority in that area.

Often, the best way to get these links is to target your content at industry influencers, such as journalists, bloggers, or conference organisers. These influencers are often content creators themselves and can help you to achieve links from keyword-targeted pages and those within your sector. The trick is to look at their content and identify any gaps within it – filling these gaps may earn you the links you need.

Finding and filling these gaps is not easy. With so much content being produced for every niche, your content must stand out. Maximise your chances by producing interesting content such as:

- Statistics and data.
- Visual content.
- Contrary opinions.

Influencers are always looking for new angles or arguments to bring forward, and data adds credibility to their assertions. Providing the relevant statistics for them is a start, but also make sure it is easy for them to share. Add 'feel free to share or link this' to increase your chances.

When you are a content marketer, a speaker at an event, or an author or blogger, you need visual content that will help catch the eye. It's often easier to get someone else's visual content, simply cite your source and link to it than it is to create visual content of your own. Therefore, producing visual content such as infographics can be an effective way to get links from others.

25. Social signals

Social media has become a key part of our online experience. But what about SEO? How much influence does a link to your site from a social media account make on your page or search rank? Unfortunately, from a PageRank point of view, it contributes nothing.

By default, all social media platforms implement the rel="nofollow" attribute on all external user generated links. So if you were thinking about getting links from Twitter, Facebook, or LinkedIn as a means to build authority, you're going to have to work harder than that!

That said, securing your social media profiles should be a fundamental part of your digital strategy. They are your distribution and amplification network. They might not influence your authority directly, but they increase the visibility of your content which increases the likelihood of achieving links in the long term.

Social media tips for SEO:

- Secure your social media profiles before someone else does.
- Select the most relevant social channels to engage with your audience.
- Optimise your social media profiles.
- Link back to your website from profiles.
- Post updates regularly (quality versus quantity).
- Share your website content via social media.
- Get your team and wider network on-board to share and engage with your content.
- Optimise the titles of your blog posts and other content to engage users on social channels.
- Include social sharing widgets on your website.
- Include calls to action on your pages to encourage people to share.

But, most importantly, be active and be human. Engage with your audience, listen and learn.

26. User engagement as a ranking factor

Like social media, user engagement is a controversial topic among digital marketers. The discussion here is around whether or not Google looks at the behaviour of a user when they engage with your content. For example, what if a website ranked at the top of Google for a particular query and no one ever clicked that result? Or if they did and then always returned to the search results and went on to click another website? Over time these behaviours might give Google the impression that the page does not fulfil the needs of the query and lead to Google changing the website's ranking position.

Again, the truth is that we don't 100% know. But we do know that ignoring user engagement for SEO is foolish. This goes beyond organic rankings, links, or even search engines. User engagement should be at the forefront of every digital marketer's mind. Longevity of ranking will only ever be achieved if the content we provide fulfils the current and future needs of the user. The secret to achieving this is meticulous attention to understanding and fulfilling user needs and intent.

Local SEO

If you are a business that provides local services you need a local SEO strategy.

A whopping 56% of on-the-go searches have local intent. People looking for products, business hours, and business locations are twice as likely to convert after a local search. As a local business, you need to be visible to tap into this.

Building local exposure

For the vast majority of local queries, or queries with local intent, the search results include listings from Google Maps. As a result the process starts with claiming and taking ownership of your Google My Business Listing(s).

Once secured, the listing should be carefully optimised and maintained to help increase the likelihood of ranking in local search queries.

Use the following tips to get the most your of your Google My Business Listing:

- Verify your Google My Business listing(s) – don't use a personal Google account to verify, use one for the business that can be shared and doesn't get lost if a team member leaves.
- Select the most relevant categories and services for your business.
- Provide a well optimised and engaging description of the business.
- Use keywords appropriately. Don't spam.
- Link to your website – use the location page if you have multiple locations.
- Complete your contact information.
- Ensure address details are consistent everywhere.
- Use a local phone number.
- Make sure your Google Map pin is positioned in the right place.
- Include opening hours.
- Include high quality images and video content to increase engagement.
- Encourage reviews from your customers.

- Don't ignore bad reviews – answer swiftly and professionally.
- Review and respond to questions from your customers. You can also add your own FAQs and answer them directly to pre-empt customer queries.
- Utilise the Posts feature to promote offers and engage users.

In addition to your Google My Business Listing, your website's content should be optimised to maximise local exposure. Consider the following:

- **NAP (Name, Address and Phone number)**
  - The three most important pieces of content you need to publish online are: your company name, address, and phone number.
  - Ensure time(s), address(es) and phone number(s) are ALWAYS consistent.
  - Make sure they are in crawlable HTML (not embedded in an image or an inaccessible format) and are consistent across all pages on your site (exactly the same wording and format).
  - Put your NAP at the top of your Contact Us page and in the site-wide master header or footer so that humans and bots can immediately and clearly identify these key features of your business.
  - Mark up your NAP with an address schema to further assist search engine comprehension of your data.
- **Store location pages**
  - For a multi-location business (like a restaurant chain), you'll be creating content for a set of landing pages to represent each of your physical locations.
  - These should feature the same types of content that a 'contact us' page would for a single-location business.
  - They can also include extra information such as reviews, location-specific offers, social media links, interior photos and information relevant for users in that area.
- **City or regional landing page**
  - Similar to the multi-location business, a service area business (like a plumber) can develop customer-centric landing pages. These pages represent the towns, cities or regions that the business serves.
  - Although unlikely and the postie will soon realise you don't live to contain a street address, if the company lacks a physical location, they contain almost everything a 'contact us' or 'store locator' page would.
  - They can also contain location-specific information such as evidence of projects completed in that city (images, text, etc), expert advice for local consumers, reviews and testimonials, and a key call-to-action.

— Make sure that your content is tailored for each specific city or region!

In addition, develop a localised content strategy and build signals and links from other authoritative local websites.

Building local citations

Citations are key signals in your organisation's authority and credibility.

Whenever your site name, URL, or business address is mentioned on the web, even without a link, it counts as a citation to your site. Often found on review sites, yellow pages, or other similar pages, local citations can be treated as positive brand signals that add credibility to your local presence.

There are two types of citations – complete and partial:

• Complete citations include everything in a business's address. This means the business name, physical address and phone number (NAP). Including a website URL and an email address make it even stronger.

• Partial citations are any combinations of these without the full NAP.

In general, complete citations are stronger than partial, but the site they are on can also make all the difference. As with backlinks, a local citation offers more credibility if it comes from a more trustworthy site. Boost your local citations by adding your business's address to listing sites like yellow pages – it's not just the signals you'll benefit from, it's the potential referral traffic too.

> ### Activity – your local citations
>
> Use tools such as Moz's online presence tool or White spark's local citation finder to find directories you are not yet listed on or any listings that are not complete or using a consistent NAP.
>
> • https://moz.com/checkout/local/check
>
> • https://whitespark.ca/local-citation-finder/
>
> Build a list of the directories that you need to feature in, and start to get your citations listed.

Building local reviews

Reviews are another great way to signal your authority. They are also a great conversion tool.

As part of your wider marketing strategy, the business as a whole should make a concerted effort to encourage your existing clients to leave reviews.

How to collect reviews:

- Educate your team on the value and importance of reviews.
- When a customer says something nice about your business, don't be shy in asking them if they would be happy to leave a review. But don't be pushy!
- Make it easy for them – create a shortened URL that sends them directly to the message box where they can leave a review.
- Look at your existing customers and network then create a shortlist to approach.
- Make it part of your follow-up process.
- Create an email campaign or feedback survey.
- Be clear and stick to Google's guidelines.
- Don't get all your friends and family, or everyone in the office, to review your site – it is against Google's guidelines.
- Don't pay a service to leave you reviews, it is likely to backfire further down the line.
- Don't make reviews a one time activity, it looks suspicious to both search engines and your users.

Most importantly, provide exceptional customer service!

One final but very important note…

Thinking of rebuilding your website?

Migrating to a new site is exciting for any business, but without proper site build and migration support it can end in disaster. From a Search Engine Optimisation perspective, building a new site is both an opportunity and a danger.

Site build support

When you rebuild a website you want to take the roots of what made it previously successful into the new version of the site. This is where you want to be sure that you have SEO site-build support throughout the construction of the new site. This is a specialist set of skills, different to those of a website developer. This support will take into account the many technical considerations which can influence organic search visibility such as:

- Content opportunities.
- Sitemap definition.
- Navigational structure.
- Indexation.
- Crawlability.
- Keyword mapping.
- URL structuring.
- Duplication management.
- Structured data.
- And much more…

Falling behind on any of these can cause problems for search engines. This can result in a reduction of your organic reach and the traffic to your site. This is not exclusive to the launch of a totally new website or domain, it can occur at three separate situations:

1. When deploying a brand new website for the first time on a brand new domain.
2. Migrating from an existing website to a new website on the same domain.
3. If you are migrating a new or existing website to a new domain.

The secret is to build search and marketing into the core of your new build, based on all the technical SEO recommendations that have been covered in this chapter.

Migration

Imagine that you are moving house. If you don't tell the Post Office that you have moved, they will continue to send letters to your old address. After a while they will stack up. If you're lucky, the postman will realise you don't live there anymore and will stop delivering the mail. However, they won't know where to re-direct it to instead. The same principle applies to site migration.

If you are moving to a new site and you don't tell Google to redirect to your new address, then Google will soon assume you no longer exist. If this happens, it won't be long before they drop you from their rankings. This can be a huge problem. This is why you need to do what is known as site *migration*.

Make sure that when you are re-working a website all of the old pages have been redirected to the new pages using 301 redirects. Do not let a site that is in development go live without carefully considering and addressing this. If ignored it can result in decreased performance, undermining the reasons why you wanted a new site in the first place!

Chapter 16: Drive more traffic, sales, and enquiries using Pay Per Click

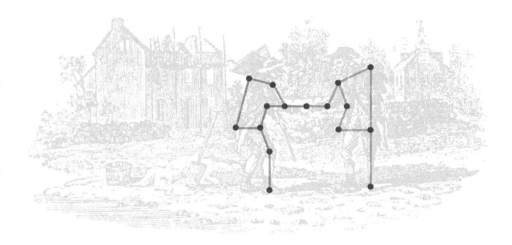

"Continuous improvement is better than delayed perfection."
MARK TWAIN

Pay Per Click (PPC) – The digital advertising option with more than one name

If you're a business, website owner, or Digital Marketing Manager looking to build your brand online, then using online adverts has probably crossed your mind. PPC – standing for Pay-Per-Click – is a very common method of online advertising. The name comes from the bidding method that makes this type of marketing especially appealing, in that the advertiser only has to pay *after* an advert is clicked on. Also called 'paid search' PPC ads can be found around the web, most noticeably as short text adverts at the top of search engine listings.

> "PPC is an online advertising model in which advertisers can display ads for their goods or services when users enter relevant queries into search engines. Advertisers are only charged when a user clicks on their ad." **WORDSTREAM**

If this sounds familiar, you might have used PPC already, but it may have been under another name. Cost-Per-Click Ads (CPC), Banner Advertising,

Search Engine Marketing (SEM), Paid Advertising, Remarketing… all of these types of online advertising are essentially different names for the same thing – they are all PPC. As is Paid Social, the term for using this method in social media channels.

To make it even more complicated, Google's PPC service, Google Ads (formerly Adwords), is so popular that some people confuse the brand name with the actual product – similar to calling all vacuum cleaners a 'hoover'. This is perhaps understandable, as Google Ads is by far the biggest player in this area, several times bigger than the nearest equivalent.

Arguably the most effective capture all phrase for this type of work is Paid Media. But for the purposes of this book we will use the most commonly accepted phrase 'PPC' to encompass all of these forms of advertising.

As a method of online advertising, PPC is a way of 'buying' traffic to your website. If done properly, the amount of revenue that this traffic generates should far exceed the amount that you spend to get those visitors. For example, if you are paying £5 per click, with 5 clicks for each order received, then you are paying £25 per order. If that order is for an average of £500, then you are making a tidy profit! It's important to understand these figures to make PPC profitable.

PPC versus Search Engine Optimisation (SEO) – what's the difference?

When considering how to get people to visit your website, one of the decisions many Digital Marketing Managers make is whether to use PPC or SEO. However, the truth is that this isn't a choice at all. They are very different methods of online marketing and there is a strong argument for using both methods, with each complimenting the other.

Renting a fancy apartment

Here, we use the 'real-estate' analogy. PPC offers the opportunity to occupy a 'property' immediately, across many platforms, but on a rolling contract that you must constantly renew. SEO, performed correctly, offers a more permanent residence, but requires a bigger down payment and a long mortgage.

With PPC, what you see is what you get. Appearing at the top of search results, PPC ads are labelled as 'ads'. You pay the going rate for your ad to appear on the first page of search results. If you are willing to pay whatever the going rate is for the keywords (searches) that you want to target, then your ad will appear on that page. SEO is more complicated, as it is based on improving the content on your site so it will rank higher on Google's 'organic' (unpaid) results.

What separates PPC from SEO?

Pay Per Click	Search Engine Optimisation
PPC is more immediate and can be activated in a matter of days – hours if need be.	SEO is a longer term strategy – it can take a few months to see an impact.
Text within the ad is quick and easy to change – it allows you to be reactive.	Listing text – the words that appear on the results page – is more difficult to amend.
It's your ad, so it says what you want it to say. Character limits mean good PPC content is succinct, compelling, and informative.	Text length is determined by the search engine, there is more flexibility over how much you write but the search engine might truncate your copy.
Advertisers pay on a cost per click (CPC) pricing model.	SEO requires ongoing investment to maintain ranking – usually charged as consultancy fees unless you have your own SEO professional.
PPC options are available on many platforms. This makes it a very attractive proposition for businesses that know their audience do not just inhabit the 'search' space, such as online communities which have become established over time on social platforms, specific websites, or even YouTube channels.	SEO is limited or non-existent on many platforms, so PPC becomes the only way to target some audiences. The space 'organic' (non-paid) listings will continue to get pushed lower and lower by paid listings.

What does Google want?

When talking about PPC, almost all the discussion revolves around the Google services, such as Google Ads. So, do the other search engines – Bing or Yahoo – not have a look in?

The short answer is no. They are in the same league, but they are mid-table at best. Google is the main player and, as far as we can tell, that's not going to change any time soon.

For Google, there are three groups that need to be taken into consideration when placing adverts on search results:

1. **Users** – the people making the search and clicking on the ad. They want fast, accurate results.
2. **Advertisers** – the companies who pay Google for every click on their ad. They want to place their ads in the most relevant position, where the greatest number of users will find them.
3. **Google** themselves – who are trying to balance the needs of users and advertisers.

The important part of this is to find the right balance between these groups. Google's aim is to create a search engine that will provide advertisers with a steady supply of clicks, while still enticing users back with excellent and speedy search results.

What is the Google Network?

When we talk about Google we often refer to the Google Network, because Google is not just a search page. As well as the page we are all familiar with, Google has connections to other websites. All of these offer marketing opportunities and can be broken down into two main areas.

1. Search

- **Search** – Google's search page, the most visited webpage in the world.
- **Search partners** – other websites that use Google within them to offer search as a facility. Examples being Amazon.com, The New York Times, and The Guardian.

2. Display

- **Display Network** – a series of websites across the globe that allow Google to show image-based ads on them.
- **Display Network partners** – including YouTube and Mobile Apps, meaning that you can use apps and YouTube to show image and video ads in your campaigns.

Why use PPC?

When you consider the reach that the Google Network offers, it starts to become clear why people would turn to it for their marketing needs. There are several compelling reasons why PPC advertising is so popular:

- It reaches the people already looking for your kinds of products or services on search engines.
- It drives immediate results.
- It's measurable.
- It's extremely targeted.
- It's not dependent on SEO or Google Algorithm changes.
- It can help you compete with larger businesses.
- It will help you break into new markets.
- You only pay when someone clicks on your PPC ad.

How does PPC work?

While the technical processes behind PPC advertising are incredibly complicated, it is surprisingly easy to visualise how PPC works from a high-level perspective.

Normally, when a user makes a search, Google's complex systems search for and rank the most relevant and focused results. This ranking forms the 'organic' listings we all see. The order in which the listings appear is influenced by the SEO efforts of each website on that list.

A similar process is applied to the PPC ads that appear at the top of the page. Just as they do with normal webpages, Google 'rates' your ad based largely on two main factors: 'bid amount,' and 'quality score'. These two factors determine if, and in what position, your ad appears on a search page.

1. **Bid amount** – This is exactly what it sounds like. It's the maximum amount you have chosen to spend for each click on your ad. When creating your campaign, you should consider the potential number of clicks you will receive and the potential ratio of clicks to orders, and then compare this with the cost of each click. This gives you a general idea of how much each click is worth to you.

2. **Quality score** – This is less black and white, and is determined by many factors including 'click through rate' (CTR) and historical data. The three main things we can control to influence quality score are: keywords, ad copy, and landing pages. If these three elements have a common theme connecting them, and they are all 'on-topic', then you should be close to getting a very healthy quality score. If one of these elements is misaligned then the quality score suffers. If you don't get any of these elements right – you don't do proper keyword research, your ad copy is weak or ambiguous, and your landing pages have bad

UX – then you will have low quality scores, resulting in high CPC (cost per click), low engagement and, ultimately, failure.

Maximising the quality score of your ad is extremely important, as it will boost the likelihood of your advert being displayed with a minimised bid amount, increasing the potential return on your investment.

When someone makes a query, Google will hold a digital auction. This auction will look at the bid amount and quality score for each advert that is supported by that particular keyword query, and then show the ads with the highest scores at the top of the search results page.

Remember – all of this is free. **You are not charged until someone clicks on your ad, hence Pay Per Click.** Whether they then carry on and buy something from you depends on how persuasive your ad is, and how well you have designed your website.

What kind of PPC should I use?

For someone new to PPC or Google Ads, the best advice is to keep it simple. One of the great things about PPC is that you are in control. Your campaigns can be as simple or sophisticated as you like and, ultimately, your goals and your audience will play a large part in how complicated your activity needs to be.

- **Start with text ads** – Easy and effective when used properly, they should be set up to appear to someone only when they are searching for the keywords that are most important to your business.
- **For e-commerce, think about using shopping adverts** – These can be a little bit trickier to set up but may eventually bring big rewards.
- **Talk to the experts** – Using a digital marketing agency to set up your PPC ads means that you can get good advice on how to use them – and support if it goes wrong!

There are many different types of PPC ads. While the most common are visible at the top of Google searches, there are more types to be seen across the web – just look for 'ads by Google' or 'sponsored link' on any ad.

Some of the most common types of PPC ads you might find are:

Text adverts. Appearing at the top of Google searches, these consist of headlines, descriptive text, and your URL. The amount of text that shows depends on how well you have created your campaign, and how well the ad is written. The aim is to be the most visible ad by taking up as much 'real-estate' on the search result page as possible, and being the ad that appears at the top of the page.

There are currently two text ad formats widely used, and encouraged by Google, each offering a different approach to your messaging. Firstly, there are Expanded Text Ads. This format is the culmination of previous iterations and allows you to be very specific with regard to your message. What you create is what will be seen on the search page. Secondly, there are Responsive Search Ads. These let you input more details, headlines, and descriptions, and the system then creates numerous ads from your information with the intention of showing the right combination of creative at any given time. Over time you will get enough data to understand which combinations perform best, and you can then make adjustments accordingly.

Dynamic search adverts. These are created automatically by Google, taking information directly from your website. You tell Google which web pages to look at when deciding if a search query is relevant to your business, Google then takes information from the page and displays it as an ad.

Mobile app engagement adverts. Found on mobile apps and websites, these encourage user engagement or action, such as playing a game.

Call only adverts. Also only appearing on mobile devices, these show a phone number. Clicking on them will take you directly to your phone's calling app.

Display adverts. These take display ads to the next level. Rather than create a finished ad, you have the ability to upload images and text, which Google then uses to create a series of ads that show across the Network.

When running Display ads consider the following best practice guidelines:

- Use high-quality images. Nothing looks more unprofessional than an ad with a pixelated or blurry image as the main focus.
- Keep your messaging on-topic, don't try to do too much. The aim is to get the person seeing the ad to go to your website and find out more.
- Be relevant. Sometimes timing is a key factor. Are your products or services seasonal? Is there a particular time of the day or week when demand would be greater? Factor this into your scheduling.

Display ads (banner ads). These are image based and appear on websites, not the Google Search Page. They are designed to appear in front of people when they are looking at a particular type of content, e.g. sport or fashion.

Video adverts. People sometimes forget that YouTube is a search engine and that it's owned by Google. It just displays results in a more visual way than the Google page. Video content that is hosted on YouTube can be easily turned into ad content and shown on YouTube channels or search pages. The principles behind the delivery of this are the same as standard search and display.

When running YouTube video ads consider the following best practice guidelines:

- Keep your videos short. 30 seconds is perfect, but anything between 15-60 seconds can work. Remember, viewers' online attention spans can be very short.
- Get to the point. Get your message across in the first seven-10 seconds. Make it interesting and engaging.
- Brand your content. Try to put your brand at the beginning and end of the video, so that people know who you are.
- Tell people what to do next. End the video with a clear call to action: visit our website, take a look at our channel, sign-up, subscribe, etc. Without an instruction you'll lose your audience!

Product shopping adverts (Google Shopping). For businesses with a large portfolio of products, shopping ads are the best way to deliver relevant content at scale, consistently, and without having to set up campaigns and ad groups manually for every product type. They rely on a spreadsheet of product information and show on specific areas of Google Search Pages.

When running Shopping ads consider the following best practice guidelines:

- Make sure the product information on your product feed (the spread-sheet you'll use to deliver ads in volume) is up to date and your product titles and descriptions are accurate and informative.
- Include offers or discount information where possible. The shopping landscape is very competitive, so whatever edge you have, make it visible.
- Ensure that your prices are accurate and comply with Google policy. Failure to do this not only makes for a bad customer experience, but you could be excluded from showing ads by Google for long periods of time!

Remarketing and remarketing lists for search ads (RLSA). Ever wondered how some advertisers know what you're interested in? Or why you're being shown ads for a pair of running shoes that you looked at last week? Well, that's remarketing. By dropping a cookie on your device when you visit a website, the advertiser is able to deliver follow-up messaging (remarketing) or even ads that reference specific items or services (dynamic remarketing).

Remarketing is a type of PPC ad that starts tracking a user when they land on a specific website. Once on the website, a cookie is dropped on that person's computer and they are included on a remarketing list. The list gives the owner the opportunity to understand that person's online behaviour in a bit more detail and give them a more relevant message in any subsequent remarketing ads. For instance, if someone visits a website and does not go on to make an enquiry or buy something, then a subsequent remarketing ad can be shown to that person to encourage them to make a phone call or incentivise them to buy something with a discount code. The ad follows the user around the web, appearing on other sites they visit, encouraging them to return to the original site.

Another remarketing option is 'remarketing lists for search ads' (RLSA). This is similar to normal text ads, except that the ads are shown to people who have already been to your website, as opposed to people who may not know about your business but are actively looking for your products or services.

The Footprint Digital PPC way – 12 steps to PPC success

When deciding to set up PPC ads it is important to develop a plan. A good plan will help you:

- Understand and anticipate what people are searching for – what are their needs?
- Address their pain points and anxieties – what problems are you solving?
- Encourage the person searching to take the next step – tell them what to do.

These three elements will go a long way to ensuring success when you put your messaging in front of a wider audience.

The great news is that you have already done the work in the previous chapters of the book! You'll recognise the issues you need to think about, the kind of information you need to gather, the questions you need to resolve, and the process you need to guide others through. So let's apply this to a PPC campaign.

Here are 12 steps to PPC success:

1. Know why your website exists

Taking a moment to reflect on the most fundamental question of all will ensure the campaign is fit for purpose. Ask yourself why your website exists. Clue: to make more money! But it's also there to showcase your brand, share information, answer customers' questions, and much more.

We're going to use a fictional example throughout this chapter. Jo's Biscuits sell delicious Gluten Free Cookies. The website is an eCommerce website that primarily exists to sell Gluten Free Cookies direct to customers. Nevertheless, it also exists to encourage retailers to stock their products as well as showcase the brand and build a list of subscribers through a recipe section on the site. We will consider these different functions of the site as we build a paid campaign.

View your website afresh from the perspective of someone responding to your ad – where on your site do you want them to land?

2. Know your CPA

Cost Per Acquisition or CPA is how much you are willing to spend to acquire a sale or lead. It is calculated by dividing the Total Spend by Total Conversions. In the case of Jo's biscuits we might say that an average order is £20. Jo is happy to invest 15% to make a sale. She is therefore happy to invest £3 for each order placed. This CPA figure will be different depending on what is being sold. But it is very important to have a good understanding of this before you consider paid advertising. Think about the number of clicks you hope to receive, the potential ratio of clicks to orders, and your typical order value, and then compare this with the cost of each click.

3. Know what you want people to do on your website

What are your goals? What do you want your customers to do? What are your conversion points? In which part of their experience do your customers typically make the shift from an enquirer to a buyer?

Answer the following questions to get you thinking about what you want to achieve and who you want to target with PPC ads.

- What is my campaign goal?
- How can I achieve that goal?
- How much am I willing to spend to achieve my goal?
- How will I measure success?
- How will I track results?

Examples of actions you might want your customers to make after clicking on your ad include:

- Newsletter subscription.
- Download.
- Watch a video.
- Email.
- Phone.
- Live chat.
- Visit your store.
- Buy.

4. Know your customers and what they want

Knowing exactly who your perfect customer is, is key to a successful campaign. We discuss this at length in chapters eight and 10 of this book, focused on brand positioning and strategy. When running a PPC campaign you can use these questions to help define your audience:

- What are people searching for?
- Who are they? What is their age, gender, etc?
- What are they interested in?
- When are they searching? What time of the day, what day of the week?
- Where are they? Which location/s will play a big part in my success?
- What devices are people using?

If you know what your customers want, you can address their interests, aspirations, and anxieties. Let's consider the customers for Jo's Gluten Free Cookies, and the kind of things they might be looking for.

- Tasty cookies
- Healthy alternatives
- Dietary advice around gluten intolerance
- Community of like minded people
- New recipe ideas
- New flavour ideas
- Beautiful instagrammable food images
- Other 'free from' inspiration
- Delivery options
- Gift packages

5. Find keywords that your customers might use to search for you

We cover effective approaches to keyword research in chapter 15 on SEO. The principles for Paid Search are the same. Use the Google Keyword Planner and everything else we reference in the previous chapter to figure out what your customers are searching for.

When you've performed your keyword research, you can think about controlling who sees your adverts by using keyword match types.

Broad Match

The default keyword match type is Broad Match. When you choose to advertise against a phrase such as 'Gluten Free Cookies' using broad match then Google will present your advert against anything that it feels is relevant to that phrase. It will allow misspellings, synonyms, and searches broadly related to that topic. For example, the search engine could show your advert if someone types the phrase 'Gluten Free Biscuits'. But this could also mean that it shows your advert to phrases that are not related to your product or that you don't want to show for such as 'Gluten Free Cookie Recipes'. It is a loose targeting option. When adding it to your keyword list you do not need to add any formatting to the word.

Negative Keywords

One way to reduce the risk of your adverts showing to people that might not be interested is to use negative keywords. This is where you can supply a list of phrases that you don't want your advert to appear against. For example, you may not want your advert selling cookies to appear against someone searching for 'Gluten Free Cookie Recipes' as you suspect that they are looking to make their own rather than purchase yours. Therefore, you might add 'recipe' or 'recipes' to your list of negative keywords. This will prevent the advert showing for people that use the word 'recipe' in their search. When adding it to your keyword list include the word with a minus in front of it: **-recipe.**

Exact Match

On the other end of the spectrum there is a keyword matching type called Exact Match. When this is used your advert will *only* show for the words that you define exactly as you write them. So if you used 'Gluten Free Cookies' as your exact match keyword it will only show when people type that in exactly. So it will not consider misspellings, the singular version, or the words in a different order. Your advert will not show for 'Gluten Free Cookie' or 'Cookies Gluten Free'. This option gives you greater control, and reduces your risk of appearing for anything unrelated. When adding it to your keyword list include the phrase in square brackets: **[Gluten Free Cookies]**

Phrase Match

This keyword match type allows you to present adverts against a specific phrase or variations of it. This means you can present the keyword 'Gluten Free Cookies' and the advert will show with related phrases or the addition of words before or after. For example 'Tasty Gluten Free Cookies to share with my friends'. But it will not show if a word is placed in the middle of the phrase, for example, 'Gluten Free Chocolate Cookies'. When adding it to your keyword list include the phrase in speech marks: **"Gluten Free Cookies".**

Broad Match Modifier

Like Broad Match, this choice of keyword match type allows the Google system some freedom to present an advert against similar search terms. However, it is slightly more targeted as you mark words that must appear in the search query with a plus sign +. So for example **+Gluten Free Cookies** will ensure that the adverts only appear when 'Gluten' is included in the query.

6. Categorise keywords by theme

Once you have understood the keywords that you think are going to be the most effective, the next step is to group these into clusters of keywords that are similar. Use five-10 keywords in each theme to minimise ambiguity.

For example:

1. Chocolate Gluten Free Cookies
2. Chocolate Chip Gluten Free Cookies
3. Gluten Free Chocolate Cookies
4. Chocolate Covered Gluten Free Cookies
5. The best chewy Gluten Free Cookies

1. Gluten Free Maple Bacon Cookies
2. Maple Bacon Gluten Free Cookies
3. Maple Syrup Gluten Free Cookies

1. Low Sugar Gluten Free Cookies
2. Sugar & Gluten Free Cookies
3. Sugar Free Gluten Free Cookies

Once you have grouped all of your keywords into sensible clusters this will form the foundation of the structure of your account.

7. Build a brilliant Google Ads Account

As with most projects, the planning stage is often critical to success. Fail to plan, plan to fail. This applies to any form of PPC campaign. If you don't have strong foundations, whatever you build will come crashing down, often with worrying economic implications.

There are four basic levels within a Google Ads account. Understanding what role each level plays is key to creating campaigns that perform at maximum efficiency to deliver the results you want.

1. **Account level** – This is the starting point. This is where your business information and billing details are held. At account level you can also allocate different levels of access to team members, depending on the role they will play in your Google Ads campaigns. This access can range from 'read-only' to 'admin'. Account level access is also where you can control the type of information and support you receive from Google.
2. **Campaign level** – This is where the creation of your marketing campaign begins. At campaign level you create the theme of your campaign, for example 'clothing', and decide on your daily and monthly budget. You also control your bidding strategies, location targeting, scheduling, and which networks (search and/or display) you want to use.
3. **Ad group level** – Ad groups sit beneath the campaign and are designed to focus on specific areas within them. For 'cookies' this could be 'gluten free cookies', 'sugar free cookies' and 'nut free cookies'. This is where you get to influence the bidding levels you wish to apply.
4. **Keywords and ads** – At the bottom of this structure, supporting everything, are the keywords and ads. These are the fundamental elements which will dictate who you're showing ads to (keywords) and how well they respond to your message (ads).

Approaching any campaign with an understanding of each level will ensure efficiency, minimal waste, and success.

Here's an example:

Account	Jo's Biscuits
Campaign	Cookies
Ad Group	Gluten-free cookies
Keywords	[gluten free cookies], +gluten +free +cookies

8. Create interesting adverts

You have created clusters of keywords and decided on your account structure. This is the moment where you can show the world how fantastic your products are by creating highly relevant ads.

A simple text ad has to do a lot more than just showcase a product or service. The best ads take into account the intent behind the search that is being performed, the barriers, anxieties, or problems that might be behind the search, and then offers a solution. When the person creating an ad can recognise these points, they are able to include them in the ad that is being delivered.

It can be looked at as a simple step-by-step process:

- **Keyword in the first title** – The title needs to match the search as closely as possible. Being able to anticipate this and include it as the first things that someone will see is vital.
- **Sales message in the second title** – Throughout the ad there needs to be an element of instruction, often this is supported by a USP.
- **Address an anxiety / solve a problem in the description** – If you can help put someone at ease, and immediately offer to help them, they are more inclined to spend time with you. This is true of ads. Anxieties can range from health & safety issues to fast or free delivery options. Including your solution shows you can help.
- **Finish the description with a Call to Action** – Never forget to tell people what you want them to do. Instruct them! If you don't you could be undoing all the other good work in the ad.
- **Use all the extra fields** – Different ad formats allow for various volumes of content in your ad creation. Use it all!
- **Include Ad Extensions** – Take up as much room on the search pages as Google allows. The best way to do this is by using Ad Extensions. These include Sitelinks, Callouts, Location, Price Ad Extensions, and Structured snippets. If you have a portfolio of brands, a range of styles or services, then Structured Snippets can be used to showcase these. This Ad Extension is also designed with particular verticals in mind. For instance, there is a 'Destinations' option which can be particularly useful to businesses

in the travel sector, and a 'Courses' option for education and learning website.

Desktop

This is Where the Keyword Goes | This is The Sales Message
[Ad] footprintdigital.co.uk/More/Keywords 01206803614
Solve a Problem or Address an Anxiety · Then Tell The Viewer What You Want Them To Do Now! Some Information About Why You Are The Best There Is · Generic Message or Offer Details.
Google Partner · Digital Specialists · Results Driven · Dedicated Manager

SEO Management Services
Expert Search Engine Optimisation
Contact the Experts Today

Digital Marketing Audit
Full Marketing Audit just £500
Contact the Experts Today

PPC Management Services
Expert Pay Per Click Services
Contact the Experts Today

Conversion Optimisation
Conversion Rate Optimisation
Contact the Experts Today

Best practice in text ad design

- Try to focus the headline on your product or service.
- Include the keyword within your ad where possible, as it will be bolded.
- Include a call to action to tell the user what to do!
- Detail USPs where possible.
- Include the product within the display URL.
- Capitalise important words.
- Do not capitalise stop words: a, and, is, on, of, or, the, was, with.

Here's the content we might use to advertise 'Delicious Gluten Free Cookies' using keywords related to that product.

Headline 1	Delicious Gluten Free Cookies
Headline 2	Visit Jo's Biscuits Online
Description 1	Shop for Delicious and Natural Gluten Free Cookies & Biscuits – Choose Your Favourite.
Description 2	Free, Safe & Secure Next Day Delivery Guaranteed – Place Your Order Online Today!
Display Path 1	Gluten-Free
Display Path 2	Cookies
Final URL	https://www.jos-biscuits.com/gluten-free-cookies

Here's what the completed ad would look like when it is shown on a Google Search Page. Notice, as well as the content we have created, the ad also takes up more room, or real-estate, on the page because we have used Ad Extensions. In this case we have included a Call Extension, Callout Extensions, and Sitelink Extensions.

Ad · jos-biscuits.com/Gluten-Free/Cookies ▾   1234567890

Delicious Gluten Free Cookies | Visit Jo's Biscuits Online

Shop for Delicious and Natural Gluten Free Cookies & Biscuits - Choose Your Favourite. Free, Safe & Secure Next Day Delivery Guaranteed - Place Your Order Online Today! Free Delivery. Healthy ingredients. Gifts Cards. Environmentally Friendly.

Chocolate Cookies	Delivery Information
Try our amazing tasing chocolate recipe Gluten Free Cookies	Need your cookies in a hurry? See our same day delivery option
Gluten Free Recipes	Ingredients
Take a look at some of the great gluten free recipes we swear by!	Order everything you need to bake your own gluten free cookies

---

Activity – Writing text ads

Practice writing a text ad for one of your products or services, using our best practice list above. Make sure to include a display URL and think about which page on your website somebody should land on after clicking your ad.

9. Targeting

You want to be sure that your adverts are sending people to the right place, are only showing to people that are likely to buy, and also only run at times of the day when people are likely to buy. Consider the following targeting features:

• **Landing page targeting** – Google likes relevance. They will penalise the quality scores of ads that aren't relevant to the landing page they send people to. Target the wrong page on your website, and your ad will land lower down the list and incur a higher CPC. So, make use of your keywords on landing pages. Rather than send traffic to your homepage find a location that is directly relevant to the search and if there isn't one, create one. For example, we want to send people that search for 'Gluten Free Cookies' to a page that will have information directly relevant to that phrase. We will therefore set up a page specifically for it. For example: www.jos-biscuits.com/gluten-free-cookies

- **Location targeting**– As with many features in Google Ads, the default setting for location targeting is probably not the one you want to go with. Location targeting can be used to deliver ads across any country in the world, and can be broken down to towns and cities, even individual post-codes. As a way to minimise wastage you can also include this data as a negative, so that you don't show ads somewhere. For campaigns target-ing a very specific area, on a small budget, this can be very useful. For example Jo often hand delivers her Gluten Free Cookies so we can make sure that her adverts only show within a 30 mile radius of her kitchen.

- **Targeting the appropriate time of day with scheduling** – Showing ads at the right time can make or break a campaign. You have the ability to choose when your ads show right down to the hour of the day, which is useful if your business relies on calls but doesn't have manned phone lines outside of regular weekly office hours. Over time the scheduling facility will also show you when demand is highest so you can ensure you are maximising your efforts at the right time.

10. Choose your bidding strategy

In order to get the best out of your investment in paid ads you can adapt your bidding strategy. We have explained how you can set bids for your adverts. There are different options available for these bids. This is referred to as a bidding strategy.

The bidding strategy you choose will depend on the goal of your paid cam-paign. So reflect on whether your campaign exists for maximum visibility (impressions), to drive traffic to your site (clicks), or with a focus on an out-come such as sales (conversions). Then choose from the following:

- Smart Bidding is effective if you aim to have customers take a direct action on your site and are tracking these outcomes as conversions.
- Cost-per-click (CPC) bidding is useful if your focus is generating traffic to your website.
- Cost per thousand viewable impressions (vCPM) bidding is especially useful for increasing brand awareness as it works to get the most impres-sions from your budget.
- Cost per view (CPV) or cost per thousand impressions (CPM) bidding will be a good option for increasing interactions or views of video ads.

At the time of writing, Google announced Smart Solutions – a bidding option for conversion focused campaigns with a number of different automated bid options. There are always new features being released and we would recommend reading Google's latest guidance on this before choosing. Keep an eye on these and how they might help you improve performance.

11. Make the most of remarketing and the display network

The focus of this chapter has been on the use of adverts that appear in search. If you just use that type of paid advertising you will be missing out on remarketing and the display network which includes YouTube. Remarketing or retargeting is used to describe the adverts that chase you around the internet.

Once a visitor has landed on your site you may be able to tag them using a "cookie" so that you can present adverts to them. This gives you the opportunity to target customers who have already visited your website, allows you to remind them that your business exists, follow-up on their interests, or share information about new products, sales, and discounts. These adverts appear on the Google Display Network which allows you to advertise on websites, YouTube, Gmail, and some apps.

12. Track results and refine

Whenever you make changes to an ad, or you're testing differences between ads, make sure you are measuring and comparing performance. You want to know that your ad is delivering on your investment. Alongside the Google Ads reporting interface you can use a number of tools that help give you a well rounded view of performance and more importantly, how you can go about fixing things.

Here are some of the tools you can use:

- **Google Ads Reporting** – The Google Ads interface is packed full of useful information and can be configured to show you exactly what you need to know. Delve into the range of reports you can produce.
- **Ad Preview Tool** – This allows you to see what an advert looks like in a search results page without triggering an impression. It will give you a chance to see how good your adverts look.
- **Google Analytics** – Ensure that your Google Ads account is properly linked to your Google Analytics account and enjoy the depth of data at your fingertips.
- **Bid Simulator** – This tool allows you to model potential increases in bids and predict the effect of changes you wish you make.

Measure, learn, and refine so that you continually improve performance. Here are some of the things to consider exploring:

- Learn from your successful ads.
- Experiment with ad formats.
- Refine your keywords.
- Control your daily budgets.
- Match budgets to business goals.
- Monitor how your budget is being spent.
- Invest in what works.

Here are some things you could add to your weekly check as ways of recognising quality:

- **Check cost/conversions Vs advert positions** – Look at how much you have spent on your adverts, what conversions they have achieved, and the average position those adverts have appeared in.
- **Check total revenue/cost Vs investment** – Look at the financial impact of the account. What revenue has it brought in? How much has it cost? Is it worth the investment?
- **Check best/worst performing adverts** – Find the adverts with the lowest click through rates or poorest conversion performance. Why are they performing badly? Should you amend them or remove them?
- **Check poor quality keywords** – Look at which keywords are being effective for your and which are not performing well. Make a decision on whether to keep them.
- **Check search query keywords** – The search query report will tell you what people have typed in to trigger your adverts. See if there are popular phrases or phrases that you do not want to appear for.
- **Add negative keywords** – If your adverts are showing against words you don't think are effective then add these words as negatives.
- **Check landing pages** – See whether the less effective adverts land on a page that is appealing. Take time to improve the page.
- **Check bounce rates** – take a look to see if people are landing on your page and leaving without clicking on anything.
- Bid at Keyword Level, NOT Ad Group Level.

Move into your new apartment and invite people over!

Establishing a permanent presence online, in the places you know your customers are to be found, is the holy grail when it comes to Digital Marketing.

Get that right and you're well on the way to success and making more money online. But achieving that visibility very often involves continual effort over a long period of time, it rarely happens overnight.

Your prime online location – the real estate you want to claim – is often sought after by several, sometimes hundreds of other businesses. You're in a very competitive market with some big players, with deep pockets, who prize that particular virtual plot as much as you do, and they are also making every effort to put their stake in the ground. So, while you battle it out, what do you do in the meantime? Simple, rent the best apartment on the block and invite people over!

Chapter 17: Social media

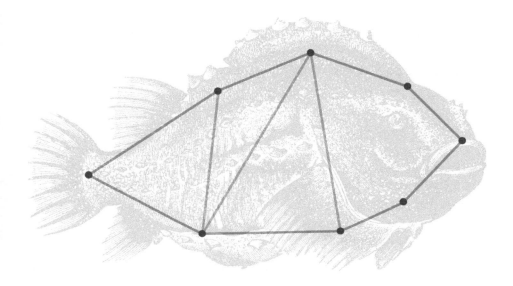

> "If fishing is interfering with your business, give up your business"
> **SPARSE GREY HACKLE**

This is water

> "There are these two young fish swimming along and they happen to
> meet an older fish swimming the other way, who nods at them and
> says 'Morning, boys. How's the water?' And the two young fish swim
> on for a bit, and then eventually one of them looks over at the other
> and goes "What the hell is water?"

This thought-provoking story is the starting point of a commencement
speech delivered by the brilliant David Foster Wallace[87]. His talk says that
*"the most obvious important realities are often the ones that are hardest to
see and talk about."* He goes on to discuss the role of a liberal arts education
as not just *"teaching you how to think"* but, more importantly, teaching you

---

87 Wallace, D, F. (2009) *This Is Water: Some Thoughts, Delivered on a Significant
Occasion, about Living a Compassionate Life'.* London, Little Brown Book Group.

what to think about. Or rather to be aware of what you spend your time thinking about as *"You get to consciously decide what has meaning and what doesn't."*

"It is about the real value of a real education, which has almost nothing to do with knowledge, and everything to do with simple awareness; awareness of what is so real and essential, so hidden in plain sight all around us, all the time, that we have to keep reminding ourselves over and over:

"This is water."

"This is water."

It is unimaginably hard to do this, to stay conscious and alive in the adult world day in and day out. Which means yet another grand cliché turns out to be true: your education really IS the job of a lifetime. And it commences: now."

Swimming in social media

Social media is the term given to a range of marketing channels through which you can distribute your message and connect with your audience. It is so embedded in our lives that it would be hard to imagine life (certainly in the business world) without it. Yet, as in the *This is Water* story, we can be so close to it that we can't objectively see the whole, let alone assess how much of our time we want to spend thinking about it. Social media can often become an obsession for Digital Marketing Managers, to the point that they neglect far more important things. The objective of this chapter is to consider how to think about social media, how to keep it in context, and to how to determine the time and resources that a Digital Marketing Manager should commit to it.

Hooked on social media

Social media is a relatively new phenomenon and has changed how we consume content, quickly becoming ingrained in our lives. In 2019, it was estimated that, globally, we each spend more than 140 minutes a day on social media platforms.[88] For many, this estimate is on the low side and it is increasingly common for people to check their social media platforms when they wake up and for it to be the last thing they do before they sleep.

---

88 Clement,J. (2020) *Daily social media usage worldwide 2012-2019* [online] available at: https://www.statista.com/statistics/433871/daily-social-media-usage-worldwide/ [Accessed 28 April 2020]

Research suggests that a fifth of young people even wake up in the night to check their platforms.[89] We are hooked. Social media has reframed how lots of people think about their own lives and there are now active campaigns (supported by social media influencers) that encourage us to 'digitally detox'.[90]

Value your time

The big challenge Digital Marketing Managers face is using their time appropriately (think back to the Head Chef syndrome in Chapter Two). Writing posts and creating content for social media is hugely time consuming and it can be an infinite game – there's no obvious limit to the volume of content you can create and share. We see so many Digital Marketing Managers spending 80-90% of their time producing social media posts to the detriment of the overall business strategy. It is vital that you assess the value of your time, ensure that you remain strategic, and don't get distracted by the shining promise of social. Instead, make sure that the content you create is part of a cohesive narrative that fosters long-term relationships, rather than something that looks flashy but soon vanishes into the ether with little engagement.

A Digital Marketing Manager's focus must remain the same: **the right message, to the right people, at the right time.** This is not to belittle the importance of social media, but rather to be careful with the best use of your time.

Social media isn't a strategy

Clearly, if a brand wants visibility, they must be where their customers are. If done well, social media campaigns are incredibly powerful. But, as staggering as the impact has been, social media itself is not a strategy (at least, not for the majority of businesses). Digital Marketing Managers need to resist the urge to conflate more platforms with greater success. The 'next big platform' should be viewed with healthy scepticism until you can be sure it is right for you and will meet your goals.

---

89 I Am Whole. (2020) *Digital Detox Day* [online] available at: https://www. digitaldetoxday.org/ [accessed 7th October 2020]
90 Digital Detox Day 2020 was a campaign by LUSH, Zoe Sugg, and mental health organisation #IAMWHOLE founded by Jordan Stephens. https://www. digitaldetoxday.org/

Finding your customers – what are they on?

The demographics of social networks are in a continuous state of fluctuation and change – Facebook *used* to be considered the social network for the young, now (in 2020) this has given way to Instagram, Snapchat, and TikTok. Was it a coincidence that, as this shift took place, older generations were installing Facebook onto their tablets and creating new accounts?

Alongside demographics, you need to consider whether you are selling directly to the customer, or to other businesses. B2C social marketing is more likely to take place on informal platforms, such as Instagram and TikTok, whereas B2B social marketing might require a stronger focus on platforms like LinkedIn. But really, it depends on your business.

Assuming you are well acquainted with your ideal customer, you will be able to combine your understanding with demographic data to work out where your customers may be. Your assumptions of who is using which social network may be wrong: beware of being a HiPPO! Most social media platforms provide insights on the volume of potential customers there may be amongst their users.

Social media: a space to serve your community

Once you've worked out the right channels for you, social media can be a very powerful way to increase your reach – to have more people see your content and engage with your brand. Often this is stated as the primary aim of social media activity. Our approach and preference is to use social media primarily as a way to encourage loyalty. The primary objective is to increase the volume of *engaged* subscribers (there are a lot of spam accounts out there), and to treat your social media as a space where you can serve your community. If your marketing is speaking to the right people at the right time, social media is a place where you can resume your conversations. Social media provides the opportunity to go deeper and more personalised into your customer base, rather than broader and wider. That is not to say that you shouldn't aspire for this to be achieved with a large reach as well.

Social media marketing as asset building

We also recommend that you avoid short-term thinking with your social media campaigns and approach them with the mindset to build a bigger asset. A well-engaged community on social media gives you a direct line to your biggest advocates and customers in an inexpensive and convenient way. A list of engaged social media followers can be one of the biggest assets you can build in a business.

It's not just 'branding' anymore

Traditionally social media was seen as a place to build brand awareness and was treated as an extension of the billboard or magazine advertising, with brands pumping money into it to achieve visibility. However, social media platforms have realised that there are many potential customers using their platforms – in fact 90% of Instagram's users follow a business account.[91] Where, in the past, it was not the medium for a direct sale, it is now possible to utilise many social media platforms as a marketplace from which you can (directly or indirectly) sell products to people. For example, Instagram now allows you to create shoppable posts where people can complete the whole customer journey – from research to purchase on the Instagram app.

Content marketing, not social

Instead of thinking about social media as a discipline in itself, we prefer to think about building a content marketing narrative which can then be distributed across all channels, including social media.

The objective is to build lists of engaged customers. To do this, you must craft a great brand story that you will deliver with consistency and, ideally, with a narrative thread that runs through everything you communicate.

Customer journey mapping

Before building the social media strategy we undertake a 'customer journey mapping' exercise. This helps us think about how a client progresses from not knowing about our brand through to research, consideration, booking, delivery, and on to post delivery. Having a clear understanding of this journey helps us understand what content we need to create, and where and when it needs to be presented to the customer.

---

91 Instagram. (nd) [online] available at: https://business.instagram.com/ [accessed 28 September 2020]

Customer Journey Mapping

Service/Product Name _____ Date _____

Stages	Research & Planning	Consideration	Booking	Delivery	Post Delivery
Touchpoints					
Consumer needs					
Consumer thoughts & decisions					
Consumer pain points					
Opportunity					

The customer's journey starts before they know they need you or your product, and it progresses through to purchase and aftercare. Each of the stages in the process will see a different customer and context that they are shopping in. How they can engage with your brand, their needs, thoughts, and pain points will be different. Therefore, so will each opportunity.

The journey mapping process does not have to be any more complicated than re-creating the grid above. Plot the journey stages across the top and then the customer variables down the left. At each cell, consider carefully what the customer may be feeling, where they are, what technology they have access to, and what might be going through their mind.

Activity – Complete the customer journey mapping for your key personas

Using the key personas developed in Chapter 10: Develop a strategy, start creating a customer journey map for each persona.

Take note of the elements you struggled to answer (where more research is needed).

Identify clear opportunities where you don't currently have content or a means to make the most of that opportunity.

This journey should, in reality, be a continuum. Once you have taken the time to locate and secure someone as a customer, it is more economical to retain them as part of your post-delivery stages and slingshot them back into subsequent consideration and booking stages. It may be best to think of the last three phases as a loop!

Think in terms of a syllabus

We would recommend, rather than creating posts and articles sporadically, that you take time to create a series of great content. Ideally you would think of this like a book or a syllabus that you will work through with your audience, keeping them engaged and giving them a reason to return to you. Once you have defined this core thread of content, you can repurpose discrete bits of content into different formats for distribution across a wide range of social media channels. You will create a content ecosystem that will foster a sense of ubiquity, a strong presence in the minds of your customers, and you'll encourage them to return to your brand even if you are not asking them to buy anything in that given moment.

'Evergreen' versus 'Prospect/Nurture/Convert' versus 'Direct sell' campaigns

There are three broad ways in which we categorise the messaging you might put out.

Evergreen campaigns are those that go on throughout the year and put out consistent messages about your brand. You generate brand awareness and loyalty with 'always on' or 'evergreen' push campaigns that build and nurture your community. 'Always on' messaging gives you visibility and consistently reminds everyone that you are there. This is a necessity in the ever-new social space – the old adage *"out of sight out of mind"* is very true on social platforms.

Prospect/Nurture/Convert campaigns look to build towards an event, sale, or product launch – creating demand over time, building to a peak. Much like a film launch, the narrative should be built to seed your product and create anticipation. Careful consideration needs to be given to the different messages you convey to different people at different stages in the buying cycle. You want to encourage people to move from one stage through to the next – from *prospect* to *nurture* to *convert*.

Direct sell campaigns generate a direct sell from someone previously 'cold'. Much like a paid search campaign or SEO activity, with this strategy you are trying to capture people that are in an active phase of wanting to purchase your product. Many social media channels offer direct selling functions within their platforms.

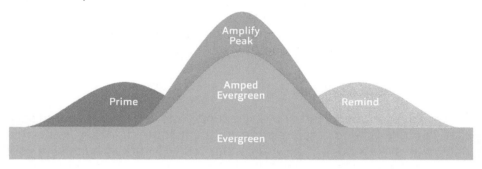

A well-rounded approach to social media incorporates all of these types of campaigns. Each of these strategies use different platforms and approaches and work best when they are carefully planned and crafted.

Delegate content creation

The success of social media comes down to how consistent and compelling the messaging from your brand is. The brand positioning document and brand lexicon (discussed in Chapter Eight: Establishing your brand's identity) are great foundations for this. As a Digital Marketing Manager you need to own them and be 100% confident in them. We also believe that you need to be very close to building the social media strategy. Once you have the brand positioning, brand lexicon, customer journey mapping, and strategy, it is then best if you can find outsourced partners or an in house social media manager to deliver the content that you need, whether this be video, animation, written word, audio, or any other format. Your role means you must remain strategic and keep a view of the whole. Beware that you do not sink your own time into a black hole of content creation.

Practical tips for managing social media

Here are some of our top practical tips to consider when managing social media:

- Set campaign goals and use them to review your marketing activity – targets for the number of likes or followers do not represent a long-term strategy, they're the by-product of a well-run one.

- If you want to succeed with 'organic' social media (non-paid), be clear what value you provide to your audiences. Build a community on something of worth and make it clear to audiences why they should want to engage with you.
- Paid-for methods of social media advertising have a broad range of purposes – they can generate brand awareness as well as revenue. BUT you need to be prepared to invest in this area and in optimising your campaigns.
- Embrace any tracking pixel your target social networks can provide – the snippet of code that shows when someone has visited a site or opened an email – and ensure that you make the most of it. Each network will provide more information that can help your campaigns run more effectively.
- Repurpose existing content and post to your social media accounts but remember that the audiences may differ. Ask yourself whether simply copying and pasting the content across the board is going to provide the most value.
- Whether you like it or not, people will use your social media pages as a customer service touchpoint. Be prepared to react quickly and positively to complaints.
- Be crystal clear on the purpose of each social engagement – what are you hoping the outcomes to be? Did you achieve them? What will you do differently?
- Follow your competitors! Social media is a great way to find out what they are doing, and you will probably find some creative ideas for your own social channels, too.

Social media is not a silver bullet

When you begin searching to understand social media marketing, you can be beset by case studies and examples of bedroom entrepreneurs who claim to be making five and six figures a month from their social media strategies. But the promise of passive income and the desire to 'go viral' needs to be measured. More often than not those that are making 'passive income' are working extremely hard for their money and those that 'go viral' are backed by marketing budgets or get very lucky. So be sure to set the expectations of those up the organisational chain. Help them understand that the 'viral' campaigns reported on the evening news are the exception, not the rule. Social media is often misunderstood, and your challenge is to demonstrate the immediate value it provides, beyond revenue.

Your social media strategy is just an extension of your content strategy, and success is unlikely to happen overnight. Be prepared to shoot the HiPPO and justify the use of your time. A community built on social networks is a highly valuable asset. But you need patience to build it and confidence that your approach will be valuable to the customers who choose to be there.

Chapter 18: Email marketing

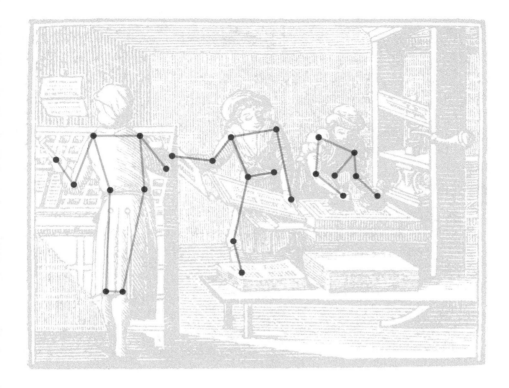

> *"Email has an ability many channels don't: creating valuable, personal touches – at scale."* **DAVID NEWMAN.**

The Blair Witch Project

In 1999, a website was set up calling for information about four young film-makers who had disappeared in the Maryland woods. Wanted posters were published and the IMDb page listed the actors as "missing, presumed dead". The mother of one of the actors even received sympathy cards.

These were the early days of the internet. Soon newsreel style interviews and police reports went viral alongside stories describing the legend of the Blair Witch. At the time this blurring of lines between fact and fiction had rarely been experienced. Such was the mystery that many filmgoers watched screenings of the film in the belief that the found footage was real. Shot with a meagre $60,000 USD budget and promoted with a virtually non-existent *marketing budget the film went on to take $248,000,000 USD at the box office.*

It almost single handedly turned the found footage style of filmmaking into a subgenre of low budget horror and has inspired countless films since. Like the Blair Witch itself, the marketing campaign has become part of folklore for its ingenuity, reach, and cost effectiveness.

We know what you might be thinking. What does a film from the late 1990s have to do with email marketing today? We think that Digital Marketing Managers can learn a lot from the Blair Witch marketing campaign, and apply the elements that made the campaign effective to the way certain types of email marketing are approached.

Don't undervalue email

Many marketers undervalue email marketing because there is a perception that email is the 'dying' channel for conversation. This is a mistake. Email is almost always 'warm' and it offers a chance to communicate with someone who already has an interest in you. It is one of the least expensive ways to build a deeper relationship with your audience and, as there is already an existing relationship, it can also be effective in driving new business. In studies[92] that assess the campaign types that deliver the greatest ROI, email campaigns always come out on top.

Email is not dead

"Are you on Email? You really have to be these days"
ELIS JAMES AND JOHN ROBINS

It is estimated that there could be 4.4 billion email users in 2023.[93] At the end of 2019, Facebook had just under 2.5 billion active monthly users[94]. So,

---

92 Charlton, G. (2014) *Email remains the best digital channel for ROI* [online] accessible at: https://econsultancy.com/email-remains-the-best-digital-channel-for-roi/ [accessed 6th November 2020)

93 Clement, J. (2020) *Number of e-mail users worldwide 2017-2024* [online] available at: https://www.statista.com/statistics/255080/number-of-e-mail-users-worldwide/ [accessed September 12 2020].

94 Clement, J (2020) *available at: Facebook: number of monthly active users worldwide 2008-2020* [online] available at: https://www.statista.com/statistics/264810/number-of-monthly-active-facebook-users-worldwide/ [accessed 6 November 2020]

irrespective of the dizzying numbers, ignore either at your peril. 90% of all email gets delivered to the intended recipient's inbox[95], anything from 20%-40% gets opened. When you compare this to the 2% of Facebook posts that are seen in a news feed, email has better visibility.

The power to outlast websites

Email predates the internet, Google, Smartphones, and all social media networks. It has remained a strong constant throughout the rise and fall of social networks and the change in computing hardware, plus it's less volatile than the impending threat of Google algorithm updates. An email marketing list has the potential to outlast websites and social media platforms.

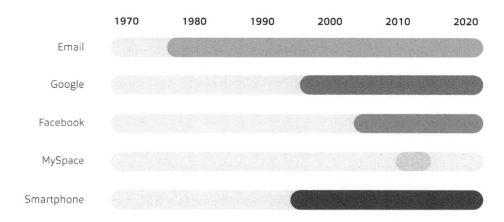

B2B versus B2C email campaigns

How you engage with email marketing will, to a large degree, be dependent on who your audience is. Are you speaking directly to customers in your emails, or to other businesses? There are a few key areas where B2B and B2C email campaigns differ and you should get to grips with these before creating a campaign.

- **Purchasing behaviour** – businesses and consumers buy things for different reasons. Often, a B2B email will land in the inbox of somebody looking to increase their ROI or give their business a USP. These people are likely to have to ask for budget for whatever it is you are selling, so

---

95 Campaign Monitor. (2019) *What Is Email Marketing? 7 Email Benefits To Grow Your Business* [online] available at: https://www.campaignmonitor.com/resources/guides/why-email/ [accessed 3rd September 2020]

the purchase process will take some time. Conversely, a B2C email will go to somebody looking to make a personal purchase and they will be more emotionally invested. They also have the power to make immediate decisions so you may see conversions much more quickly (if your email is persuasive enough).

- **Timing and frequency of send** – a B2B email will land in a business email inbox, so there's very little point sending these out after 5pm or on weekends or holidays. On the flip side, a customer may well want to see your emails during a public holiday or at the weekend (i.e. emails about Christmas recipes and gifts in the lead up to 25th December or ideas for evenings out on a Saturday). B2C emails should mark important holidays, can be sent more frequently and at different times to B2B emails.

- **Content types** – it probably goes without saying that content in a B2B email should be more professional and data driven than content in a B2C email. For B2B, keep content clear, concise and use data to prove why your product or service can help their business. The recipient can use these facts to make a business case for buying from you. In B2C emails you are looking for more of an emotional response – try storytelling, GIFs, competitions and other engaging forms of content to build a relationship.

Strategy is key

Rather than sending out emails sporadically, build a strategy that pinpoints the key moments when you need to be getting in touch with people in your database. This is different for every industry, but for B2C e-commerce businesses we can be fairly sure that your busiest email send times are going to be around Black Friday, Christmas and other important holidays. It's vital that you build an email send strategy focusing on the lead up to these key dates, and that you're thinking about targeting the right people at the right time. Here are some tips:

- Nurture your database from the moment they sign up.
- Set up automated emails to save time and strike while the iron's hot.
- Strike the balance between being actively visible in their inbox and being spammy.
- Be relevant – plan for key industry dates.
- Create a preference centre and email it to your audience (this can be a simple survey that someone fills out where they choose the types of content they want to see from you).
- Segment based on who you want to target and what your audience have told you they like through your preference centre.

- Include 'opt out' emails in your strategy where people can opt out of receiving communications at sensitive times e.g. Father's Day or Mother's Day.
- Tie in with the rest of your marketing mix – use email to compliment and promote.

Ingredients of a successful email

1. **An irresistible subject line** – Create a message which resonates with the recipient. Consider what will differentiate it from the other subject lines in their inbox. Be daring and different, but ultimately authentic.

2. **A subject relevant to the recipient** – Provide something of genuine value. Give your readers a reason to want to open your email. This isn't always easy, but if they're your audience or potential customers you need to be able to add value. Whether it's a product they need or a problem they're trying to solve, ensure their need is central to the information in the email.

3. **An immediate 'hook' in the opening** – The hook (and bait needed) depends on what you are trying to achieve with the email, but the recipient needs a reason to stick around. Popular examples include an unmissable offer, a relatable story, a pleasant surprise.

4. **A clear purpose and call to action** – The call to action in the email is driven by your goals – what do you want someone to do with the email? This could be anything from the expected – buying a product or signing up to an event – to conveying some information, sharing good news or just reminding a customer that you're there.

5. **Usher people back to your website** – Opening an email is good, clicking back to the site is great. When you see your users landing on your pages from email campaigns you know what they've looked at, you learn what they're interested in AND you can build a retargeting list around them specifically.

6. **It displays well across all devices** – Nothing is worse than opening an email on your phone only to find you have to pinch and zoom, then scroll to read it all. Ensure that your email looks good on mobile: the images need to resize appropriately, the text needs to be visible, and the calls to action have to be clickable.

7. **Only send to consenting recipients** – Email marketing cannot start without building a list of customers, prospects, partners and peers. It goes without saying, but if you're not actively collecting this information (i.e. via a sign-up form), your lists are going to grow slowly. Since GDPR, if these people are based in the European Union, they need

to have consciously opted-in to communications. If then they do, this means they're actively interested in hearing what you have to say.

8. **Tracking opens and clicks** – Mathematician, Karl Pearson, famously said *"that which is measured improves"* and this certainly applies to email marketing. if you don't accurately track your emails, how do you know if they even work and how can you improve them? Google Analytics by default won't separate emails from other marketing channels, meaning that anyone reaching your website from a campaign will be almost invisible to you.

Activity – Creating the perfect welcome email

Using the tips above, create an email to welcome new subscribers. You can then trigger this to send out to anyone who adds themself to your database. Make sure that the email conveys your brand story, clearly explains what you do, and tells subscribers what they can expect from future emails.

Approaches to email

Email usually works best if it is part of your content strategy, allowing you to reinforce messages across multiple channels simultaneously. This would be part of a grander narrative that you would look to deliver through a content marketing calendar.

The joy of email is that you can use it in any way that you like. We're going to take a look at just a few core approaches.

- **Lifecycle emails** – a series of emails that nurture customers through a journey from A to B.
- **Transactional emails** – a type of lifecycle email, these emails register specific actions such as a purchase.
- **Always on email** – the most common and least effective. Emails such as newsletters that are sent on a consistent basis to remind customers that you exist.
- **Promotional emails** – using email to build anticipation and launch a product or special offer.

We will now look at these four types of email in more detail.

Lifecycle emails

Lifecycle emails are set up to target people at every stage of their customer lifecycle – simple really! They work best when automated, reaching customers at the right moments in their journey (it would be pointless to send somebody a discount code to use on their birthday a week after the date) .

There are lots of types of lifecycle emails but some of the most common are welcome campaigns when someone first signs up, re-engagement campaigns when someone hasn't engaged with you for a while, loyalty campaigns which include personalised offers, and shopping basket abandonment emails. Each of these campaigns needs to be mapped out and emails need to be created that will be triggered at your chosen time points.

A customer journey mapping exercise (as discussed in the Chapter 17: Social media) can help you map out your customer lifecycles and determine which emails are needed throughout the Research and Planning > Consideration > Booking/Purchase > Delivery > Post Delivery phases of a customer journey.

Transactional emails

Unlike the other email types we're listing, transactional emails are not for marketing purposes. These types of email support the provision of a product or service and provide very important information at critical times in the customer journey. Without them, customers are likely to feel frustrated, concerned, and powerless. The most obvious is the confirmation email that is triggered after a purchase is made on a website. At minimum, it should include a breakdown of the order, where it is being sent, and when the person should expect it. Other reasons for sending a transactional email include tracking notifications, delivery confirmation, opt in confirmation, and password resetting.

Transactional emails should be automated to ensure that they are sent out at exactly the right time – there's nothing more concerning to a customer than purchasing something expensive and then spending ages refreshing their inbox, waiting for their receipt to appear.

In terms of design, they should provide unambiguous information that is clearly presented, otherwise misunderstanding may occur and in extreme circumstances the customer may try to cancel their order. They should also look as though they came from you. There's no need for them to be boring just because they contain important information! Make sure that your brand comes across in colours and fonts, and that any imagery is of high quality.

Transactional emails are not the best place to upsell or try to market to a customer. They have already bought from you and either don't want anything else from you right now, or will be annoyed if you present them with a product they could have added to their cart and now won't be receiving in their order! However, you can include a preference centre link and a 'sign up to our newsletter' banner to find out more about these customers and move them into your marketing database.

It's also worth sending transactional emails from a separate email address to your marketing emails as this means they are less likely to end up in junk or promotional inboxes.

Always on email

Instead of targeting specific people at specific moments with specific content, always on email is an ongoing approach that isn't campaign focused. It pushes messages out frequently to entire databases in the hope that some people will bite. These emails can be quite reactive, for example a Digital Marketing Manager could see that sales are down so sends out a blanket email including some of the products they want to improve sales for. This is unlikely to create much engagement and just feels spammy to customers.

Always on email *can* work, but only if you already have a good relationship with your customers and the content you are sending out is top notch. Otherwise they're likely to feel bombarded and will hit that unsubscribe button. We suggest that you beware of being always on, and instead focus on building strong lifecycle campaigns and memorable promotional campaigns.

Promotional email campaigns

The principles for success with this approach can be explained using the example of a new film campaign – like the promotion of the Blair Witch. Whenever a new film is launched it never arrives without warning. Instead, film marketers craft long campaigns that tease, build anticipation, and take fans on a journey to the eventual premiere and launch. It is common that the first time people know something is coming is when an actor 'accidentally' posts a picture on social media with a future co-star. This subtle and vague initial tease, much like the Blair Witch Project wanted posters, starts the rumour mill with fans beginning to speculate about what it is all about. The marketing department will then slowly release snippets of clues to build excitement and pick up by third parties. This will often include a launch date, a teaser trailer, some controversy over a lead actor, a full trailer, a testimonial style video with fan reactions, all the way up to the glitzy and flamboyant star studded premiere.

The idea of promotional email marketing is to build a similar type of antic-ipation and it can be applied to any product, service, or announcement no matter how big or small. A core component of this involves creating a moment of scarcity or reason to purchase at a particular point in time. Incorporate early bird pricing into your email campaign, tell people when product stock is low, and that you expect it to sell out. Make them under-stand that this product or service will not be available forever.

Promotional emails in action

We will use the promotion of this book as an example, and explain how we moved from an early announcement to build anticipation to a moment when the book is launched. Below is a simple schedule and rough draft emails which formed the basis of the book launch campaign. Alongside the email campaign, we produced videos to tease the book and to showcase testimonials, a trailer, an unboxing video, and a thank you video to take our audience on the journey with us. We used content across social media to reinforce the messaging in each of the emails, and set up a PPC remarket-ing campaign and Facebook retargeting campaign.

Tuesday April 28th	1st tease	The book manuscript is done. Anyone up for proofing it?	Email plus to camera video on social channels
Tuesday June 23rd	Which cover wins?	Big news! Our first book is nearly done! Help me pick a cover	Email with pick a cover survey
Tuesday July 7th	This cover won	Thank you. The reaction has been great to the upcoming book. The winning cover is... Also include some testimoni-als from first proofers.	Email
Tuesday July 13th	My lessons from writing a book	Finally the book is back from the proofers and is off to the printers! Here are my lessons for writing a book.	Email with link to 'What I learned writ-ing a book' article
Tuesday July 28th	Official unboxing	It's back from the printers! How exciting. Can't believe it's in my hands. Countdown to launch. Pre-order here.	Email with embed-ded link to unboxing video
Tuesday August 4th	Trailer	Here's what makes the book so great.	Email with embed-ded link to trailer

Monday August 10th	Tomorrow's the day!	It's happening, it's actually happening!	Email
Tuesday August 11th	Launch	It's live! Please buy it!	Email with embedded link to promotional video & Amazon Link
Tuesday August 18th	Thank you!	Wow, thanks for the fantastic response. We can't believe how well received it's been. Thank you! Tease the online course.	Email with embedded link to thank you video plus CTA to order a copy

Structuring, segmenting, and cleaning

A well segmented list of email addresses gives you the opportunity to send personalised content – information, offers, and propositions that are relevant to each customer at that moment. We have already mentioned preference centres, and would really recommend spending some time setting one up in order to segment your data lists based on what they want to see. Highly relevant, targeted messages are more successful and lead to a better experience – everyone wins here.

Depending on the data you collect when somebody subscribes to your list, you could segment your email list on any number of things. Some of the most common segmented lists are:

- Gender (very important for clothes shops etc)
- Age
- Purchase amount and type
- Birthday month (great for loyalty and re-engagement by giving people unique voucher codes)
- Engaged and frequent clicker

If you are sending a similar email out to several segments at once, make sure that for every email you send you exclude people who have already received an email from you that day. This will stop people who appear in multiple segments from receiving multiple similar emails.

As well as segmentation, it is important to regularly clean up your data to remove any spam accounts and ensure that people who have unsubscribed are not still receiving communications from you. Firstly, use a double opt in to make sure that people who sign up to you are providing real email addresses, and that they have access to those accounts. This will prevent a lot of spam and stop you having to clean out these accounts in the first place.

Secondly, run a re-engagement campaign to separate engaged subscribers from those who no longer open your emails. Keep openers on your list, and give non openers several chances to open your emails before letting them know you will be removing them from your list.

Building an email template

Before you get cracking with sending emails, you need to make sure that the emails you send reflect your brand and tone of voice. This is especially important if you've got more than one person working on email marketing, as they may have very different ideas about what a good email looks like.

The solution to this? An email template.

Some email marketing platforms will help you build an email template, but if you're working on a good platform it should be easy enough to build one yourself.

The template should be a generic email, with your company's branding and colour scheme, providing an outline of what all of your future emails will look like. The most important things to consider when building a template are:

- What font type and size your header and body content text will be.
- Where your logo will sit.
- What links will be in your email navigation banner.
- Where your social buttons will be.
- What your CTA buttons will look like.
- What ratio of copy to imagery you will have, and how this will be arranged.
- How much white space there will be – don't make your template too busy.
- What will be in the email footer – hint always have an unsubscribe option here.
- Will you include any banners?
- Anything else that is relevant to your industry, e.g. awards, accreditations, etc.

Once you've built a template, get some eyes on it. Other people might be able to point out areas for improvement – or glaring mistakes.

We're not suggesting that every email should look like a carbon copy of your template – how boring would that be! But it should act as a guide to keep your brand message and appearance consistent. The template should also not be set in stone – as new trends and information arise, go back to your template and see if it needs tweaking.

Everything's a test!

As with everything in the world of digital marketing, if you're not testing it, you're not making the most out of your email marketing strategy. Treat each email you send as an experiment, with the goal that you learn more about what your recipients enjoy seeing and responding to. Here are some things you can test:

- **Subject lines and preview text**

  Subject lines are THE most important thing to get right and the first thing that you should test. This is the short snippet of copy that shows up in your inbox, and tends to be followed up very quickly by another email's subject line, which may or may not draw your attention away.

  The hard truth is that if you write bad subject lines, you'll have a bad open rate and all the work you put into the rest of your email will go to waste. When you create an email, set up an A/B test and play different subject lines off against each other. Find out which messages get people's attention and work with these.

- **Email headers**

  Once you've achieved that all important click through, the first thing your recipient will read is your header – so make it a good one! Headers can be informational (does what it says on the tin), inspirational (makes the reader feel a certain way) or instructive (tells them what to do next).

  Try setting up three versions of the same email, using an informational, inspirational, and instructive header, and see what results you get.

- **Email body content**

  Does your audience engage more with lengthy copy or short and snappy soundbites? Are they more likely to click on eye-catching images, quirky GIFs, or links embedded into copy? Do they like inspirational quotes, thought-provoking statistics or original infographics? You won't find out unless you test different types of content in your emails.

It goes without saying that not every type of content will work for your brand, but pull a list together of the types that do and start testing them out.

- **Calls to action**

  Every email needs to have at least one call to action, which should click through to a dedicated landing page on your website. (If the landing page is irrelevant, or 404s, then your whole email is wasted).

  Spend some time putting together a list of CTAs that fit your tone of voice, and then test these in your emails. See which ones get the most engagement and lead to conversions. You can also test the CTA button size, style and colour, but each of these things should be investigated separately.

- **Email send time**

  There's already a plethora of research on when the best time to send an email is. Take a look at your inbox and you'll see that lots of emails are sent to you just before the morning commute, while hardly any appear after 4pm on a Friday. Some marketers swear that certain days yield higher click through rates, but to truly understand when your audience is engaging, you'll need to test send times yourself.

> **Activity – Create your own test ideas**
>
> Using the welcome email that you created in the previous activity, think about some of the ways that you could test it.
>
> - Write two subject lines and preview text for each
>
> - Write two different headers for the email
>
> - Write two main calls to action that you could test

One thing at a time

While testing is vital, it's important not to get carried away. If you're testing multiple things in one email, you're unlikely to know which new thing worked – or if anything worked at all.

Instead, build a testing timeline into your email strategy. This could be as simple as testing subject lines and preview text for the first three months, then moving on and testing email content for the next three months, CTAs for the next three, and send times after that. Whatever works for you.

Remember to make full use of the data from each testing period to improve your emails for the next period. You'll learn things that can inform your email strategy and you'll tweak your email templates for the better. By the end of the year, you'll have amalgamated a huge amount of knowledge about your email recipients, and your campaigns will be performing better and making you more money.

Chapter 19: What can you do about climate change?

We choose to go to the Moon. Achieving the impossible.

'We choose to go to the Moon in this decade, not because that will be easy, but because it will be hard – because that goal will serve to organize and measure the best of our energies and skills, because that challenge is one that we are willing to accept, one we are unwilling to postpone, and one which we intend to win.'
PRESIDENT JOHN F. KENNEDY, SEPTEMBER 1962

Kennedy's mission of putting a man on the Moon by the end of the decade is similar to the one we are now facing with climate change. His speech inspired people to make the impossible possible. It also led to a space mission that *has contributed to a complete change of people's perception of and relationship with the planet Earth.*

On Christmas Eve in 1968, astronauts Frank Borman, Jim Lovell and Bill Anders were orbiting the Moon on Apollo 8, a mission to find the best spot for a future landing. They were equipped with high resolution cameras to capture images of the Moon's surface. At one point, Bill Anders saw the Earth 'rising' from behind the lunar horizon and took a photo. Little did he know that this photo named 'Earthrise' would become "the most influential environmental photograph ever taken", as declared by nature photographer Galen Rowell in Life's "100 Photographs That Changed The World"[96].

The power of the 'Earthrise' photo was in its depiction of the beauty of our planet from a perspective previously unseen by all but a few astronauts. As Anders noted, "people realised that we lived on this fragile planet and that we needed to take care of it." It also inspired the poet Archibald MacLeish who wrote, "to see the Earth as it truly is, small and blue and beautiful in that eternal silence where it floats, is to see ourselves as riders on the Earth together, brothers on that bright loveliness in the eternal cold." Earthrise inspired many environmental movements and helped us realise that Earth is the only home we have.

Ignoring the warnings

Our climate has been warming since the beginning of the Industrial Revolution, around 1850, when we started burning fossil fuels to create energy for manufacturing, heating, and transport. As far back as 1965, a report prepared by America's Presidential Science Advisory Committee[97] made politicians directly aware of the devastating impact that burning fossil fuels has on the planet. For decades, we've been ignoring these warnings and happily focusing on economic growth and high living standards. However, since the start of the century we have been witnessing the impact of our actions through extreme weather events including intense rainstorms, heat waves, powerful hurricanes, severe droughts, bushfires, and melting glaciers. All of these events are causing the sea level to rise and coastal areas to flood, destroying homes and disrupting vital ecosystems on our planet.

---

96 Life editors. (2003) *100 Photographs That Changed The World*. New York City, Time Warner International

97 The Economist. (2019) *The past, present and future of climate change* [online] Available at: https://www.economist.com/briefing/2019/09/21/the-past-present-and-future-of-climate-change [accessed 28 April 2020]

Together we can make a difference

The man-made climate crisis is no longer something we can ignore. It is too late to deny scientific facts. Every small step towards a sustainable future can make a big difference on a global scale. People all over the world have been waking up, using their voices and making better choices to secure a better future on this planet. We must all contribute to protecting our environment. We can still change things and avoid even more devastating consequences of climate change. But to do that, we must work together.

The internet's role in climate change

You might be wondering why you've been reading about digital marketing up until now and all of a sudden we've switched to climate change. How does this fit into a Digital Marketing Manager's role?

Some of us may feel bad for taking a flight or driving a petrol car because of the impact we know this has on the environment. However, few of us consider any of our digital activities as harmful! You might be shocked to discover that the internet is responsible for approximately 2% of global greenhouse gas emissions.[98] That is a similar share to the entire aviation industry. With the ever-increasing number of internet-connected devices, this percentage continues to grow every year.

Digital carbon footprint

All the information that we exchange online requires electricity to travel between data centres, networking infrastructure, and end-user devices. The problem is that about 80% of electricity is generated by burning fossil fuels.[99] Therefore, all of our digital actions contribute to global greenhouse gas emissions. Every video we watch, every song or podcast we listen to, every article we read, every search, every 'like', every tweet... all of this has a carbon footprint. To illustrate why this matters, let's discuss two specific examples: page views and emails.

––––––––––

98 Vaughan, A. (2015) *How viral cat videos are warming the planet* [online] Available at: https://www.theguardian.com/environment/2015/sep/25/server-data-centre-emissions-air-travel-web-google-facebook-greenhouse-gas [Accessed 28 April 2020]
99 IEA. (2014) *Fossil fuel energy consumption (% of total)*, [online] Available at: https://data.worldbank.org/indicator/EG.USE.COMM.FO.ZS All rights reserved. [Accessed 28 April 2020]

What's the carbon footprint of a page view?

According to Wholegrain Digital, the average web page currently emits 1.79 grams of CO2 per page view, roughly the weight of an almond. If you think about it, an almond is equivalent to quite a sizeable volume of carbon emission every time someone loads a page on their devices. By reducing the size of our websites and individual web pages, we can reduce the carbon emissions released into the atmosphere each time someone visits them. Every *byte* matters.

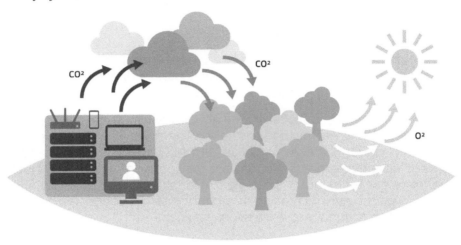

What's the carbon footprint of an email?

The second example is email. OVO Energy published research about the environmental impact of sending unnecessary emails[100] in collaboration with Mike Berners-Lee, an English researcher, author of several books about carbon footprints and climate change, and brother to Tim Berners-Lee, best known as inventor of the World Wide Web. OVO Energy calculated that the average carbon footprint of an unnecessary email (an email with up to four words) is approximately 1g of CO2.

Here are the top 10 unnecessary emails regularly sent:

---

100 OVO Energy. (2019) *'Think Before You Thank'* [online] Available at: https://www. ovoenergy.com/ovo-newsroom/press-releases/2019/november/think-before-you-thank-if-every-brit-sent-one-less-thank-you-email-a-day-we-would-save-16433-tonnes-of-carbon-a-year-the-same-as-81152-flights-to-madrid.html [Accessed 28 April 2020]

1. Thank you	6. Have a good evening
2. Thanks	7. Did you get / see this?
3. Have a good weekend	8. Cheers
4. Received	9. You too
5. Appreciated	10. LOL

The research calculated how many tonnes of carbon emissions would be saved if every internet user living in the UK sent just one less unnecessary email a day for one whole year. The results were astonishing. One less email a day would save 16,433 tonnes of carbon dioxide a year. That is an equivalent to halting 81,152 flights from Heathrow to Madrid or taking 3,334 diesel cars off the road.

Whilst the carbon footprint of a single email isn't huge, the example above illustrates the impact of our digital interactions on the environment.

Technology as a driver for a more sustainable world

> *"The first step in solving a problem is recognising there is one."*
> **WILL MCAVOY**

The digital world plays a big role in climate change, but it can also be a part of the solution. As Digital Marketing Managers, we need to acknowledge that the digital space in which we operate and communicate with our customers has a carbon footprint. However, recognising the environmental impact of our digital interactions shouldn't stop us from using the technology that is available to us. We just need to learn how to use it in a more efficient way.

Technology has always been the leader in innovation. If we all help to make the internet more sustainable, we can accelerate the shift from fossil fuels to clean energy. Therefore, a sustainable internet can be a part of the global mission to solve the climate crisis. That is one of the reasons why we are so proud to work in this industry.

Top 10 things Digital Marketing Managers can do to reduce carbon footprint

We encourage you to become part of the global mission to make the internet greener. Here's how you can help:

1. Be a sustainability champion

> *"No one is too small to make a difference."* **GRETA THUNBERG**

The best thing you can do is become a sustainability champion in your organisation. Speak to your colleagues and try to create a more sustainable working environment by reducing the negative and maximising the positive environmental impact in all aspects of your organisation. Be the change and empower others to make positive changes within and beyond your organisation.

2. Know the carbon footprint of your website

> *"If you can't measure it, you can't manage it."* **PETER DRUCKER**

Knowing the carbon footprint of your website is the first step to understanding how you can reduce it. But the rule of thumb generally is that the bigger the site, the more emissions it generates. Reducing the size of your site to a minimum will not only reduce its carbon footprint, it will also increase your page speed. Wholegrain Digital is a UK-based web design agency that developed the world's first carbon calculator for web pages. If you'd like to test your pages, visit https://www.websitecarbon.com/. They also developed a Carbon Badge[101] which you can install for free to the footer of your website to raise awareness about the digital carbon footprint and also be transparent with your customers about your own approach to this issue.

We are extremely proud to have collaborated with Wholegrain Digital on a brand new **Carbon Reporting Tool** for websites which was launched in November 2020. This tool allows you to calculate the carbon footprint of your entire site. Using real-time data from Google Analytics, the toll will

---

101 Wholegrain Digital. (2020) *Website Carbon Badges.* [online] available here: https://wholegrain.gitlab.io/website-carbon-badges/ [accessed 12 August 2020]

show you which pages are the most polluting ones and, crucially, what's causing it so that you can make positive changes. Visit https://www.web-sitecarbon.com/ to find out more.

3. Switch to green hosting

Make your website more sustainable by switching to a green hosting provider. There are companies that recognise the importance of this and are switching to 100% renewable energy, such as Google, Apple, and Microsoft. Find out who your hosting provider is, where are they based, and how they power their computing systems. You can be part of the mission to make the internet sustainable by using a website hosting powered by renewable energy. If you're unsure where to find one, visit https://www.thegreenwebfoundation.org/, which offers the largest Green Hosting Directory.

4. Reduce digital waste (improve load speed and reduce file sizes)

Every element on your site is data that needs to be loaded each time someone visits your site. The more elements you have, the longer it takes to load them all. If any element on your website significantly slows it down, consider removing it or resizing it. If you want to share images on your site, reduce their pixel size to a minimum first. There is no need for expensive software, you can use free online tools that will do this for you. Try https://tinypng.com/ or https://www.reduceimages.com/. This will help increase your page speed and reduce the amount of data to load the whole page (great for users as well as the environment). Try to do the same with videos or any downloadable files to make sure your site is fast and easy to load.

5. Choose quality over quantity (invest in SEO, UX, and great copy)

> *"Make everything as simple as possible, but not simpler."*
> **ALBERT EINSTEIN**

By optimising your website for search engine rankings (SEO), improving site navigation and accessibility (UX), and creating great content, you are helping people find what they want quickly and easily. This helps them spend less time browsing the web and, therefore, consume less energy. Follow best practice and you will increase website efficiency and reduce consumption of energy.

6. Reduce travel for business meetings

Today's technology allows us to connect with people anywhere in the world, which can help us significantly reduce the CO2 emissions from travel as well as save us a lot of time. Coronavirus made us aware, more than ever before, that it's possible, and sometimes even more comfortable, to join meetings and events from the comfort of your home. Once things go back to the new normal, try to stick to conference calls whenever possible. You can use tools such as Hangouts, Webex, Zoom, Teams, or Skype.

7. Choose sustainable and ethical branded merchandise

There is a sea of branded plastic keyrings, badges, pens, and many more products that no one *really* needs. Research shows that 88% of consumers want brands to be more environmentally friendly and ethical.[102] People care, and you can show them that your company cares too. Don't fill customers' lives with stuff they don't need. If you do use promotional merchandise, choose an environmentally friendly option.

8. Include sustainability in your events, meetings and training

When you run any events, meetings, or training, cut down any waste by avoiding plastic water bottles and use reusable ones instead. If you serve food, try to have at least 50% plant-based options. This is important because meat-centric Western diets account for a fifth of all global greenhouse gas emissions.[103] Having plant-rich diets is ranked as the fourth best solution to solve climate change, according to Project Drawdown[104]. Every small step towards a sustainable future matters. It shows you care and sets a good example for your colleagues and clients.

---

102 Townsend, S. (2018) *88% Of Consumers Want You To Help Them Make A Difference* [online] Available at: https://www.forbes.com/sites/solitairetownsend/2018/11/21/consumers-want-you-to-help-them-make-a-difference/#29b180696954 [Accessed 28 April 2020]
103 Project Drawdown. (2020) *Plant-Rich Diets* [online] Available at: https://www.drawdown.org/solutions/plant-rich-diets [accessed 28 April 2020]
104 Project Drawdown. (2020) *Table of Solutions* [online] available at: https://www.drawdown.org/solutions/table-of-solutions [accessed 28 April 2020)

9. Join a movement

Climate change is everybody's business. We're in this together and it is up to all of us to build a better future for everyone. Join those who are using their voices and choices to make a difference.

- Sign the **Sustainable Web Manifesto** and declare your commitment to create a green web.
- Become a **B Corporation** and publicly commit to reducing your carbon emissions to net zero by 2030.
- Join **Extinction Rebellion** to compel government action to avoid fast-approaching tipping points in the climate system, biodiversity loss, and the risk of social and ecological collapse.
- Be part of **The Climate Reality Project** to move the conversation about climate change forward and turn awareness into action.
- **Join The Countdown**, a movement powered by TED and Future Stewards, to get informed and spread the word about the climate crisis.
- Use the **Sustainable Development Goals** by the United Nations as guidelines to create a better world by 2030 by ending poverty, fighting inequality and addressing the urgency of climate change.

10. Support those who are making a difference

"The wise man does not lay up his own treasures. The more he gives to others, the more he has for his own." **LAO TZU**

Being able to *give* is a gift in itself. It's a selfless act that is good for others and for our physical and mental wellbeing. There are many organisations and charities that are working hard to make a difference and if we're lucky enough to be able to help them, we really should. Below are our top choices (related to climate change) but there are many, many more causes you can support. Pick the one that's closest to your heart and take it from there.

- Join **1% for the Planet** and commit to giving back to credible, environmental causes.
- **Cool Earth** is a charity that works with local people to halt deforestation and climate change.
- **SolarAid** combats poverty and climate change by providing access to solar lights in some of the most remote regions of Malawi and Zambia.

- **Building Malawi** helps build sustainable schools, libraries and the largest sports complex in the country. They also collaborate with the local permaculture centre to teach local children how to plant trees and take care of them.
- **All Hands and Hearts** helps families and communities recover from increasingly frequent natural disasters around the globe by building safe, resilient schools, homes and other community infrastructure.
- **4Oceans** is on a mission to end the ocean plastic crisis by cleaning the ocean and coastlines and helping to change consumption habits.
- **Rainforest Alliance** works with farmers, forest communities, companies and consumers to create a world where people and nature thrive in harmony.

Our pledge – we want to be 100% regenerative

The time to act is now. Being carbon neutral is no longer good enough. We will take regular action to reduce our carbon emissions *and* commit to absorbing DOUBLE the amount of carbon emissions that we produce to become 100% regenerative.

100 trees for every tonne of CO2 emissions

A typical tree can absorb as much as 48 pounds (about 21.8 kg)[105] of carbon dioxide (CO2) per year. Therefore, to absorb one tonne of CO2 emissions, we need to plant about 46 trees to become carbon neutral or at least 92 trees to become 100% regenerative.

As of 2020, Footprint Digital annual CO2 emissions are approximately 12 tCO2e (tonnes of carbon dioxide equivalent) or about 800 kg per employee per year. So we'd need to plant about 36 trees per employee to be carbon neutral or at least 72 trees to become 100% regenerative.

Since we like round numbers, we made a pledge to plant 100 trees for every tonne of CO2 we emit as a business to become 100% regenerative.

---

105 Stancil, J, M. (2019) *The Power of One Tree - The Very Air We Breathe* [online] available at: https://www.usda.gov/media/blog/2015/03/17/power-one-tree-very-air-we-breathe [accessed 28 April 2020]

The tax we're happy to pay

We're hoping that this self-imposed 'carbon tax' will help contribute to a better planet and also support projects that make society better for all. This is the tax we're happy to pay.

Be part of the global mission to help solve the climate crisis and encourage your company to be 100% regenerative as well!

Congratulations

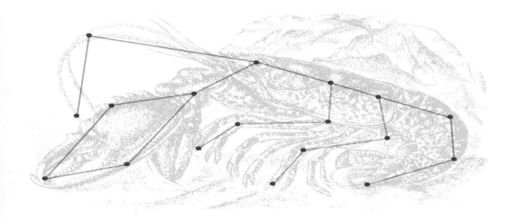

Thank you, well done, and congratulations for finishing the book! We are thrilled you made it this far.

We hope you have learned lots of practical ways to improve your online presence and thrive in your marketing career. And of course, shoot the HiPPO. Whilst we may never meet in person we feel that by reading this book we are friends, partners and like lobsters, mates for life.

Whenever we deliver our courses in person attendees are rewarded with a packet of smarties and a graduation ceremony. Whilst we can't offer you that, we invite you to reward yourself, and tag us in a picture of your Shoot The HiPPO 'graduation'! Use the hashtags #FootprintDigital #ShootTheHiPPO.

If you have questions about anything in the book, or if we can support you in the future, then please contact us.

We'd love to hear your stories, so please stay in touch (we mean that!)

Happy hunting,

Tom Bowden & Tom Jepson

Footprint Digital

Website: footprintdigital.co.uk   Instagram: @footprintdigital.ltd

Twitter: @footprintdigit   Facebook: @FootprintDigital

LinkedIn: Footprint Digital LTD

It's a jungle out there.

Our online course helps you stay ahead of the pack.

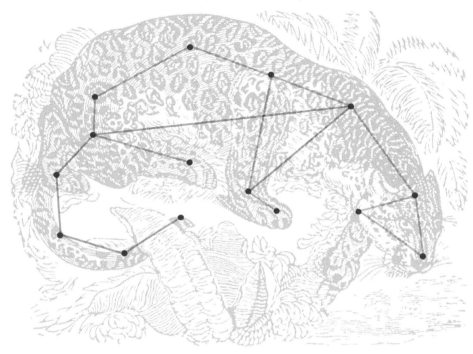

If this book has made you excited to dive even deeper into the world of the Digital Marketing Manager you are in luck...

We have launched an online version of the course through which we deliver the lessons lecture-style with supporting seminars, calls, and quizzes to help you deepen your understanding. Digital does not stay still. The beauty of the online course is that alongside the content featured in this book we regularly update it with practical and tactical content in line with the very latest developments across digital marketing. It also includes many bonus 'how-to' sections that walk you through features in Google Analytics and other tools that change almost daily.

Find out more about the course here: www.footprintdigital.co.uk

Glossary

ALGORITHM A program of rules or processes that computers use to problem solve. For example, search engines use lots of algorithms to determine your website's ranking position.

ALT TEXT Search engines can't read images, so don't know if they are relevant or not to users. Alt Text is a description of the image, in text, that a search engine can read to understand the image. It can also be displayed if the image doesn't load so people know what they should be seeing.

ANCHOR TEXT – In a piece of copy online, the anchor text is anything that you can click that takes you to another page (all of the pink text on this page). It's a hyperlink, and this text is important for search engines because it helps them to understand the topic on the page that you're linking to (so don't use 'search engine optimisation' as anchor text for a page about puppies – it'll confuse things!)

BACKLINK This is when another website inserts a link to your website on theirs (they are linking back to you – hence, backlinks!) Getting backlinks from quality sources (i.e. good websites, relevant to your industry) is very important for search engines to trust you.

BACKLINK AUDIT A backlink audit takes a detailed look at your current links (also called your link profile) analyses them, and determines whether they are good for your website or not. After an audit, it is customary to try to have any negative links removed.

BACKLINK PROFILE All of the backlinks that are currently pointing towards any page on your website.

BOUNCE RATE The rate of users who land on a specific webpage, and then bounce right off and leave the website without clicking on any more of its webpages. Different webpages can expect different bounce rates – for example the homepage should usually have a lower bounce rate than extremely detailed blog pages.

ccTLDs A country code top level domain appears in the end letters of a URL. For Footprint Digital, the ccTLDs is 'uk'. It shows users and search engines where your website is registered (i.e. which country or state). They are important for SEO, because they show a search engine that your website is specifically targeted to a location.

CITATION Citations and backlinks sometimes get confused. A citation is NOT a backlink (because it's not clickable and hence is not linking back), it is a reference to your website or business's name, address and phone number on another website – often in directories. Like backlinks, citations are important for search engines to understand the online authority of your website.

CONTENT DUPLICATION A problem in the eyes of search engines, content duplication is when the same content appears on two or more web pages. Internal duplication is when the same content appears on two or more of your own pages, whilst external duplication is where it exists on your website, and another website (potential plagiarism). Both are frowned upon because search engines give users the best search results for their search term, and think it's unhelpful for users when the same content is in several places.

CMS A content management system (e.g. WordPress, Joomla...) is part of the back-end system of the website. It's specifically created so that an administrator can make changes to content on the website without getting bogged down in the technical coding stuff.

E- COMMERCE A website that is specifically created to deal with online sales.

EXACT DUPLICATION Also called scraping, this is when content is copied, word for word, from a webpage onto another. Plagiarism like this is never good, because search engines want to give users unique, interesting content that they haven't read multiple times before.

GOOGLEBOT Google's 'spiders' which are used by the search engine to rank pages.

HREFLANG Hreflang is a tag that you can put into your on-page markup to tell search engines what language you are using on a particular webpage. This helps the search engine show your page to people using that language. It's useful if you are creating a version of your webpage for people in another country (e.g. if your business is expanding globally) and you want to make sure that they see the right version.

HTML Hypertext Markup Language (HTML) is a uniform system for tagging and coding text files on a website to achieve effects such as colour, listing, font changes, graphics, and hyperlinks.

IMPRESSION An impression is when a user looks at your website – also called a page view.

IP ADDRESS IP stands for Internet Protocol and it is a unique number given to every device active on the internet. It is used to identify devices from each other when they are using the internet, if you are unsure of what your IP address is, type in '**What's my IP address?**' into Google and it'll tell you – clever, huh?

KEYWORD The phrase that somebody types into a search engine when they are looking for something. A keyword is often not just one word – it is a phrase. People often use longtail keywords when they search – these are a keyword that contains several words i.e. 'the best pizza in town' rather than just 'pizza' or 'best pizza'.

KEYWORD CANNIBALISATION Using the exact same keyword on too many of the same pages on your website. Doing this means that search engines don't know which page is the most important one to show to users. This often happens if you have overlapping information on pages, or if the topic/ theme of a page is too similar to another.

KEYWORD RESEARCH The process of finding out which keywords should be targeted on specific webpages and in PPC ads. There are tools (such as Google Ads Keyword Planner) which can be used to research keyword search volumes.

KEYWORD STUFFING Keyword stuffing is a content no-no. It's essentially cramming your webpage content full of the same keyword to try to rank higher for that word, and creates a poor user experience. It was used in the early days of SEO to manipulate search engines - but search engines are too clever for keyword stuffing now. If there are too many of the same keyword on a page (so that it reads unnaturally) then search engines will rank it down.

LANDING PAGE A landing page is any page on your website that acts as the initial entry point for a user. A common misconception is that people always land on your homepage, but they rarely do after making a search! It can be any page on your site, depending on which of your pages a search engine decides to present to a user when they make a keyword search, or which page you direct people to after they click a PPC ad.

LINK ACQUISITION/ BUILDING Link building is the strategy of working to get other (relevant and trustworthy) websites to link back to your website. It's not an easy task, but it is incredibly useful and will help search engines to see you as an authority in your field.

LINK OPPORTUNITY The decision over whether or not you will be able to get a link back from a website. Some websites are great opportunities (i.e. your own contacts in the industry) others are not (huge businesses that you don't know, or businesses/ website that are irrelevant to your topic).

META DESCRIPTION The meta description is the short snippet of text that appears underneath the title in a search result. It is around 320 characters, and summarises what is on the webpage. It has no bearing on your ranking position, but it can entice users to click on your search result over competitors.

ORGANIC SEARCH PERFORMANCE How well (or how badly) your website does in search engine results pages (often shortened to SERPs). SEO is the process of improving your organic search performance.

PAGE TITLE TAG This is not the main title in the actual content of the webpage (that's an H1 tag). The title tag is an HTML title, that appears at the top of each search engine result, and in the tab. It's vital for both SEO and user experience (because it explains what the page is about to a search engine and to users).

REFERRING DOMAIN A referring domain is a website that is linking to you on one or more of their pages. It can also be called a ref domain.

ROBOTS.TXT Code that gives search engine 'robots' instructions about crawling your website – i.e. whether they can crawl or not.

SCHEMA - Schema markup (or just Schema) is code that, if added to your HTML, can help to improve how your webpage is understood by search engines and how they present it in their results pages. Schema creates a rich snippet which is then shown in your search engine result, providing users with more information, and making it more likely that the right users will click onto your webpage. Schema can be used for lots of things including: events, businesses, recipes, reviews, and videos.

SITE MAP - Every website should have a site map for search engines to crawl and users to look at if they need to. It is often a webpage that lists all of the unique webpages on the website, mapping them out in hierarchical order to make them easier to crawl.

URL - A URL is a unique web address for a resource held on the internet, and it stands for Uniform Resource Locator. Every page has a different URL.

WEB DESIGN - Planning and creating the aesthetics of the website – the front end parts that users will see. This includes graphic design, the website's interface, navigation, layout, user experience, usability, and many more things.

WEB DIRECTORY - A web directory (or link directory) is a collection of websites, held online. It catalogues a part of (or all of) the world wide web. Usually, each listing includes the name of the website and a link to it, alongside any other key information.

WEBSITE EXPOSURE - The amount of times your website is viewed by users. SEO attempts to increase your website exposure by pushing it higher up in the search engine results pages (SERPs). Webpages that appear on page one will have much greater website exposure than webpages lower down.

Bibliography

Agile Business Consortium (2014) *The DSDM Agile Project Framework, 2014 Onwards.* DSDM Consortium.

Ash, T. (2012) *Landing Page Optimization: The Definitive Guide to Testing and Tuning for Conversions.* Sybex.

Bower, M. (1966). *The Will to Manage: Corporate Success Through Programmed Management.* New York, McGraw-Hill.

Brook, Q. (2017) *Lean Six Sigma and Minitab (5th Edition): The Complete Toolbox Guide for Business Improvement.* Winchester, OPEX Resources Ltd.

Brown, B. (2011) *The Power of Vulnerability* [online] available at: https://www.ted.com/talks/brene_brown_the_power_of_vulnerability [accessed 9th November 2020]

Brown, B. (2018) *Dare to Lead: Brave Work. Tough Conversations. Whole Hearts.* London, Vermilion.

Brown, B. (nd) Dare to Lead with Brené Brown [podcast] Parcast Network. available at: https://open.spotify.com/show/3oEPsPKDhPVoNNL7pH5db6?si=x-4dw5xBKROO5pdA3Lodb1A [accessed 9th November 2020]

Buchanan, L, Inc. (2020) *Welcome to the Church of Fail* [online] Available at: https://www.inc.com/magazine/201311/leigh-buchanan/nixonmcinnes-innovation-by-celebrating-mistakes.html [Accessed 28 April 2020]

Campaign Monitor. (2019) *What Is Email Marketing? 7 Email Benefits To Grow Your Business* [online] available at: https://www.campaignmonitor.com/resources/guides/why-email/ [accessed 3rd September 2020]

Campbell, J. (1949) *The Hero With a Thousand Faces.* Princeton, Princeton University Press, N.J.

Carnegie, D. (2006). *How To Win Friends and Influence People.* London. Vermilion.

Carroll, L. (1991) [1871]. *2: The Garden of Live Flowers. Through the Looking-Glass* (The Millennium Fulcrum Edition 1.7 ed.). Project Gutenberg. Retrieved 26 September 2017.

Charlton, G. (2014) *Email remains the best digital channel for ROI* [online] available at: https://econsultancy.com/email-remains-the-best-digital-channel-for-roi/ [accessed6th November 2020)

Cirker, B. (1962) '1800 Woodcuts by Thomas Bewick and His School'. New York, Dover Publications, inc.

Clegg, D; Barker, R (1994). *Case Method Fast-Track: A RAD Approach.* Boston, Addison-Wesley.Bender, L. et al. (1997) *Good Will Hunting.* Buena Vista Home Entertainment.

Clement, J (2020) *available at: Facebook: number of monthly active users worldwide 2008-2020* [online] available at: https://www.statista.com/statistics/264810/number-of-monthly-active-facebook-users-worldwide/ [accessed 6 November 2020]

Clement, J. (2020) *Number of e-mail users worldwide 2017-2024* [online] available at: https://www.statista.com/statistics/255080/number-of-e-mail-users-worldwide/ [accessed September 12 2020].

Clement,J. (2020) *Daily social media usage worldwide 2012-2019* [online] Available at: https://www.statista.com/statistics/433871/daily-social-media-usage-worldwide/ [Accessed 28 April 2020]

Collins, J and Porras, J. (1994) *Built to Last: Successful Habits of Visionary Companies. New York,* HarperBusiness.

Doran, G. T. (1981) *There's a S.M.A.R.T. way to write management's goals and objectives.* Management Review. Volume 70, Issue 11, Pp 35–36.Bezos, J. (1999) *Jeff Bezos In 1999 On Amazon's Plans Before The Dotcom Crash* [online] Available at: https://www.youtube.com/watch?v=GltlJO56S1g [Accessed 28 April 2020]

The Economist. (2019) *The past, present and future of climate change* [online] Available at: https://www.economist.com/briefing/2019/09/21/the-past-present-and-future-of-climate-change [Accessed 28 April 2020]

Edmonds, G. (2000) *The Good Web Site Guide 2001: A-Z of the best 1000 web sites for all the family.* London, Orion.

Edmonson, A. (1999) *Psychological Safety and Learning Behavior in Work Teams.* Administrative Science Quarterly, Volume 44, Pp 350-83).

Edmondson, A. (2018) *The Fearless Organization: Creating Psychological Safety in the Workplace for Learning, Innovation, and Growth.* New Jersey, Wiley.

Encyclopedia Britannica. *Determinism.* [online] Available at: https://www.britannica.com/topic/determinism [Accessed 28 April 2020]

Flynn, G, cited by Sinek, S. (2020) *The Tail Can Wag the Dog.* [online] Available at: https://www.youtube.com/watch?v=Qg7smyaXdrl [Accessed 28 April 2020]

Gerber, M. (2001) *The E-Myth Revisited.* New York, Harper Business, Harper Collins.

Goldsmith, J et al. (2000) *What Women Want.* Paramount Pictures.

Google (nd) Google Analytics In Real Life - Online Checkout [online] available at: https://www.youtube.com/watch?v=3Sk7cOqB9Dk

Google (2020) *Announcing mobile first indexing for the whole web. [online] available at:* https://webmasters.googleblog.com/2020/03/announcing-mobile-first-indexing-for.html [accessed 30 April 2020]

Guardian (2017) *Tim Berners-Lee: I invented the web. Here are three things we need to change to save it* [online] available at: https://amp.theguardian.com/technology/2017/mar/11/tim-berners-lee-web-inventor-save-internet

Hancock, J et al. (2013) *Saving Mr Banks.* Walt Disney Studios.

Harari, N.Y. (2016) *Homo Deus: A Brief History of Tomorrow.* London, Harvill Secker.

Harley, S. (2013) *How to Say Anything to Anyone: A Guide to Building Business Relationships That Really Work.* Texas, Greenleaf Book Group Press.

Henrich, J., and Gil-White, F. J. (2001) *The evolution of prestige: Freely conferred deference as a mechanism for enhancing the benefits of cultural transmission.* Evolution and Human Behavior, Volume 22, Pp 165–196.

Hsieh, T. (2010) *On a Scale of 1-10, How Weird are You?* [online] The New York Times, accessible at: https://www.nytimes.com/2010/01/10/business/10corner.html [accessed 9th November 2020]

I Am Whole. (2020) *Digital Detox Day* [online] available at: https://www.digitaldetoxday.org/ [accessed 7th October 2020]

IEA. (2014) *Fossil fuel energy consumption (% of total),* [online] Available at: https://data.worldbank.org/indicator/EG.USE.COMM.FO.ZS All rights reserved. [Accessed 28 April 2020]

Instagram. (nd) [online] available at: https://business.instagram.com/ [accessed 28 September 2020]

Iqbal, M. (2019) *App Download and Usage Statistics.* [online] available at: https://www.businessofapps.com/data/app-statistics/ [accessed 28 April 2020]

Ishiguro, K. (1989) *The Remains of the Day.* Boston, Faber.

Johnson, S. (1998) *Who Moved My Cheese?: An Amazing Way to Deal with Change in Your Work and in Your Life.* New York, Putnam

Kaushik, A. (2020) *Occam's Razor by Avinash Kaushik* [online] available at: https://www.kaushik.net/avinash/digital-marketing-and-measurement-model/

Kaushik, A. (2006) *Seven Steps to Creating a Data Driven Decision Making Culture. Occam's Razor.* [online] available at: https://www.kaushik.net/avinash/seven-steps-to-creating-a-data-driven-decision-making-culture/ [accessed 28 April 2020]

Karpman, S. (1968) *The Karpman Drama Triangle - Fairy tales and script drama analysis* [PDF] available at: https://karpmandramatriangle.com/pdf/DramaTriangle.pdf [accessed 6th November 2020]

Kawai, K. (1950) *Mokusatsu, Japan's Response to the Potsdam Declaration.* Pacific Historical Review. Volume 19, Issue 4.

King, M. (2017) *Moriori: A People Rediscovered.* New Zealand, Penguin Random House.

King, S. (2012) *On Writing: A Memoir of the Craft.* London, Hodder.

Koski, J et al. (2015) *Understanding Social Hierarchies: The Neural and Psychological Foundations of Status Perception* [online] Available at: https://www.ncbi.nlm.nih.gov/pmc/articles/PMC5494206/ [Accessed 28 April 2020]

Krug, S. (2014) *Don't Make Me Think, Revisited: A Common Sense Approach to Web Usability.* San Fransisco, New Riders.

Lewis, M. (2004) *Moneyball: The Art Of Winning An Unfair Game.* New York, W.W.Norton.

Life editors. (2003) *100 Photographs That Changed The World.* New York City, Time Warner International

Looby, N. (2017) *Modern Zombies: How to Stay Ahead of the Horde and Communicate Your Way to Incredible Success.* London, Feet on the Ground Training Ltd.

Lucas, G et al. (1977) *Star Wars: Episode IV – A New Hope.* 20th Century Fox.

Lundin, S. et al. (1998) *Fish!* New York, Hyperion.

Masanobu, F. (1978) *The One Straw Revolution.* New York, New York Review Books Classics.

Maslow, A, H. (1943) *Hierarchy of Needs: A Theory of Human Motivation.*

McDowell et al. (2016) An examination of retail website design and conversion rate. Journal of Business Research, Volume 69, Issue 11, Pp 4837-4842.

Moore, G, E. (1965) *Cramming more components onto integrated circuits* (PDF). intel.com. Electronics Magazine. Retrieved April 1, 2020.

Original Source Unknown. (2020) *Where Do You Sit? Above The Line Or Below The Line?* [online] Available at: https://peopleleaders.com.au/above-or-below-the-line/ [Accessed 28 April 2020]

Orwell, G. (1946) *Why I Write.* London, Penguin Books.

OVO Energy. (2019) *'Think Before You Thank'* [online] Available at: https://www.ovoenergy.com/ovo-newsroom/press-releases/2019/november/think-before-you-thank-if-every-brit-sent-one-less-thank-you-email-a-day-we-would-save-16433-tonnes-of-carbon-a-year-the-same-as-81152-flights-to-madrid.html [Accessed 28 April 2020]

Pederick, C. (nd) *Web Developer.* [online] available at: https://chrispederick.com/work/web-developer/ [accessed 28 April 2020]

Project Drawdown. (2020) *Plant-Rich Diets* [online] Available at: https://www.drawdown.org/solutions/plant-rich-diets [accessed 28 April 2020]

Project Drawdown (2020) *Table of Solutions* [online] available at: https://www.drawdown.org/solutions/table-of-solutions [accessed 28 April 2020)

Raimi, S et al. (2002) *Spiderman.* Sony Pictures Releasing.

Rosling, J. (2013) *More money More time Less stress.* London, 1Fish 2Fish.

Rowling, J.K. (1997) *Harry Potter and the Philosopher's Stone.* London, Bloomsbury Publishing PLC.

Sakaguchi, M. (2019) *Creating Psychological Safety in the Workplace. A Think with Footprint guest lecture.* [online] Available at: https://www.youtube.com/watch?v=H0-2Wfk8n3M [accessed 28 April 2020]

Schawbel, D. (2016) Gary Vaynerchuk: Managers Should Be Working For Their Employees. [Online] available at: https://www.forbes.com/sites/danschawbel/2016/03/08/gary-vaynerchuk-managers-should-be-working-for-their-employees/?sh=205afca62008 [accessed 28 April 2020]

Schmidt, E. et al. (2014) *Google: How Google works* (First edition.) New York, Grand Central Publishing. Sinek, S. (2020) *The Tail Can Wag the Dog.* [online] Available at: https://www.youtube.com/watch?v=Qg7smyaXdrI [Accessed 28 April 2020]

Search Engine Journal. (nd) *60+ Mind-Blowing Search Engine Optimization Stats. [online] available at:* https://www.searchenginejournal.com/seo-101/seo-statistics/ [accessed 18 April 2020]

Sinek, S. (2009) *Start with why: how great leaders inspire everyone.* London, Penguin.Syed, M. (2020) *Diversity and creative thinking - the power of rebel ideas* [Podcast] Available at: https://podcasts.apple.com/gb/podcast/eat-sleep-work-repeat/id1190000968?i=1000471564042 [Accessed 2 May 2020]

Stancil, J, M. (2019) *The Power of One Tree - The Very Air We Breathe* [online] Available at: https://www.usda.gov/media/blog/2015/03/17/power-one-tree-very-air-we-breathe [Accessed 28 April 2020]

Stanley, A. (2011) Tweet on @AndyStanley account [online] available at: https://twitter.com/AndyStanley/status/103841035108630528 [accessed 9th November 2020].

Tolkein, J.R.R. (2013 [1937]) *The Hobbit.* New York, HarperCollins Children's Books.

Townsend, S. (2018) *88% Of Consumers Want You To Help Them Make A Difference* [online] Available at: https://www.forbes.com/sites/solitairetownsend/2018/11/21/consumers-want-you-to-help-them-make-a-difference/#29b180696954 [Accessed 28 April 2020]

Trefis. (nd) *Alphabet's Revenues: How Does Alphabet Make Money?* [online] available at: https://dashboards.trefis.com/no-login-required/HMtQjcWW/Alphabet-s-Revenues-How-Does-Alphabet-Make-Money-?fromforbesandarticle=goog191224 [accessed 2 August 2020]

Vaughan, A. (2015) *How viral cat videos are warming the planet* [online] Available at: https://www.theguardian.com/environment/2015/sep/25/server-data-centre-emissions-air-travel-web-google-facebook-greenhouse-gas [Accessed 28 April 2020]

Wallace, D, F. (2009) *This Is Water: Some Thoughts, Delivered on a Significant Occasion, about Living a Compassionate Life'.* London, Little Brown Book Group.

Welch, J; Welch, S. (2005) *Winning.* New York, HarperBusiness.

Wholegrain Digital. (2020) *Website Carbon Badges.* [online] available here: https://wholegrain.gitlab.io/website-carbon-badges/ [accessed 12 August 2020]

Wikipedia, the free encyclopaedia. (nd) *Red Queen Hypothesis*. [online] available at: https://en.wikipedia.org/wiki/Red_Queen_hypothesis [accessed 28 April 2020]

Wikipedia, the free encyclopaedia. (nd) *PageRank*. [online] available at: https://en.wikipedia.org/wiki/PageRank [accessed 28 April 2020]

Wiseman, R. (2019) *Shoot for the Moon: How the Moon Landings Taught us the 8 Secrets of Success*. London, Quercus Publishing.

Wohlleben, P. (2017) *The Hidden Life of Trees*. Glasgow, William Collins.

Further reading

Avinash Kaushik – *"Web Analytics: An Hour a Day"*

Donald Norman – *"The Design of Everyday Things"*

Dr Karl Blanks – *"Making Websites Win: Apply the Customer-Centric Methodology That Has Doubled the Sales of Many Leading Websites"*

Eric Schmidt and Jonathan Rosenburg – *"How Google Works"*

Greta Thunberg – *"No One is too Small to Make a Difference"*

Jeff Walker – *"Launch"*

John Hegarty – *"Hegarty on Creativity: There are No Rules"*

Matthew Syed – *"Rebel Ideas: The Power of Diverse Thinking"*

Michael Watkins – *"The First 90 Days"*

Michael L. George, John Maxey, David Rowlands, Mark Price – *The Lean Six Sigma Pocket Toolbook: A Quick Reference Guide to 100 Tools for Improving Quality"* and *"Speed: A Quick Reference Guide to 70 Tools for Improving Quality and Speed"*

Mike Warren – *"The Exit Formula"*

Nancy Duarte – *"Resonate: Present Visual Stories that Transform Audiences"*

Paco Underhill – *"Why We Buy: The Science of Shopping"*

Rand Fishkin – *"Lost and Founder: A Painfully Honest Field Guide to the Startup World"*

Rod Judkins – *"The Art of Creative Thinking"*

Steve Krug – *"Don't Make Me Think"*

Seth Godin – *"Purple Cow"*

Simon Sinek – *"Start With Why: How Great Leaders Inspire Everyone to Take Action"*

Steve Peters – *"The Chimp Paradox"*

Yvon Chouinard – *Let My People Go Surfing: The Education of a Reluctant Businessman"*

About the authors

Tom Bowden

Tom is coming to terms with the reality that he is the guy that wrote a book about marketing. He'd always imagined that he'd write one about something a bit more nourishing to the soul. Nevertheless, he has worked alongside so many brilliant people over the years and gleaned from them a great deal of knowledge. He thought he ought to write it all down.

His biggest interest in life is providing opportunities for young people in Malawi. He does this as trustee of Building Malawi (http://www.buildingmalawi.com/) and throughout the last 18 years of his life has built four libraries, two schools and the first and largest sports academy in the country's capital, Lilongwe. If someone could write a cheque to enable Building Malawi to build more, please do it. The world is grossly unfair to young people in that part of the world and you have the power to make life better for them. So give us your effing money! (All profits from the sale of this book will go to Building Malawi.)

He has lots of the fearsome big-hitter-businessy accolades that you would expect from an author of a marketing book. He is managing director of a digital marketing agency, he has developed global strategies for clients you will have heard of (Sony, Motorola, Cartoon Network, Google, Legal and General etc etc) and has delivered lectures for universities, trade bodies, and governments.

The thing he likes most about running a digital agency is supporting his team to learn, play, and grow both personally and professionally. He also quite enjoys occasionally doing the tea round and if you ask for a green tea he will always present it with a plate and a spoon so you can decide for yourself how stewed you would like it.

Tom is the person to talk to if you are interested in understanding the most effective way to build a team capable of adapting to the fast changing digital world (Culture), develop a winning strategy (Strategy), generate business through paid advertising (PPC) and improve the conversion rate of your website (CRO).

Tom Jepson

Tom was one of the pioneers of the service that is now known as SEO and, through 20 years of experience, he has seen search engines become part of everyday life. His intrinsic understanding of how they work has enabled him to help hundreds of companies thrive online and has made him one of the leading minds in the industry. Which is made ever more impressive by the fact that he grew up as the only English guy in his school in Serrekunda, The Gambia. The school only had blackboard and chalk and Tom didn't get his hands on a computer until he was 14. It may also make him the only industry leading SEO who also speaks Wolof.

Nominative determinism is the theory that the name we are given influences who we become. I'm not sure if there is a similar term for people inhabiting the characteristics of people they look like. Tom is the spitting image of Mowgli and embodies this by being resourceful, free spirited, and enthusiastic. He is obsessed with understanding how things work and combines his superb technical knowledge and analytical approach with his exceptional ability to communicate in a way that businesses can understand. He bridges the technical, analytical, and creative and has a fierce reputation for getting results.

He is a Director at Footprint Digital, a husband, and the proud father of two beautiful girls; the centre of his world.

Tom is the person to talk to if you are interested in understanding the most effective way to invest online (Google Analytics) and improve your site rankings in Google (SEO).

Chris Green

Chris has been obsessed with digital marketing for over ten years. He's an author, experienced Marketer, Strategist, and Technical SEO. He has an impressive beard and an even more impressive hairline for someone who has dealt with Google algorithms all of his life (most industry peers have torn theirs out).

When Chris delivers a webinar he uses a different voice, something akin to the one your Mum used to use when she answered the phone to someone in authority. His warm encouraging tone makes even the most terrifyingly technical topic approachable and fun.

What is rare and special is that, unlike lots of tech geniuses, who prefer to ferret their extensive knowledge away in their own private vaults, Chris loves to share and teach everything he knows to anyone that will listen. Those who do are well rewarded.

Head of Marketing Innovation at Footprint Digital, Chris Green has worked in Digital Marketing & Search marketing for the last decade. Chris's core focuses have been Technical SEO, Web Analytics, Paid Search, and Digital Strategy. He has spoken at industry events such as BrightonSEO, State of Digital, Search Norwich, Search LDN, and Optimisey and worked with household names, SMEs and one man bands. Chris is a certified trainer for SISTRIX, an Ambassador for OnCrawl, and a contributor for State of Digital.

Michael Scanlon

Once a year, on boxing day, Michael runs naked into the sea. It is a chastening experience, not least for those that are present when he does it, but, also for those that have had the misfortune of picturing it in their mind's eye. It is a form of penitence ritual, something to do with the Irish catholic guilt he carries from his youth.

It must be that same Irish blood that makes him proficient at all things Google. Sadly Michael's accent is somewhat undercut by the guttural sounds of his Coventry upbringing, but he is bloody good at paid search campaigns, to be sure, to be sure.

Michael believes that digital can encourage communication, creativity and, ultimately, make the world a better place.

Head of PPC at Footprint Digital, Michael is the person to talk to if you are interested in the unconventional percussion choices in the music of the late Buddy Holly, the career goals to game ratio of Peter Ndlovu, or the precision of a well formed PPC account.

Marketa Benisek

Marketa Benisek leads the way in Footprint Digital's drive to make the internet more sustainable. A top of her class marketing phenomenon Marketa has degrees, awards, and successes spilling out of her ears.

Marketa is a certified Climate Reality Leader, and she maintains a blog called *Everyday Choices* (https://www.everydaychoices.life/) which helps people understand what they can do to contribute to a better future for our planet and ourselves and start making a difference today. She believes we can solve the climate crisis together but, to do so, we must act quickly. Behind her back the team affectionately refer to her as MarGRETA Funberg, Al GOREgeous or, at times, Sir David Quick-hide-your-single-use-plastic-batternburg. She also sometimes writes book chapters on digital sustainability.

Marketa is the person to talk to if you want to reduce your website carbon footprint (Sustainability) and is the person that will whack-a-mole you with a placard if you don't.

Alex Eade

Chief editor of this book Alex Eade once tried to escape Footprint Digital. She ran away to London for two years to work in the marketing department at Gordon Ramsay's restaurants. Footprint gave chase. Unable to compete with discounts on delicious cuisine we instead offered the impossible-to-resist opportunity to open up a London office and lead the Footprint marketing team. Schooled by the master of dishing out foul mouthed obscenities Alex was well equipped to cope with the proof readers' feedback on the author's first draft.

Alex has lived the entire Footprint lifecycle. After graduating from her masters in business she attended an early version of the Shoot the HiPPO course. On completion she joined the team and ran the content department. She then left. (But please don't mention it because we're still not fully over it). She then returned. Alex understands the text from all perspectives and like a good chef has found balance with the diverse flavours within the book to make it palatable and satisfying to all.

She's a self-confessed book worm, and not even the process of editing Shoot the HiPPO has put her off spending far too much money in Waterstones. She is a champion chocolate eater (we can confirm that levels of consumption have dramatically increased during the editing process) and loves nothing better than a long walk, usually to Richmond Park, to spot the deer or fawn over other people's dogs.

Lightning Source UK Ltd.
Milton Keynes UK
UKHW050729160921
390672UK00002B/15